BLUEPRINTS FOR 9 THEATRE PERFORMANCES BY ONTROEREND GOED

# CONTENTS

Ontroerend Goed is a theatre performance group.

At the core of all our work is the belief that the world is inevitably doomed but also the belief that every action matters, every interaction is worthwhile.

The performances we create deal with how people, as individuals, cope with the world around them, with its problems and the high probability of a bad outcome on the one hand and on the other hand, how everything people do, all their interactions as human beings, are extremely valuable and important. We embrace the tension between these two beliefs in every idea we try to communicate. We look for the ideal form to convey each idea.

A girl tries to write down everything that's wrong in the world. Teenagers shut themselves away in an attempt to rebel and make their lives meaningful. Humans try to make sense of the history of everything of which they are only a miniscule part. Individuals try to keep up in a manipulated crowd. People find out the world around them is a projection of their inner world. Two strangers explore truth and lies in first encounters.

The black box of the theatre is our free space, where every form is possible. No other medium is as immediate as theatre. In our work, we cherish the direct communication between creator and visitor. For both performers and audiences, life goes on during performances.

We use the word 'we' because each performance is made by a group of people. Theatre is essentially a shared experience, in every aspect.

# PERSONAL TRILOGY

# THE SMILE OFF YOUR FACE

A sensory 25-minute-journey of the imagination for one visitor and eight performers.

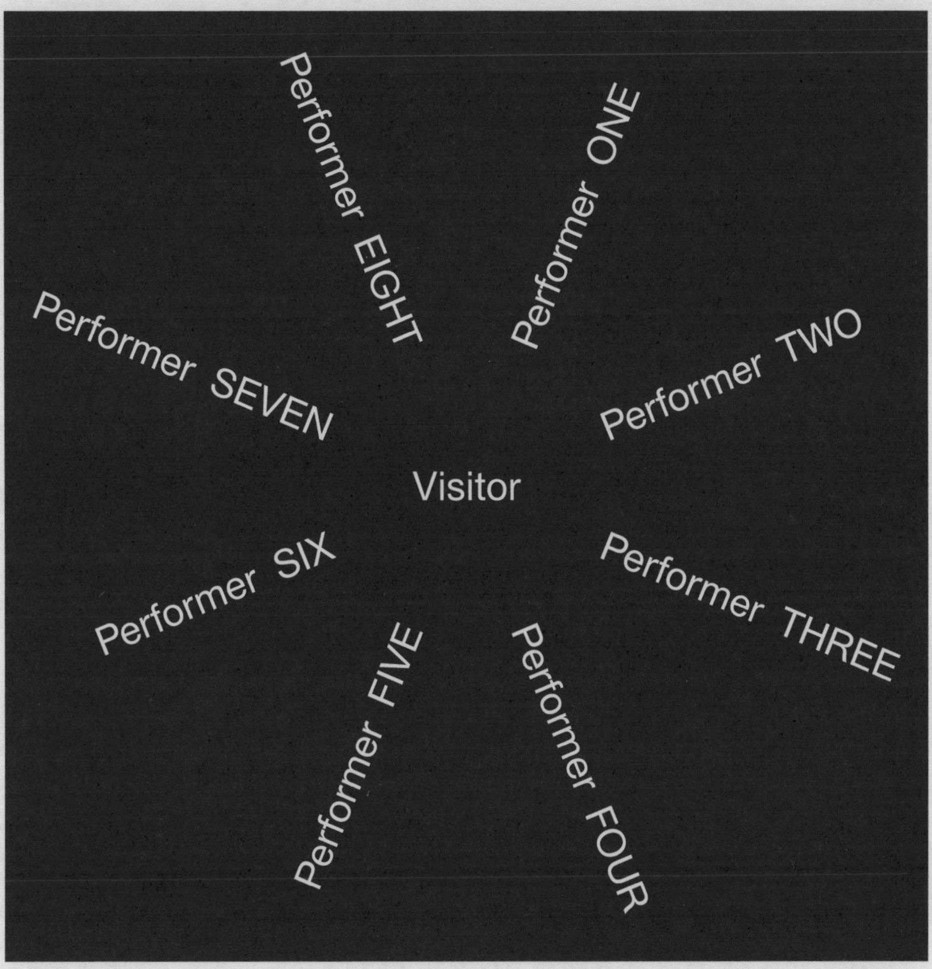
Performer ONE
Performer TWO
Performer THREE
Performer FOUR
Performer FIVE
Performer SIX
Performer SEVEN
Performer EIGHT
Visitor

# OUTLINE

'The Smile Off Your Face'
is a one-on-one sensory
experience for individual
visitors. They enter alone in
a wheelchair, hands tied and
blindfolded. The play is set
in the mental space between
stimulation and imagination.
The audience is invited to
surrender and explore physical trust and intimacy. The
performance has been called
'a massage of the imagination', 'aroma therapy', 'a
confessional' and 'a deconstruction of theatre.'

'The Smile Off Your Face'
is the first part of the
Personal Trilogy

- · A darkened space.
- · A polaroid camera.
- · A bed.
- · A ramp and small platform.
- · A throne-like chair.
- · A Saint-Nicolas costume (cfr. Santa Claus).
- · Chocolate, marzipan, a peeled carrot.
- · Six wheelchairs.
- · Six blindfolds.
- · Six small ropes.
- · Optional elements such as spices, lighters, an alarm clock, a Chinese lightbox photograph with waterfall sounds, musk, lots of mints and eye-care products.

## CREDITS

**Created by**
  Joeri Smet
  Sophie De Somere
  Bob Stoop
  Aurélie Lannoy
  Alexander Devriendt

**First performed**
  January 30th, 2004
  De Singel, Antwerp, BE

**Originally produced by**
  Ontroerend Goed
**And thereafter with**
  Richard Jordan
    Productions Ltd.
**With the support of the**
  Province of East-Flanders
  City of Ghent

# CREATION

'The Smile Off Your Face' starts from an unusual position for the audience member: he or she is alone, in a wheelchair, hands tied and blindfolded. This is the way people enter the performance and the starting point from which the whole show was devised. 'The Smile Off Your Face' dismisses the distinction between stage and seating area and immerses the spectators into the progression of the 'play'. The blindfold encourages them to imagine their surroundings and construct a story of their own, stimulated by scents, sounds and gentle touches. The wheelchair forces them to surrender control and explore physical trust and intimacy.

'The Smile Off Your Face' was created in 2004 and since then, it has traveled the world, from Australia to the USA, Singapore to Israel, Morocco to Sweden. These wanderings have had a profound influence on the show, since it obliged the format to function in different cultures with distinct approaches to intimacy, physical contact and social interaction. At times interpreted as a 'massage of the imagination', 'aroma therapy', an elaborate 'confessional' or a thorough 'deconstruction of theatre', 'The Smile Off Your Face' has kept fascinating and dazzling audiences, because of its profound emotional impact and personal treatment of the visitors.

As the opener of the Personal Trilogy, it's been called a 'warm bath' compared to the more challenging and dissecting shows that follow it.

As our first one-on-one performance, almost accidentally born from experiment, the creation of 'The
Smile Off Your Face' was a bumpy road. It took about
a year and a half before the show reached its present
form. Scenes were added and skipped, performers
were engaged, then replaced, but, crucially, it, was
only through this consistent exploration that we were
able to discover the core strength of the concept.

The story began in the summer of 2003, when
we got an invitation to create a performance for a
Happening in a museum. It would be a one-time
event and since we had little space, no stage and a
moving crowd, we decided to do something different.
As we had made it our trademark to explore the
boundaries of the medium of theatre, we came up
with a formally bold idea: what if the audience
would move on their chairs, instead of the actors on
stage? We started messing around with office chairs,
building a closed set in which the performers – all
four of them in character – would jump up and
scare the audience, like in a haunted house. After
two weeks of rehearsal, we presented our work in
the museum and it was a flop. The audience felt the
'installation' was either weird or ridiculous. But they
all loved the idea of being tied in a chair.

At the time, we believed in fixing a failed
project. So we went back to the chairs, replaced
them with more practical wheelchairs and thought
the whole thing over again. Essentially, we were
depriving the audience of their mobility. So why not
deprive them of their eyesight? Enter the blindfolds.
Moreover, we singled them out, so this meant every
performance would be a unique, individual experience. Putting these elements together, we figured out
that we needed the audience to imagine the show
themselves. We would merely provide the stimuli.

The second series of rehearsals consisted mainly
of playful experiments with blindfolded people in

wheelchairs. This would be the basis for the trajectories of the rollers – using scents, subtle sound effects and gentle touch. In this phase, the acts were still premature: we had a shower scene, with the audience as a peeping voyeur, a miniature puppet show – performed in front of the tied-up visitor – and a tapdancer, weary of her act, who told the audience everything about her complicated relationship status.

We were offered another showcase, on a literary Happening in Antwerp, and this time, 'The Smile Off Your Face' was a huge success. Quite by accident, a Moroccan programmer attended the performance and invited us to his festival in Chefchaouen. We were overwhelmed, but apart from the cultural differences we had to consider, there were some practical and artistic issues. Moving the audience around in wheelchairs, in the system we had devised, was complicated and demanded a lot of people. On top of that, we weren't convinced of every single act. We needed to trim the cast and purify the concept. In the end, only one act from this 'pioneering' period would survive: Santa Claus. It was the only scene in which the blindfold was essential. It related directly to the main concept of the audience imagining things unseen, and the riddle-structure of the text proved both funny and mysterious. The act became like a blueprint for further development.

Many audience members had described the experience in Antwerp as 'intimate'. We decided to use this feedback as a guideline. We dropped the puppet show and the shower scene and developed the idea of a bed scene – a blindfolded conversation lying down with a stranger asking personal questions. Another new act was inspired by our tour in Morocco. At first it we thought of a Middle-Eastern fortuneteller – some sort of psychic searching the audience's 'soul'. This evolved into taking pictures of the visitors to capture their presence. The performer

would then confront them with the image and ask
them to smile. Every time the act was performed,
it became very emotional. The performer got either
angry or started crying. This added intensity to
the show, so we included the tears (not the anger)
as a fixed part.

Our trip to Morocco turned out to be revela-
tory. There were some restrictions: feeding the
audience sweets and fruit, dressed up as a catholic
saint, was deemed too close to an attempt at conver-
sion, and adult male strangers touching young,
unmarried and unsupervised muslim girls proved too
precarious. But in essence, the performance worked,
and communicated a message, even though the
majority of our Moroccan audience wasn't exactly
familiar with experimental theatre. For us, however,
it was liberating to see how people made sense of
their experience, regardless of the (Western) tags
'art', 'performance', 'therapy' or 'religious ceremony'.
We felt the performance had, in effect, crossed the
boundaries of theatre. In the end, our Moroccan
spectators called it a 'massage of the imagination.'
We returned home with the knowledge that this
performance could appeal to many people in many
different countries and cultures.

The breakthrough for 'The Smile Off Your Face'
came when it was programmed as a side-act in the
Belgian-Dutch Theatre Festival in August 2004.
Sometimes we had to perform for more than eight
hours a day, as audiences kept pouring in, fueled by
word of mouth. New bookings resulted from this and
we needed to tighten the performance even more.
The core story of 'The Smile Off Your Face' was not
the sensory exploration, nor the topic of intimacy.
It was the journey of a blindfolded person, being
allowed to use his imagination to construct the plot,
the setting, and the meaning of the show. The acts
had to serve this overall purpose. We skipped the

tapdance act and reduced the show to a triangle of essential moments: the picture and the crying, the bed, and Santa Claus. These were the important steps of gradual revelation that would lead to the finale: taking off the blindfold and confronting the visitor with the real, physical space and the machinery of theatre, defying the imagined space in his mind. In between, there would be the sensory journey, carried out by a minimum of rollers. This formula would prove seaworthy.

In spite of its un-economic setup – a crew of nine, maximum capacity of sixty visitors a day – 'The Smile Off Your Face' turned out Ontroerend Goed's biggest door-opener and we've kept it on the playlist for almost ten years. Curiously, we never knew what the performance was about, but what it *did* proved more than satisfactory. We believed it was our best shot at conquering an international audience in the 2007 Edinburgh Festival, and we were right. Throughout the years, many performers have taken on the roles of criers, Santas and girls-on-the-bed. Maybe one day, the show will be performed without anyone from the original cast, perhaps even by other companies. We'd love to come and experience it ourselves.

# SCRIPT

There are three acts in 'The Smile Off Your Face', performed by four performers. The circulation of visitors in wheelchairs is taken care of by 'rollers'. On the left, we will describe the experience of a visitor, using masculine pronouns. On the right, we will describe the performance from the point of view of the performers and rollers.

00.

**THE VISITOR**
**I'm waiting outside the performance space among the other**
**visitors. We're chatting, a little nervously. There are a few**
**chairs and a guestbook, for after the show. I've seen people**
**coming out, some were quite emotional. The guy with the**
**wheelchairs is calling me.**

> *THE PACKER*
> I call in the visitor. I take him to a wheelchair.
> I tell him to take a seat. I say:

*I'm going to blindfold you and tie*
*your hands.*

**THE VISITOR**
**I take a seat in a wheelchair. The guy takes a small rope and**
**ties my hands. I'm being blindfolded. Someone moves my**
**wheelchair, probably the same guy.**

> *THE PACKER*
> I roll the visitor into the space and hand him
> over to the 'lighter'.

TIMER: 0'00"

01.

THE VISITOR
My wheelchair has stopped moving. I'm inside. I hear music, voices and people walking around.

> *THE LIGHTER*
> I take a cup filled with aniseed and hold it above the visitor's head. I shake it gently, it makes the sound of gravel or pebbles on the beach.

THE VISITOR
I hear a grinding sound. I'm not sure where it comes from.

> *THE LIGHTER*
> I move around the visitor's head, so it gets difficult to locate where the sound comes from. This is to sharpen the visitor's hearing and attention. I play hide-and-seek with the visitor, when he's moving his head towards the cup. At the end, I hold the cup under his nose so he smells the aniseed.

THE VISITOR
I smell aniseed.

> *THE LIGHTER*
> While I keep on shaking the cup, I turn on the music on my ipod: Pippilotti Rist's version of 'Wicked Game' by Chris Isaac. It starts with the creaky sound of a record.

1'00"

**THE VISITOR**
Someone puts on a record. I recognize the tune. It's Chris Isaac's 'Wicked Game'. But a woman is singing it.

*THE LIGHTER*
I take a lighter and light it. I bring it near the visitor and go over his body with it. Not too close, just enough to feel the heat. After hearing, smelling, this heightens the visitor's sense of touch. There's also a risk involved. I could burn him. This is the first moment the visitor really needs to trust us, the performers.

**THE VISITOR**
The woman sings the words 'I was on fire...' and someone lights a lighter near me. I can feel the heat. The flame passes by my face, my neck, my arms, my legs, my chest. I say: 'Hi', to make contact. But nobody responds.

*THE LIGHTER*
If the visitor asks something, I don't say a word. In this phase, all communication is non-visual and non-verbal. When the first chorus sets in, I start pushing the wheelchair into the space.

**THE VISITOR**
As the woman sings the chorus: 'No I...don't wanna fall in love', the wheelchair starts moving. It feels like the journey has started.

2'00"

### THE LIGHTER

I push the wheelchair in straight lines through the open space. Not too fast, so the visitor doesn't get dizzy. When I turn, I try to make sharp angles, so it feels as if we're turning around a corner. I use the objects hanging from the ceiling to produce sounds, close to the visitor's ear.

The aim is to desorientate the visitor as much as possible and to create an illusion of the space as either very large or labyrinth-like. Of course it's the visitor's imagination producing this illusion.

## THE VISITOR

While I'm gently moving on, in the warm, relaxing soundscape, I hear someone leafing through a book, a waterfall and tweeting birds, although they sound very electronic, sloshing water, the ticking of a clock, muffled voices having conversations, footsteps, busy people, like in a factory.

### THE LIGHTER

I stop the wheelchair on the mark near the cryer. I fasten the brakes. I step away, loud enough for the visitor to hear my footsteps. This is to make sure that he knows there will be another person attending to him.

NOTE
Up till now, this was a 'prelude' to massage the visitor's senses and bring him fully into the atmosphere of the performance. The length depends on the timing of the whole show. If there is a delay or a gap in the circulation, the Lighter might decide to make it shorter or longer.

3'00"

02.

**THE VISITOR**
**My journey has come to a halt. The person who guided me here, leaves. I'm alone.**

> *THE CRYER*
> **I lean over the wheelchair and bring my face close to the visitor's face. I breathe in his face.**

**THE VISITOR**
**I can sense someone's close to my face.**

> *THE CRYER*
> **I touch the visitor's nose with my nose.**

**THE VISITOR**
**He – or she – is touching me.**

> *THE CRYER*
> **We gently rub noses. I step over the wheelchair, so that I'm facing the visitor. I'm almost sitting on his lap, but I take care not to touch him.**

**THE VISITOR**
**I can sense the warmth of a body very close to me.**

> *THE CRYER*
> **I move my upper body along his nose, so he can smell the musk I've put on. I take his hands and bring them to my face.**

4'30"

THE VISITOR
He – or she – takes my hands and puts them on his face. His face, because I can feel a beard now.

*THE CRYER*
I let him feel my cheekbones, my eyes, my neck…or wherever his hands go.

THE VISITOR
I'm feeling him. He starts feeling me.

*THE CRYER*
I'm copying his movements on his face, touching him in the same way he touches me.
I slowly lift his feet from the foot rests and pull him out of the chair.

THE VISITOR
I'm standing up. He's still holding my hands.

*THE CRYER*
I guide him. First only by the hands, then I put my arm around his shoulders. Step by step, we move towards the wall.

THE VISITOR
He's bringing me somewhere. I follow his steps.

*THE CRYER*
I rock him back and forth, meanwhile turning his back towards the wall. I let go of him.

**THE VISITOR**
Suddenly he's gone. I try to reach out and feel whether he's still there. For a moment I'm standing alone, blindfolded, in an unfamiliar place. It's awkward.

>*THE CRYER*
>I grab his shoulders and push him against the wall. While he's still recovering from the surprise, I fetch my polaroid camera and take a picture. I let him hear the sound of the camera rolling.

**THE VISITOR**
Someone pushes me roughly against a wall. I assume it's him. He takes advantage of my confusion to take a photo.

>*THE CRYER*
>I hold his hands, embrace him. I slowly guide him back to the chair. The roller assists me and puts the chair behind him.

**THE VISITOR**
He brings me back to the wheelchair and I sit down.

>*THE CRYER*
>When he's seated, I keep holding his hands. The roller pulls him back. There's a little trial of strength when he tries to keep hold of my hands, against the roller's power. (Sometimes, when it's a tiny person or a very expressive one who dances or shows great flexibility, I lift them up in my arms and carry them to the next act).

**THE VISITOR**
I'm being pulled away. He's still holding my hands. I don't want to let go. It's like a tug-of-war. Finally I release the grip. I'm being pushed to the next destination.

**NOTE**
By the time this first act is finished a new visitor is waiting for the same thing to happen.

6'00"

03.

*ROLLER No. 1*
**I bring the visitor to the bed.**

**04.**

> *THE GIRL ON THE BED*
> I hold the visitor's hands and bring them to my
> neck. I lift his feet from the foot rests and make
> him stand up. I turn him with his back towards
> the bed.

**THE VISITOR**
Again, someone holds my hands. This time, it's a girl. She gets
me up and guides me, similar to the man before her.

> *THE GIRL ON THE BED*
> I make him sit on the bed. Then I throw myself
> on him so he has to lean back and lie down.

**THE VISITOR**
I'm not sure what I'm sitting on, but the girl forces me to
recline. I fall back. This is how I find out I'm on a bed.

> *THE GIRL ON THE BED*
> I'm on top of him. I whisper in his ear:

> *Left or right?*

> I'm aware this is the first time someone speaks
> to him. Usually, I have to repeat the question.

**THE VISITOR**
The girl is very forward. I've barely met her and she's all over me. I say: 'Left.'

> ### *THE GIRL ON THE BED*
> I lie down next to him, on his left side. I wrap one leg around his legs. My head is close to his ear. I do everything to make it comfortable, like putting a pillow under his head. I start asking questions, at first, simply:

> *How are you doing?*

**THE VISITOR**
I tell her I'm fine.

> ### *THE GIRL ON THE BED*
> I continue:

> *What are you doing?*
> *How was your day?*

**THE VISITOR**
I tell her how my day has been so far. I didn't expect finding myself in this situation. She seems to pick up on this.

### *THE GIRL ON THE BED*

*Are you relaxed now?*

**THE VISITOR**
I feel I ought to be relaxed. So I try to ease down. I tell her I'm relaxed.

### *THE GIRL ON THE BED*

*You feel well.*

By now, he should have adapted to the situation. I try to make him feel safe and secure, so he'll open up.

*Do you laugh a lot?*

*What makes you laugh?*

**THE VISITOR**
**I tell her how often I laugh and what for.**

### *THE GIRL ON THE BED*

*Are you worried about things?*

**THE VISITOR**
**I tell her my worries. She enquires into them, makes me put them into words. The blindfold helps me to imagine what I'm talking about, to dig deeper into my mind.**

### *THE GIRL ON THE BED*
**I ask questions about the things that occupy his mind. I try to be critical but not judgemental, at times suggesting solutions or offering different perspectives. Then I turn to the situation in the here-and-now:**

*Do you find this intimate?*

**THE VISITOR**
**I tell her what I find intimate. It makes me think of what real intimacy means.**

*THE GIRL ON THE BED*

*Are you in love?*

**THE VISITOR**
**She asks me if I'm in love with her. At least, that's my first interpretation.**

*THE GIRL ON THE BED*
**I repeat the question.**

**THE VISITOR**
**I figure out she means it in a more general way. Then I ask myself if I'm in love. It's a difficult question to answer. What does it mean, 'being in love'?**

*THE GIRL ON THE BED*

*Would you like to be in love?*

**THE VISITOR**
**I tell her I'd like to be in love.**

### *THE GIRL ON THE BED*

*What is beautiful to you?*

**THE VISITOR**
**I tell her what I find beautiful. Somehow, I've created an image in my head of how she looks, what she's wearing, the colour of her hair, her eyes, how tall she is, how old. I could be wrong – I'm probably wrong – but the image sticks to my mind. It's the only one I have right now.**

### *THE GIRL ON THE BED*

*Friendship.*
*What does it mean to you?*

**THE VISITOR**
**I tell her my ideas about friendship and how important it is to me.**

*THE GIRL ON THE BED*

*Do you get irritated?*

**THE VISITOR**
**I'm not sure if she's implying my friends irritate me.**

*THE GIRL ON THE BED*

*Do you keep your promises?*

**THE VISITOR**
**I tell her how I deal with promises.**

*THE GIRL ON THE BED*

*Why?*

This question can be interpreted in two ways. If the visitor keeps his promises, the question suggests that sometimes it's necessary to break them. If he doesn't, the question appeals to his moral conscience. My next question elaborates on this by exploring regret:

*Do you feel sorry for something?*

**THE VISITOR**
I tell her how I deal with regret.

**THE GIRL ON THE BED**

*Do you cry a lot?*

**THE VISITOR**
I tell her how often I cry.

*THE GIRL ON THE BED*

*When was the last time?*

**THE VISITOR**
**Involuntarily, I recall the last time I cried.**

*THE GIRL ON THE BED*

*What makes you happy?*

**THE VISITOR**
**She forces me to name the things that make me happy. It's hard to put them into words. I feel the next question coming.**

*THE GIRL ON THE BED*

*Are you happy?*

THE VISITOR
Now that I've named what makes me happy, I have to consider
whether I am truly happy. I can't help comparing the ideal
with the reality. Answering this question honestly with 'yes' or
'no' is quite a challenge.

### THE GIRL ON THE BED

*Thank you very much.*

I slip out of the bed, ready for the next visitor.

THE VISITOR
I don't feel the girl anymore. She's gone. I wonder when she
left, if I was talking to myself for a while.

12'00"

05.

> ROLLER No. 2
> I take the visitor's hands and lift him up.

THE VISITOR
Someone puts me back in the wheelchair.

> ROLLER No. 2
> I roll the visitor up the ramp for his encounter
> with Santa Claus.

THE VISITOR
I'm going fast suddenly. It's like a fairground attraction: I'm
rolling uphill, onto some sort of platform.

> ROLLER No. 2
> I put the brakes on for safety.

THE VISITOR
I'm standing still.

**06.**

*SANTA CLAUS*
I'm sitting on a bar stool next to the ramp, close to the visitor. I'm dressed up as Sinterklaas, but I don't try to make my voice sound old or manly. On the contrary, I'm trying to sound as sensual and feminine as possible.

*Hello. I'm happy to see you.*

NOTE
'Santa Claus' is not the correct name for the part, but in Anglosaxon countries the original name 'Sinterklaas' doesn't ring a bell. 'Santa Claus' is the closest to what we intend. In the low countries, Sinterklaas is a folkloristic character, originally a catholic saint, who became some sort of sugar daddy to children, bringing the good ones toys and candy and punishing the bad ones. He is said to ride a white mare and his assistant is a black man named Zwarte Piet – 'Black Pete'. All of the elements in the text refer to typical attributes of Sinterklaas and would be recognizable to virtually everyone who is familiar with the tradition. Around the 6th of December, Sinterklaas' official nameday, it's a custom to stage children's meetings with the 'holy man' at schools, in shops and other public occasions.

**THE VISITOR**
A woman with a French accent whispers in my ear. I say 'hello' but she seems to ignore my intervention.

*SANTA CLAUS*
I don't ignore the visitor's reaction, I just don't respond, to create a mysterious atmosphere.

**I squeeze his shoulder:**

*Don't be afraid, I'm your friend.*
*What's your name?*

**THE VISITOR**
**I tell her my name. It's the first time someone asks me. She**
**says it's a lovely name.**

*SANTA CLAUS*

*Have you been a good boy?*

**THE VISITOR**
**I tell her about my behaviour in the past year.**

*SANTA CLAUS*

*Can I touch your leg?*

**THE VISITOR**
**I give her permission to touch my leg.**

*SANTA CLAUS*
**I touch his leg. I start touching his head. I ask:**

*Can I touch your hair?*

**THE VISITOR**
**She's already touching my hair before she asks permission.**
**But I tell her she can do it.**

*SANTA CLAUS*

*Do you want to sit on my lap?*

**Before or during his response, I add:**

*No, that's impossible.*

And I burst into laughter, at first with him, but I continue even after he has stopped. Maybe he feels mocked, but I soothe him:

*I like to laugh. I'm always cheerful.*
*I wear a red dress. And lace. Touch.*

**THE VISITOR**
**She lets me feel her dress.**

*SANTA CLAUS*

*Nobody knows what I'm wearing*
*under my dress.*

I fetch my box with chocolates, marzipan and tangerines. I put it on his lap.

*Here's your present.*

**THE VISITOR**
**A metal box is thrown on my lap. I touch it, unable to open it.**

*SANTA CLAUS*

*Let me help you.*

**THE VISITOR**
**She opens the box. I smell candy.**

*SANTA CLAUS*

*I like sweetness. Chocolate that
melts on the tongue.*

**THE VISITOR**
**She pushes a piece of chocolate in my mouth. I eat.**

SANTA CLAUS

*Sugar in my mouth.*

THE VISITOR
I get a piece of tangerine.

SANTA CLAUS

*Marzipan. Especially in the shape*
*of little fruits.*
*Apples. Pears. Bananas.*
*But most of all, I like marzipan in*
*the shape of little pigs.*

THE VISITOR
She forces a piece of marzipan into my mouth. I'm chewing.

SANTA CLAUS
I step away from the platform and declaim:

*I like to be alone with animals.*
*Carress the shiny coat of my horse.*

**THE VISITOR**
**As she's talking about animals, the woman strokes my back as**
**if I was a horse.**

*SANTA CLAUS*

*My horse eats carrots. Peeled*
*carrots. Because they are softer.*

**I take a big carrot and move it up and down in**
**his folded hands. The metaphor is obvious.**

**THE VISITOR**
**As I'm holding a giant phallic object, she asks me if I like**
**African people.**

*SANTA CLAUS*
**I say:**

*My best friend is an African.*

I take the carrot from his hands, adjust my
costume and tell him it's time, that I have to go.
I take off his blindfold.

THE VISITOR
For the first time in almost 20 minutes, I'm allowed to see. I need
some adapting to the light. Slowly I start to discern an image.
Santa Claus, sitting on a throne. Not what I expected. He…
No, she nods.

18'00"

07.

*ROLLER No. 3*
As Santa Claus nods, I put the visitor's blindfold back on from behind. I pull him back from
the platform and push him towards the photo
wall. As I approach the wall, I slow down, until
I've reached the central chair.

THE VISITOR
I'm blindfolded and on the road again.

*ROLLER No. 3*
I remove the blindfold.

08.

THE VISITOR
After a short trip, someone takes my blindfold off again. This
time, I'm in front of an empty chair and a huge black wall full
of polaroids portraying blindfolded people.

> *THE CRYER*
> I approach the visitor from behind. My silhou-
> ette is visible on the wall in front of him, so he
> can see me coming. I take a seat on the chair
> facing him. I pull him closer.

THE VISITOR
A man is sitting very close to me. He's wearing a tank top and
ripped jeans. He looks me straight in the eyes.

> *THE CRYER*
> I ask him how he's doing.

THE VISITOR
I tell him I'm ok.

> *THE CRYER*
> I ask him if he enjoyed the performance. If he's
> been afraid, able to relax.

THE VISITOR
I try to describe how I felt during the performance.

### THE CRYER
I ask if I scared him, when I pushed him against the wall.

THE VISITOR
I realize this is the guy who pushed me against the wall. I tell him how it felt.

### THE CRYER
I ask if he noticed I took a picture of him. I tell him I can show it.

THE VISITOR
The man turns around facing the wall and looks for my picture. When he finds it, he points at it. It's close to his chair. I take a look at it.

### THE CRYER
While he's studying his picture, I rub my eyes. I touch the eyeballs with my finger. From now on, I stop blinking. I tell him to come closer.

THE VISITOR
When I look back at the man, he's staring at me in a funny way. He pulls me closer.

### THE CRYER
I ask him to produce a smile.

THE VISITOR
I try to smile. It's hard. It feels fake.

> ### THE CRYER
> I ask him to make it real.

### THE VISITOR
His remarks make me laugh.

> ### THE CRYER
> When he laughs, I ask him to hold that expression. Sometimes I tell people they have a beautiful smile. Sometimes I tell them it's important to keep smiling. As I stare into the spotlight, without blinking, tears roll down my cheeks.

### THE VISITOR
He starts crying. I don't know why. The tears are real. I don't know how to react to this.

> ### THE CRYER
> I give a signal to the roller to pull him back.

21'00"

09.

*ROLLER No. 3*
I pull the visitor back. Slowly at first, then
faster, like a camera zooming out.

THE VISITOR
I'm being pulled back. Bit by bit, I get an expanded view of
the wall, it's huge and full of polaroids. I get to see the whole
space. The bed, Santa Claus, other blindfolded visitors being
moved around in wheelchairs, just as I was a few moments
ago. The crying man is still looking at me. Before I realize,
I'm out. Back in the waiting room.

*ROLLER No. 3*
I leave the visitor behind to be liberated.

10.

### THE PACKER
**I untie the visitor's hands and invite him to leave a note in the guestbook** •

NOTE
Sometimes people ask about the meaning of 'The Smile Off Your Face'. Very often, the performance leaves the visitors feeling emotional, and they want to know why. There is no clear-cut answer to this question. The strength of the performance is what it does, not what it means.

'The Smile Off Your Face' works like an assembly line producing stimuli that trigger the imagination. In the end, the whole 'factory' is revealed, exposing theatre as a machine that processes emotions, thoughts, memories and aesthetic impressions. However, as one critic pointed out, the mental space belongs to the visitor.

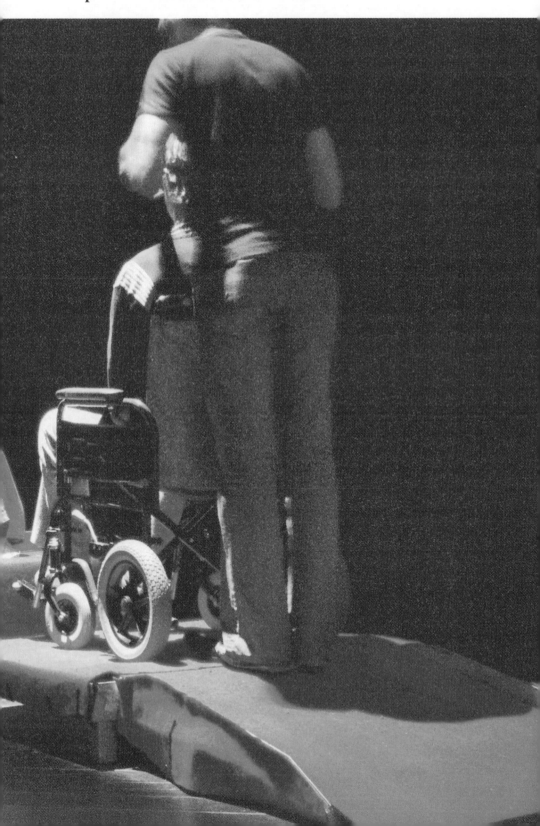

A one-on-one performance for five visitors and five performers:

Visitor ONE
Visitor TWO
Visitor THREE
Visitor FOUR
Visitor FIVE

Performer FIVE
Performer FOUR
Performer THREE
Performer TWO
Performer ONE

# OUTLINE

'Internal' investigates the
possibility of a meaningful
relationship with a stranger
within a theatrical setting.
The time is limited to 25
minutes. The individual
visitors are invited to engage
personally in the progression
of the piece. They experience an intimate encounter
with a performer which is
then shared with the other
'couples'. The show con-
structs a metaphor for real
life intimate encounters and
the level of truth and lies
within them.

 'Internal'
 is the second part of the
 Personal Trilogy

## REQUIREMENTS

- · Five actors.
- · A darkened space.
- · Slightly cheesy, sentimental orchestral music.
  We used Mantovani's
  arrangements of 'Send
  in the Clowns', 'Some
  Enchanted Evening',
  'A Lovely Way to Spend
  an Evening', 'Torna A Sor-
  rento' and 'Try to Remember', but any music that
  conveys a sense of old-
  fashioned romance will do.
- · Classy evening dress.
  One actor should be able
  to take off her top in the
  blink of an eye.
- · Ten folding chairs.
- · Five bottles of liquor
  with five pairs of assorted
  drinking glasses.
- · The desire to have intimate
  conversations with strangers twelve times a day.

## CREDITS

**Created by**
  Alexander Devriendt
  Joeri Smet
  Aurélie Lannoy
  Sophie De Somere
  Nicolaas Leten

**First performed**
  September 14th, 2007
  KC België, Hasselt, BE

**Originally produced by**
  Ontroerend Goed
  KC België
  Vooruit
  Inkonst
**And thereafter with**
  Richard Jordan
    Productions Ltd.
**With the support of the**
  Flemish Community
  Province of East-Flanders
  City of Ghent

# CREATION

In this performance, we investigate the possibility of a meaningful relationship with a stranger,
and how this can be translated to a theatrical
setting. The time is limited to 25 minutes.

As in 'The Smile Off Your Face', audience
members experience the performance from
within. They are invited to engage personally
in the progression of the piece so that every
trajectory is different, according to the visitor's
individuality and willingness to open up.

'Internal' sparked a lot of controversy due
to the combination of real-life details provided
by the visitors and the premeditated script
followed by the actors. The performance constructs a possible reality that acts as a vivid
metaphor for real life intimate encounters and
the level of truth and lies within them.

Early in 2007, our manager David felt that
Ontroerend Goed needed another side-project,
a small, out-of-the-box performance, that would
complement our official playlist. Obviously,
he had a second 'The Smile Off Your Face'
in mind, but he didn't say it out loud. We all
got the message, though. In our meetings, we
referred to the project as 'the internal thing',
since rehearsals would be informal, with a
limited number of people, and no clear goal
or any form of pressure. Nevertheless, David
asked for a promotional text, so we knew he
had high hopes. Completely unaware of what

we were going to create, we faked a 'leaked' internal mail, telling him we didn't feel like making this show. This was our promotional text and we dubbed the project 'Internal'.

We gave ourselves one month of rehearsals to come up with an idea. All of the performers in the space had been in 'The Smile Off Your Face', either as creators or replacements. We reckoned our experience with one-on-one theatre would come in handy, but still we didn't know how a sequel to 'The Smile' would look – what it would *be*. We only had the title, which sounded exciting, so we started fantasizing a performance that would fit it. Our first interpretation of 'internal' was physical, as in 'internal organs'. We imagined a very visceral performance, with the audience on hospital beds or transported over an assembly line, following the template of 'The Smile'. However, at some point, we had to face the fact that we had already done the sensory thing. We realized that creating a sequel to 'The Smile' also meant defying the expectations. After all, no audience member had anticipated the blindfolds or the wheelchairs, so why would we go the same way in this new show?

Our second interpretation of the word 'internal' yielded more inspiration. What if we would look for internal information of the visitors, personal stuff, private thoughts and feelings? All the people in the room were good at winning the trust of strangers. We started experimenting among ourselves, inventing scenarios for conversations, creating intimate atmospheres, assigning roles to each other, of the seducer, the therapist, the professional blind-dater. We checked how far we could push each other to reveal personal information and how we could project an image of sincerity.

Yet the question remained: where's the performance? If our private talks were comparable to

a speed-dating session, what did we need to drama-
tize the information we got out of it? This is where
we came up with the metaphor of a group talk. We
would create a theatrical 'simulacrum' of a relationship – five relationships – discussed in a therapeutic
gathering, using the material from the private talks.

In a way, 'Internal' gave birth to our notion of
'possible reality', since we decided to use real life
data from the audience in a fictional setting. In the
bed of 'The Smile Off Your Face', people told us
their secrets and emotional concerns, but they were
kept safe and private. In 'Internal', we would take
it one step further: the revelations and confessions
would be processed – edited, twisted, taken out of
context, paraphrased...and made public. We were
walking a thin line and it would always remain a
thin line. We suspected the experience could become
blurry for some visitors, but we wanted to take the
risk. Our first try-outs, with people plucked from the
street, proved that our concept was confusing but
also fascinating. We were onto something.

After a two-month break, we picked up the
process again. We created a script for the group
talk, organized in slots, which would be filled with
the specific details of our 'partners'. There were
five of us, all in need of a visitor, so we had to let
the audience enter in small groups of five. In order
to pick our perfect match, we would start with a
line-up. We would then swap places to show our
preference. Our set designer made five booths, each
with a different mood and lighting, accompanied by
strong liquors to loosen the tongues. We selected
some cheesy music that would fit the timing for
the conversations. It felt as if we were organizing a
dating event, but the stakes were much higher than
superficial encounters. After one month and a half
of rehearsals and improvisations, we were ready to
put the whole thing to the test.

The first performances of 'Internal' were quite rowdy. It felt as if we had unleashed uncontrollable forces – a couple broke up after the show, a man suffering of unrequited love plunged into a dark mood, another one had a crush on one of the female performers and stalked her afterwards. It was scary and exhilarating at the same time, but it worked. We had a show that could get under people's skin, though not without risk. In a way, we needed this experiment to explore the boundaries of one-on-one theatre, to find out how personal we could get with our visitors without losing the theatrical footing. But the audience had to know where it stood as well. At one point, we did wonder if we were making it too hard for people to distinguish reality from fiction, when a woman told us she had made some drastic life decisions after being in the show. Our gut feeling said we weren't responsible for that, but it was tricky anyway. Did we want to make a show that literally changed people's lives? Maybe not. The woman, however, didn't blame the performance. She said anything could have triggered her decision: a movie, a family dinner, a remark in a pub. In this case, our theatre show was the catalyst. And it continued to fulfill that role, from time to time. 'Internal' has had a deep impact on many people involved.

# SCRIPT

To give an accurate impression of
the performance, we will present two
parallel stories, one from the point
of view of a visitor and one from the
point of view of a performer.

00.

**THE VISITOR**
**There are five of us, waiting for the usher to let us in. We are**
**guided into the space through a dressing room. We see a table**
**with mirrors and the actors' personal belongings: a hairbrush,**
**lipstick, envelopes and stamps, black and white clothes neatly**
**arranged on a rack.**
    **We enter a dark space. The usher asks us to stand on**
**white marks and face the black curtain in front of us. We're**
**in a line-up.**

                ***THE PERFORMER***
        **I stand in the line-up in front of the black**
        **curtain, with the four other actors. I can hear**
        **the visitors talking on the other side. We've**
        **been told how many men and women there are,**
        **whether there are any couples.**

**THE VISITOR**
**The curtain goes up. We are facing five actors. They stare at us.**

                ***THE PERFORMER***
        **The curtain goes up and I'm facing the line-up**
        **of visitors. I look into the eyes of the one in**
        **front of me. Then I look at the others. We have**
        **an agreement: the girls choose the men accord-**
        **ing to their taste, one male actor takes the**
        **prettiest girl or woman. Another actor takes**
        **the person who looks the most troubled or has**
        **something to hide.**

THE VISITOR
The actors swap places, each chooses one of us.

> *THE PERFORMER*
> We swap places until we're in front of 'our' visitor.

THE VISITOR
I shake hands with my actor. He says hello.

> *THE PERFORMER*
> I shake hands with my visitor. We say hello.

THE VISITOR
We turn around and in the dark space behind us, five booths light up, and nostalgic music starts.

> *THE PERFORMER*
> I take my visitor to my booth, my arm around his shoulder.

THE VISITOR
The actor takes me to a booth. We sit down at a small table with a shaded lamp. He pours me a drink and introduces himself. I tell him my name.

> *THE PERFORMER*
> I ask my visitor to take a seat at the little table in my booth. I introduce myself and offer him a drink.

## THE VISITOR
## He starts asking me questions.

**NOTE**
At this stage, the five visitors
have a different conversation
and/or experience, depending on the actor they're with.
The conversations last about
eight minutes. The music
serves as a timer.

01.                    *PERFORMER ONE*

                   *THE NEGATIVE ONE*
I ask my visitor how old he is.

VISITOR 1
I tell him my age.

                   *THE NEGATIVE ONE*
I compare his age to mine and calculate the
difference. If there's a difference of more than,
say, ten years, I say:


            *Well, that's something…but not*
                  *impossible, is it?*


Usually, it takes a few seconds before the visitor
comes up with an answer, but then I quickly add:


            *It depends what for, of course.*


This is an ice-breaker. I ask whether he's
attracted to older or younger people.

**VISITOR 1**
I tell him I'm attracted to younger people.

*THE NEGATIVE ONE*
I ask:

*Are you in a relationship?*
*With an older or younger person?*
*For how long?*

I try to figure out whether they're a happy couple and what his philosophy of love is. This is
the point in the conversation where my visitor
should relax and talk freely. I observe the way
he talks, whether there's something he is hiding
or avoiding. I try to pick up on a sense of trou-
ble or frustration.

**VISITOR 1**
I tell him about my relationship, the rough patches, what keeps
a couple going.

*THE NEGATIVE ONE*
I ask about his first impression of me.

**VISITOR 1**
I tell him what my first impression of him was.

                        *THE NEGATIVE ONE*
               **I tell him what my first impression of him was.**
               **I try to be vague enough, but not too general,**
               **so he really feels I've 'read' him.**

**VISITOR 1**
**He tells me what his first impression of me was.**

                        *THE NEGATIVE ONE*
               **I ask whether people have told him these things**
               **before and whether this first impression is**
               **correct. The answer will reveal something about**
               **my visitor's self-image. I ask him to imagine**
               **how his best friends would describe him.**

**VISITOR 1**
**I tell him what my best friends would say about my person-**
**ality. Good things**…

                        *THE NEGATIVE ONE*
               **I ask him what they'd say if I told them to be**
               **critical.**

**VISITOR 1**
…**and bad things.**

                        *THE NEGATIVE ONE*
               **While he's talking, explaining why his friends**
               **would criticize him for this or that, I interrupt**
               **him with the question:**

*Have you ever wished someone dead?*

**The surprise at this weighty question is in itself
telling, and so is the speed of the response. This
part is a good gauge of sincerity or spontaneity.**

**VISITOR 1**
**I tell him that I once wished someone dead.**

**THE NEGATIVE ONE**
**I ask him who.**

**VISITOR 1**
**But I don't tell him who.**

**THE NEGATIVE ONE**
**If the visitor doesn't want to answer a question,
I don't push. In the long run, respecting his
wish to keep things for himself will pay off. It's
gaining trust. If I feel the reticence isn't strong,
I suggest things like:**

*Was it someone close?*
*At work?*
*In your family?*

Even if the visitor doesn't answer the question, his reactions to the suggestions might be revealing. In rare cases, this question makes people cry. If so, I don't panic, but I try to calm them down and show some understanding and compassion. Basically, anything a normal, sensitive person would do in this situation.

**VISITOR 1**
I ask him if this is a real conversation. He says it is.

### THE NEGATIVE ONE
If meta-questions arise, such as 'are you an actor?' or 'are you following a script?', I confirm that I'm an actor, that this is a performance, but the conversation we're having is real. I even tell people that the questions I ask are prepared, but the answers genuinely interest me. This is not a lie. Sometimes I invite people to ask me something personal, and I respond truthfully. But I quickly turn to the next question, since time is limited.
I ask him whether he gets angry easily, and how he expresses anger.

**VISITOR 1**
I tell him how I express anger.

### THE NEGATIVE ONE
I ask him what his greatest fear is. It's significant whether the fear involves other people

or just himself. Most parents would mention
something happening to their children. Most
ambitious people would say: failure. People
who feel quite happy and secure in their lives
would mention a minor fear such as 'spiders'
or 'being trapped in an elevator'. Disease, loneliness and old age also top the list.

VISITOR 1
I tell him what my greatest fear is.

THE NEGATIVE ONE
If there's still time left, I ask him whether he
remembers his dreams. Does he have any
recurring ones?

VISITOR 1
I tell him my recurring dream.

THE NEGATIVE ONE
I ask whether I can hold his hand.

VISITOR 1
I let him hold my hand.

NOTE
The closing-eyes-part is a
fixed exercise that happens
in every booth, except for the
Silent One. If there are any
variations, they will be mentioned. But from now on,
the performer will just state:
'I play the eye-game.'

*THE NEGATIVE ONE*
I ask him to close his eyes.

VISITOR 1
I close my eyes.

*THE NEGATIVE ONE*
I ask him to imagine a place that's not here.

VISITOR 1
I imagine I'm in a different place.

*THE NEGATIVE ONE*
I ask him to describe the place, how it feels,
what he's doing there, who's there with him.

VISITOR 1
I imagine what I'm doing there, whom I'm with.

*THE NEGATIVE ONE*
I ask him if I'm there.

VISITOR 1
I imagine the actor there, at that place.

*THE NEGATIVE ONE*
I ask what we're doing there.

VISITOR 1
I imagine what we're doing, together.

**THE NEGATIVE ONE**
I tell him to open his eyes.

VISITOR 1
I open my eyes.

**THE NEGATIVE ONE**
The split second he opens his eyes, I ask him
whether he likes me.

VISITOR 1
I tell him I like him.

**THE NEGATIVE ONE**
I ask him if he could imagine us being friends,
good friends.

VISITOR 1
I tell him I imagine we could be friends. Good friends.

**THE NEGATIVE ONE**
I ask him if it would last long, the friendship.

VISITOR 1
I tell him how long the friendship could last.

**THE NEGATIVE ONE**
I propose a toast to the potential of friendship.

VISITOR 1
We bring a toast to our imaginary friendship.

*THE NEGATIVE ONE*
I tell him we are being expected outside the
booth. I take him out into the open space.

02.                          *PERFORMER TWO*

### THE SILENT ONE
I take my visitor to my booth. I show him his
chair. We sit down.

**VISITOR 2**
The tall woman in the black evening dress takes me to a cabin.
She offers me a chair at a little table. The light is warm, like a
candle. We sit down opposite each other.

### THE SILENT ONE
I pour a drink. It's a sugary liquor. I don't
speak. I raise my glass, we drink.

**VISITOR 2**
She pours my glass. I drink. I ask her name. She doesn't respond.

### THE SILENT ONE
I don't answer his questions. If he keeps
talking, I say:


*I don't need to talk.*
*Shall we try silence?*


**VISITOR 2**
She tells me to shut up, in a gentle way. She stares at me.

> ### THE SILENT ONE
> I look into his eyes, copy his facial expressions.
> I slip my hands closer to his.

VISITOR 2
Her hands come closer. Mine are on my lap. Without uttering a word, she makes me put my hands on the table.

> ### THE SILENT ONE
> I touch his hands, subtly.

VISITOR 2
She touches my hands, I start touching hers.

> ### THE SILENT ONE
> I let him touch me.

VISITOR 2
I feel free to touch her arms.

> ### THE SILENT ONE
> I turn my head away, tuck my hair behind my ear. I caress my neck. I take his hand and put it on my neck.

VISITOR 2
She lets me touch her neck.

> ### THE SILENT ONE
> If he's gentle and I like him, and he's pulling me closer, I give in. Sometimes, lips touch.

**If I'm not sure whether he finds me beautiful or not, I ask him:**

*Do you think I'm beautiful?*

**VISITOR 2**
**I tell her she's beautiful.**

                    *THE SILENT ONE*
**I guide him out of the booth, into the open space.**

03.                           *PERFORMER THREE*

*THE CRITICAL ONE*
I ask how old she is.

**VISITOR 3**
I tell her my age.

*THE CRITICAL ONE*
Since I'm a young woman, most of my visitors
are older than me. Very often, there's even a
generation gap. I calculate the difference in
age and then ask her where she was, all those
years ago.

**VISITOR 3**
She asks where I was when I was her age. I tell her what I was
doing at that time, what my life was about, the people I was
involved with.

*THE CRITICAL ONE*
I have a little chat about her life as a young
woman. I try to picture how she was, how she
looked, what she might have lost or gained on
the way. I try to sense if she's talking with nos-
talgia about the past. Since most people were
students at my age, I ask her what she studied,
and if her degree is useful for her current job.

**VISITOR 3**
I tell her to what extent my degree is relevant for my job.

#### THE CRITICAL ONE
I ask her whether she still feels challenged.

##### VISITOR 3
I tell her how I feel about challenges in my life.

#### THE CRITICAL ONE
I ask her whether she feels she's still growing,
evolving. I ask her about her current ambitions,
if she still has them.

##### VISITOR 3
I tell her my ambitions for the future.

#### THE CRITICAL ONE
I ask her whether she's planning to fulfill
her ambitions. This is an important issue for
me because I have a strong personal belief
that happiness is also determined by actively
working on the realisation of dreams. This
involves risks, so I ask her whether she'd
change her job if it got boring.

##### VISITOR 3
I tell her how I think about changing jobs if boredom slips in.

#### THE CRITICAL ONE
I ask her if she takes care of herself.

**VISITOR 3**
She asks me if I take care of myself. I don't understand what she means by that.

> *THE CRITICAL ONE*
> I ask her what it means to her, taking care of herself.

**VISITOR 3**
I tell her what I understand by taking care of myself, physically and mentally.

> *THE CRITICAL ONE*
> I ask her whether she does it for herself or for others.

**VISITOR 3**
I tell her I take care of myself for myself.

> *THE CRITICAL ONE*
> I ask about her love life. Whether she's in a relationship, I ask her if she's giving herself fully to her partner. If she's not, I ask her if she has given herself fully in previous relationships, and if she believes she could do that again in the future.

**VISITOR 3**
I tell her about my relationship. I tell her I don't give myself fully to my partner. She seems slightly disapproving.

> ### THE CRITICAL ONE
> I ask her if she makes compromises.

### VISITOR 3
I tell her about the compromises I made in my life.

> ### THE CRITICAL ONE
> I play the eye-game with her.

### VISITOR 3
With my eyes closed, I imagine us together. I imagine what we're doing.

> ### THE CRITICAL ONE
> I tell her I'd like to do something else than she suggests. I ask her if she'd like to go my way.

### VISITOR 3
She wants to do something else. I tell her that's fine by me. I tell her I like her, that I can imagine us being friends. We drink to friendship.

> ### THE CRITICAL ONE
> I guide her out of the booth, into the open space.

**NOTE**

There are three versions of the Critical One. The part was created by Nicolaas Leten, who had a checklist involving income, fidelity, physical attraction, taste etc. The conversation felt like a gentle cross-examination, very close to the format of speed-dating. At one point, Nicolaas showed his visitors three nude pictures of him and asked them which one they preferred. It was a test to see whether they'd chose the one he liked best. Karolien De Bleser created a new 'critical' version, focussing on beliefs: in soul mates, in God, in eternal love, in perfection. She also asked whether the visitors were afraid of death. The above version was created by Charlotte De Bruyne.

This is an important aspect of the ownership we strive for. We strongly believe that the performer, even if he or she replaces another actor, needs to feel the part is his or hers. Charlotte and Karolien moulded the 'critical' part to their own interests, adapting it to their personality and appearance. In the end, if they're going to ask the same questions to hundreds of people, they'd better be the ones they get really excited about.

04.                    *PERFORMER FOUR*

*THE FEMALE SEDUCER*
I smile at my visitor, make him feel comfortable
and relaxed. I try to create a casual atmosphere.
I ask him simple questions: whether he's from
the neighbourhood, what he does for a living.

**VISITOR 4**
I tell her where I'm from, what my job is.

*THE FEMALE SEDUCER*
I ask him whether he enjoys his job. If he doesn't,
I ask him what he'd prefer to do instead.

**VISITOR 4**
I tell her how I feel about my job.

*THE FEMALE SEDUCER*
I raise my glass and say cheers:

*To us.*

**VISITOR 4**
We bring a toast 'to us'.

> ### THE FEMALE SEDUCER
> I ask about his love life. If he's in a relationship,
> I ask whether he's still in love. If he's single,
> I ask if there's anything he misses – I suggest
> intimacy.

**VISITOR 4**
I tell her about my relationship, about the feeling of being in love.

> ### THE FEMALE SEDUCER
> I ask him whether he believes in love at first
> sight and whether he has ever experienced it.

**VISITOR 4**
I tell her what I think about love at first sight.

> ### THE FEMALE SEDUCER
> I ask him if he believes in first impressions. I get
> him to talk about his first impression of me and
> I tell him mine.

**VISITOR 4**
We talk about our first impressions of each other.

> ### THE FEMALE SEDUCER
> I ask him to imagine how people close to him
> would describe him. How his partner would
> describe him.

**VISITOR 4**
I tell her what my closest friends and relatives would say about me. What my partner would say about me.

>*THE FEMALE SEDUCER*
>I ask him if he thinks these things are true.

**VISITOR 4**
I tell her how many of those things are true.

>*THE FEMALE SEDUCER*
>I ask him if there are things people don't notice about him. Things he wishes they'd noticed more.

**VISITOR 4**
I tell her the things about me that go unnoticed. I tell her I wish they'd be noticed more.

>*THE FEMALE SEDUCER*
>I ask him if he's the sort of person people turn to when they feel bad.

**VISITOR 4**
I tell her what I do when a friend is in distress.

>*THE FEMALE SEDUCER*
>I ask him about the most romantic thing he has ever done for someone.

VISITOR 4
I tell her about a romantic thing I once did.

> THE FEMALE SEDUCER
> I ask him about the most spontaneous thing he
> did in the past year.

VISITOR 4
I tell her about a moment in the past year when I did something unpremeditated.

> THE FEMALE SEDUCER
> I ask him what he finds beautiful in a woman,
> what attracts him in women.

VISITOR 4
I tell her what makes a woman attractive to me.

> THE FEMALE SEDUCER
> I play the eye game. I ask him to take me to a
> special place.

VISITOR 4
I imagine a special place where I can take her.

> THE FEMALE SEDUCER
> I ask whether we're alone, close.

VISITOR 4
I imagine I'm alone with her, close.

> ### *THE FEMALE SEDUCER*
> I ask whether it's romantic, whether we're
> kissing. If we do, I ask whether it's passionate.

**VISITOR 4**
She suggests a kiss. I make a choice.

> ### *THE FEMALE SEDUCER*
> I ask him whether he likes me, whether we
> could be friends.

**VISITOR 4**
I tell her I like her and we could be friends. We cheer to
friendship.

> ### *THE FEMALE SEDUCER*
> I guide him out of the booth, into the open
> space.

05.                    *PERFORMER FIVE*

**THE MALE SEDUCER**
**I behave like a gentleman from start to finish.**
**It starts with the way I offer my woman the**
**chair. She needs to feel well-treated. I try to be**
**flirtatious in a subtle way. Otherwise, the effect**
**is intimidating or a downright turn off.**

**I ask about her day. Whether she has done**
**something special, how she feels.**

VISITOR 5
I tell him how my day has been so far.

*THE MALE SEDUCER*
**I ask her what she does for a living.**

VISITOR 5
I tell him about my job.

*THE MALE SEDUCER*
**I ask what she likes doing in her spare time.**
**I look for common interests.**

VISITOR 5
I tell him how I spend my spare time.

*THE MALE SEDUCER*
**I ask her how her intimate friends would**
**describe her.**

VISITOR 5
I tell him how my friends would describe me.

> THE MALE SEDUCER
> I ask about her passions. What makes her
> happy. This part of the conversation may take
> a while. I show a lot of interest, ask a lot of
> additional questions depending on what she's
> willing to share.

VISITOR 5
I tell him about my passions, the things that make me happy.
He's asking a lot of questions and he seems interested. I can
tell he's trying to make me feel special.

> THE MALE SEDUCER
> I ask her if she has any bad habits. If she's
> reluctant to name any, I give an example of my
> own. I act as if it will be our little secret.

VISITOR 5
I tell him one of my bad habits.

> THE MALE SEDUCER
> I ask her what she finds important in a
> relationship.

VISITOR 5
I tell him what's important in a relationship.

> ### THE MALE SEDUCER
> I play the eye-game with her. I push to be alone with her in her fantasy.

### VISITOR 5
I imagine him and me alone.

> ### THE MALE SEDUCER
> I ask her whether I can come closer, whether I could kiss her.

### VISITOR 5
I have to decide to let him come closer. I have to choose whether or not I let him kiss me. I tell him I like him. I tell him I can imagine us being friends.

> ### THE MALE SEDUCER
> I guide her out of the booth, into the open space.

06.

**NOTE**
**In the middle of the space there is a circle of chairs. All the performers take their visitors to the circle and offer them a seat. There is a fixed seating plan; the visitors always sit to the performers' right. The music fades out and the booth lights are dimmed. There's only a cold light on the circle.**

**THE VISITORS**
**We're sitting in a circle, next to our actor. We're looking at each other. We don't speak.**

*THE PERFORMERS*
**We are preparing what we're going to say about our visitors. We have five slots to make statements, so we're trying to build an arc. When we've finished, we look up, which is the signal for the critical one to open the group session.**

## 07.　ROUND I

### THE CRITICAL ONE
I welcome everyone. I say my name and I
introduce my visitor.

### THE PERFORMERS
We say hello to the visitor, all together.
We make it sound monotonous like in a
ritual. We repeat this every time a visitor is
introduced.

### THE FEMALE SEDUCER
I introduce myself and my visitor together,
using the phrasing 'we are...'.

### THE MALE SEDUCER
I introduce myself and my visitor.

### THE NEGATIVE ONE
I introduce myself and my visitor.

### THE SILENT ONE
I introduce myself and I say I don't need to
know my visitor's name.

### THE CRITICAL ONE
Since I've opened the group conversation,
I take the lead. In this case, I welcome the
silent one's visitor, just to make sure he's
comfortable.

## 08.   ROUND II

### THE CRITICAL ONE
I state three positive points about my visitor.

### THE FEMALE SEDUCER
I state what I have in common with my visitor, preferably concerning our ideas about relation-ships or beauty.

### THE MALE SEDUCER
I state my visitor's passions and interest, focus-ing on the ones we have in common. I state what she finds important in relationships.

### THE NEGATIVE ONE
I state that my visitor has wished someone dead. If this is not the case, I tell the group how my visitor deals with anger. If anger is not an issue, I tell the group about my visitor's greatest fear.

### THE SILENT ONE
I say I'm beautiful.

### PERFORMERS
We all look at the silent one's visitor, for a brief moment, acknowledging that he finds her beautiful.

## 09.   ROUND III

### THE FEMALE SEDUCER

I start the third round with a statement about my visitor's way of being romantic or adventurous. I use the information about the most romantic thing he has ever done, or the most spontaneous thing he has done in the past year.

### THE NEGATIVE ONE

I add another negative point to my first comment. For this second statement, I might choose issues of jealousy, the criticism of friends, or the topics fear, anger, resentment, if I haven't already dealt with them in the first slot.

### THE CRITICAL ONE

Looking at the negative one, I say another positive point about my visitor, stressing the word 'positive' to indicate that the negative one is somewhat off track. The positive point is about my visitor indulging me, which I take from the eye game.

NOTE
In the other versions, the same fixed interaction takes place. Nicolaas states that his visitor can stare at him for a very long time, referring to the nude pictures. The Negative One asks if that's scary. In the Karolien-version, the positive point is about perfectionism. The Negative One asks if perfectionism is considered a positive thing.

### THE NEGATIVE ONE
As a fixed interruption in the script, I reinterpret the critical one's positive point. I say that the visitor is apparently easily influenced.

### THE CRITICAL ONE
I correct the negative one: my visitor was just taking care of me.

### THE MALE SEDUCER
I tell the story of me and my visitor in the fantasy. I conclude with the kiss. There are several variations: 'I tried to kiss her, but she wouldn't let me', 'I kissed her, but she didn't kiss me back' or simply 'we kissed'.

### THE SILENT ONE
I say:

*We touched each other in a dark room.*

### THE FEMALE SEDUCER
As opposed to the silent one's focus on the physical aspect, I play up the mental connection between me and my visitor. I use the fantasy of the eye game to prove how we get along.

## 10.   ROUND IV

### *THE CRITICAL ONE*
**I say:**

*That's all very well, but now it's time for the negative points.*

### *THE FEMALE SEDUCER*
**I say:**

*X (the negative one) has already started.*

### *THE NEGATIVE ONE*
**I ask my visitor:**

*Am I being too negative?*

## VISITOR 1
I give my actor feedback on his representation of me.

### THE CRITICAL ONE
I state one of my visitor's negative points.
I draw on the topics of happiness, taking care,
compromises, risk-taking or willingness to give
herself fully in a relationship. For instance,
I could say my visitor doesn't take care of
herself. I could say she's too afraid to engage
fully in a new relationship. I could say she
doesn't have any ambitions anymore.

### THE SILENT ONE
If I had a nice experience with my visitor, I say
I don't have any negative points. I add that
he has been very respectful and attentive, or
that he knows how to treat a woman, that he's
sensual or tender. One of my favourite lines,
with young men, is 'I like the fragility of young
boys.' If my visitor was rude, forward or licen-
tious, then I state that he's been disrespectful.

### THE MALE SEDUCER
I reveal my visitor's bad habit. I try to make it
sound cute and forgivable.

### THE NEGATIVE ONE
Bearing in mind that my visitor wants me to be
more positive, I state an underlying problem in
his life and try to suggest a way out.

*THE FEMALE SEDUCER*
**During the negative one's slot, I copy my visitor's posture.**

## 11.   ROUND V

### *THE FEMALE SEDUCER*
**I say to the negative one:**

> *I don't know what happened*
> *between the two of you, but we*
> *had a great time. We are very*
> *comfortable with each other.*

### *THE CRITICAL ONE*
**I add:**

> *Yes, you look very relaxed together.*

### *THE SILENT ONE*
**I say:**

> *Yes, look at the legs and the arms,*
> *it's the same.*

### THE NEGATIVE ONE
**I say:**

*Yes, you look comfortable together,
but I don't think it would last
between the two of you.
I don't think you're the kind of
man who could handle her.*

### THE FEMALE SEDUCER
**I whisper to my visitor:**

*He's just being negative.*

### THE SILENT ONE
**I say:**

*We could have something together,
because we don't need words to
understand each other.*

**If my visitor talked too much, I say:**

*We couldn't be together, because*
*he needs too many words and*
*I prefer silence.*

*THE CRITICAL ONE*
**I ask the negative one about his 'relationship'.**

*THE NEGATIVE ONE*
**I use the fantasy of the eye game to describe the potential friendship. I use the word 'surprise' or 'disappointment', depending on the level of intimacy and involvement between us in the fantasy. If my visitor didn't let me in, I'm disappointed. If the fantasy was imaginative and we were on the same wavelength, I'm surprised.**

*THE CRITICAL ONE*
**I use my visitor's ability to make herself happy as a gauge for potential friendship.**

## 12.  ROUND VI

### *THE FEMALE SEDUCER*
I ask the critical one to score her visitor on happiness.

### *THE CRITICAL ONE*
I give my visitor a mark out of ten for happiness.

### *THE FEMALE SEDUCER*
I ask the visitor how high she'd mark herself.

**VISITOR 3**
I give myself a score out of ten for happiness.

### *THE MALE SEDUCER*
I say to my visitor:

> *Do you want me to tell you what
> I think about you?*

I take her out of the circle, into a corner of the space. I whisper to her:

*Could you wait here until I give
you a sign? Then you can return
to the circle.*

I return to the circle, alone, and call the group
closer. I tell everybody what I think of my
visitor. I try to anticipate and mirror what she'll
say about me. I give her the sign to return.

## VISITOR 5
I allow my actor to say what he thinks about me. He takes me
into a corner of the space, asks me to wait there until he gives
a sign for me to come back. I'm standing in the corner while he
returns to the circle. I hear him whispering to the others. Then
he gives me the sign and I return to the circle.

### THE MALE SEDUCER
As my visitor returns to the circle, I walk away.

### THE NEGATIVE ONE
I ask the visitor what she thinks of the male
seducer. Whether she could trust him, whether
she'd like to get to know him better.

## VISITOR 5
I tell the group what I think of my actor.

### THE MALE SEDUCER
I return to the circle.

### THE NEGATIVE ONE
I ask my visitor if I can give him a hug.

**VISITOR 1**
I agree to a hug.

### THE NEGATIVE ONE
I hug him.

### THE FEMALE SEDUCER
I ask my visitor if we had a 'click' – a connection.

**VISITOR 4**
I tell the girl I believe we had a connection.

### THE CRITICAL ONE
I say to Visitor 4:

*You don't have to say 'yes', you
don't have to indulge her.*

If he insists that there was a connection,
I say:

*Then I want to see it.*

### THE SILENT ONE
I challenge them to show the connection.

### THE FEMALE SEDUCER
I propose a kiss. If I notice my visitor is very uncomfortable with this, I suggest a hug. In case there's no connection or too much hesitation, I walk away.

## VISITOR 4
I respond to my actors' suggestions.

### THE FEMALE SEDUCER
I reveal my visitor's relationship status to the group.

### THE SILENT ONE
I unbutton my top and show my breasts to my visitor. I say:

*Is this what you wanted to see?*

Sometimes I say, before I take it off:

*I'll give you something to think about.*

**VISITOR 2**
I tell the actress how I feel about seeing her breasts.

> ### THE SILENT ONE
> I put my top back on. I get up, stand in the middle of the circle. I reach out for my visitor. He gets up, we look into each other's eyes. When the music starts, I dance with him. A slow. We spin around.
>
> ### THE PERFORMERS
> We look at the silent one dancing with her visitor. One by one, we invite our visitors to join in. While we dance, we ask for our visitors' addresses. We offer them a piece of paper to write it down.

**THE VISITORS**
The actors ask for our addresses. Some of us write it down.

> ### THE PERFORMERS
> We take our visitors back to the line-up. We say goodbye.

**THE VISITORS**
The actors take us back to the marks on the floor from the beginning. We kiss goodbye.

> ### THE PERFORMERS
> The curtain drops.

**THE VISITORS**
**The usher comes and leads us out. The light in the dressing room has changed. We see a wall full of letters. We get only a few minutes, enough to figure out we're looking at letters written by previous visitors to their actors.**

*THE PERFORMERS*
**We return to our cabins, write down some key words about our visitors. We clean our glasses for the next group. We gossip about our visitors.**

**'THE END'**

**THE VISITOR**
**I receive a handwritten letter from my actor.**


**THE END ·**

# A GAME OF YOU

A 25-minute journey through a mirror palace of personal projections:

Visitor

Avatar

Visitor

Avatar

# OUTLINE

'A Game of You' is a one-on-one labyrinth of mirrors and projections. A single visitor is guided through rooms and corridors, where he meets both real and virtual people, who gradually create a character out of him or her, based on the projections of others as well as their own. It's about the subjectivity of self-image and how the world is a projection of our own experience.

'A Game of You'
is the third part of the
Personal Trilogy

## REQUIREMENTS

- A darkened space.
- Four booths, identical in size, interconnected by corridors.
- Red curtains.
- Lightbulbs and shaded lamps.
- A two-way mirror.
- A microphone to record voices.
- A webcam.
- Writable CD's.
- A projector.
- Two handset telephones.
- Laptops, a surround soundsystem.
- Quicktime.
- Playmobil figurines, notepads, pencils, (four identical) jars of water.
- The four booths should look similar in design, but different in atmosphere.
- For the visitor, they ought to be recognizable as variations on the same basic room.
- Although the structure of the space looks simple on paper, the visitors should feel like they're in a labyrinth.

## CREDITS

Created by
  Alexander Devriendt
  Charlotte De Bruyne
  Kristof Coenen
  Nicolaas Leten
  Maria Dafneros
  Joeri Smet
  Eden Falk
  Aurélie Lannoy
  Sophie De Somere

First performed
  January 29th, 2010
  KC België, Hasselt, BE

Originally produced by
  Ontroerend Goed
  BAC (Battersea
    Arts Centre)
  National Theatre Studio
  Vooruit
  KC België
  Inkonst
  Richard Jordan
    Productions Ltd.
With the support of the
  Flemish Community
  Province of East-Flanders
  City of Ghent

# CREATION

Before the first rehearsals of 'A Game of You' started, we already knew quite well what we wanted to achieve with this project.

Our first two individual shows had taught us a lot about working one-on-one. 'The Smile Off Your Face' had been performed for five years, 'Internal' had just won three awards at the Edinburgh Festival. We had encountered thousands of visitors in an immersive theatre setting, so we felt we had gained a great deal of expertise in constructing a play for a single audience member.

In exploring the boundaries of the relationship between performer and visitor, 'Internal' had been a challenge. The show blurred the distinction between reality and fiction, at the risk of confusion and too emotional an impact on the visitor. From the outset of 'A Game of You', we felt we wanted to protect the visitor more. Physically – after tying people up in wheelchairs and blindfolding them or pairing them up with a performer as a companion and guide, we wanted to give them as much freedom as possible – but also mentally: we wanted to relieve them of emotional stress and any pressure of expectation. We challenged ourselves to create a performance that would work even for the least engaging or cooperative spectator.

Another issue was the social dimension of the performance. In 'Internal', the sharing of personal information among other visitors was perceived by some audience members as a breach of privacy. Whenever this aspect of the show had leaked, we noticed some visitors felt compelled to raise their guard, which made the experience less rewarding. In 'A Game of You', we made sure the visitors met only performers, which allowed us to be more confronting without them feeling exposed.

During our journeys with the two previous immersive shows, sometimes in themed one-on-one festivals, we felt that for many audiences and programmers, individual theatre was synonymous with 'intimate' theatre. 'The Smile Off Your Face' lived up to the expectation of a tactile, sensory experience involving physical contact and personal care, but we became convinced that the one-on-one form could communicate broader themes. We shifted our focus from the intimate to the individual. Even 'one-on-one', set in a labyrinth of mirrors and projections, was redefined as 'one-on-oneself'. The very idea of confrontation with oneself became the centre point of the creation process.

Two ideas were pivotal for the performance:

· A dream of the director in which he encountered three versions of himself. The tension this produced seemed worth exploring.

· The philosophical speculation that everything you perceive around you is a projection of your inner world. Intellectually, it's easy to accept this as an objective truth, but on a practical, everyday level, the consequences for your view on reality are devastating and impossible to consider.

# SCRIPT

As in the previous one-on-one performances, we will describe the experience of the visitors and the experience of the performers separately. We will call the performers 'avatars' – this is the term we use in the performance. At the centre of the performance is the Dungeon Master who keeps an overview of everything.

The visitor we describe here is, of course, fictional. We use his voice not only to give an impression of the trajectory, but also to express the deeper layers of the performance. Real visitors rarely get the insights we describe instantaneously, but we assume they seep through after the performance.

00.

### AVATARS
### DUNGEON MASTER
### & USHER

Before the performance starts, we make a list
of avatars, from 1 to 5. The order decides on
which avatar can see another avatar perform.
For the rest, it's a random order since we
cannot choose a visitor, we just take the next
one who comes in.

When we're ready to begin, the Dungeon
Master starts the soundscape. It's a recording
of different voices describing people, with an
eerie, ambient tune underneath. The Dungeon
Master remains seated at his table in the
middle of the labyrinth during the whole show.

When it's time, the usher fetches the first
visitor. Avatar 1 takes a seat behind the mirror
of the first room, the waiting room, so he can
observe the visitor coming in.

## THE VISITOR
I'm waiting in a darkened room, alone. An usher comes and gets
me. He takes me to another dark space, with a small red curtain
closing off a doorway. There's light shining from inside.

## 01.   WAITING ROOM

**THE VISITOR**
The usher moves the curtain away and reveals a tiny room
with a big mirror on the wall, two chairs facing it and a little
table with playmobil figurines, a jar of water, plastic cups, a
notepad and a pencil. He tells me to sit on the first chair and
help myself to a glass of water.

> *DUNGEON MASTER*
> I start recording the scene in the waiting room
> from a webcam underneath the mirror.

**THE VISITOR**
The usher leaves. I'm alone again, in front of the mirror.
Nothing happens.

> *AVATAR 1*
> I'm obversing my visitor from behind the mirror.
> I copy his posture, his movements and gestures.
> While I'm copying, I select at least three remark-
> able actions that I will reproduce later on. The
> waiting room is an ideal place for observation:
> people have no purpose or knowledge of what's
> going to happen, so the way they 'kill time'
> already reveals something about their nature.

> *AVATAR 2*
> At 1'20", counting from the moment the visitor
> entered, the usher lets me into the waiting room.

**THE VISITOR**
A woman enters the room and takes a seat next to me. She
starts talking. I'm not sure if she's a visitor or a performer.

> *AVATAR 2*
> Sitting next to the visitor, facing the mirror,
> I start talking about myself. First I tell him how
> I feel about the room, the situation, as if I was
> another visitor. I talk about the mirror, how it
> makes me feel, the things that strike me about
> my appearance. I explain my body language, the
> meaning of my gestures and postures. I tell him
> about my inner life, how I feel about myself.
>      At 3'00", the dungeon master gives a horn
> signal. I introduce myself. I use a man's name.

**THE VISITOR**
After she's been talking for a while, she introduces herself
with a man's name. It's clear to me she's a performer. I tell her
my name. She repeats it.

> *AVATAR 2*
> I tell him about my job, my relationship, my
> friends. I tell him about my ambitions, doubts,
> desires. I tell him the truth about myself.

> *AVATAR 1*
> I memorize the visitor's name and leave the
> space behind the mirror. In the backspace, on
> my way to the copyroom, I quickly write down
> my visitor's name and a few characteristics

I want to remember on a notepad. I walk around the set to prepare for the copy room.

### AVATAR 2

Everything I told him, refers to an existing person. It's not me. I play that person.

At 4'15" the dungeon master gives the second signal, a bell. I say:

*I'm talking about myself, but it's not only about me.*
*I think it should be about you too.*
*I think it's time for you to go inside.*

### THE VISITOR

The woman pulls back the curtain opposite the entrance and urges me to go in. I see a corridor lined with red curtains, illuminated by a light bulb. As I walk in, I see a person walking up to me.

### AVATAR 2

After my monologue, I get out of the waiting room and install myself behind the mirror, waiting for the next visitor to come in.

> ### *AVATAR 1*
> I'm facing my visitor in the red corridor. As he comes near, I mimic his movements.

### THE VISITOR
The man is imitating me. I try some movements to see how my 'mirror' image copies them.

> ### *AVATAR 1*
> When my visitor gets that I'm mimicking him, I freeze and ask him to come with me.

### THE VISITOR
He stops the game and brings me to another room.

## 02.   COPY ROOM

**THE VISITOR**
**I take a seat. Through a big open frame the size of the mirror**
**in the previous room, I see a space that looks exactly like the**
**waiting room: white wall, red curtains, light bulb, even the**
**table with the figurines and the water are identical. The man**
**who just imitated me comes in.**

> ### *AVATAR 1*
> **I enter the copy room and take a seat. From**
> **the start, I imitate the movements and postures**
> **of my visitor during the time he spent in the**
> **waiting room. Sometimes I repeat movements**
> **or exaggerate them, but never in a mocking**
> **way. I start asking questions about the motives**
> **and thoughts behind his body language. I ask**
> **if the visitor likes to talk to strangers. Is he the**
> **first to start a conversation? Or does he wait**
> **for others to talk to him? I use the formula 'you**
> **did this...', 'why?' or 'what were you thinking?'**
> **I pay special attention to the visitor's reactions:**
> **does he deny his behaviour, is he embarrassed**
> **about it? Has he analysed it before? Sometimes**
> **the visitor is completely unaware of his body**
> **language or tics. All of this yields significant**
> **information.**

**THE VISITOR**
**I'm being impersonated. The man seems to have observed me**
**closely, the way he mimics my gestures is very accurate. He**

asks me about my thoughts and feelings while I was waiting,
I try to put them into words. It feels as if we're trying to figure
things out together. He's obviously a performer, but the way
we interact is very natural, almost casual. Seeing him 'do'
me, I can't help thinking of the way I come across. It's quite
confronting.

### AVATAR 1

I remind the visitor of the moment when the
other avatar came in. I copy his physical interaction with her: leaning forward or backward,
smiles, nods, sudden changes in posture. I ask
him when he felt most comfortable: when he
was by himself or when he got company. I ask
him what he remembers of the conversation,
whether he liked her or not, if she told him
things he recognized in himself or in people he
knows. Usually, if there was any recognition,
visitors start talking about their own concerns
or views on life.

### THE VISITOR

The man makes me recall the conversation I had with the
woman in the waiting room. I tell him what comes to my
mind. He points out what my body language suggested during
the conversation. I tell him if that's correct. Again, I'm forced
to think about the relation between my outward appearance
and what's going on inside. Somehow, it seems impossible
to align these two. Or does my body reveal truths I'm not
conscious about?

> *AVATAR 1*
> At the 3'00" signal, time is up. I remind the
> visitor of the moment the avatar sent him
> through the red curtain, and I leave the copy
> room in the same way. Now I approach the
> visitor from behind. I open the curtain behind
> him and invite him to turn around. The first
> thing he sees is a projection.

**THE VISITOR**
The man opens a curtain behind me. As I turn around, I'm
facing video footage of me sitting in the waiting room, projected onto a white wall. Immediately, I can verify whether
the man's impersonation of my body language was correct.
But I'm mostly fascinated with my own image. Film is very
different from a mirror and in this footage, I'm unaware of
the camera, so it's seducing to think that this is 'the real me'.
I stare at the screen for a while.

> *AVATAR 1*
> I ask the visitor if he likes looking at himself.
> If he's happy with what he sees. I ask him if the
> image is different from what he imagines. I ask
> if there's something he'd like to change about
> himself.

**THE VISITOR**
I tell the man how I feel about looking at myself on screen.
I tell him what's different about the image compared to the
way I think I look. I tell him the things I'm not satisfied
about and what I would like to be different.

*AVATAR 1*

I ask him if he has a lot of mirrors in his house
and what's the first thing he focuses on when
he looks into them. I ask him whether he looks
into his own eyes sometimes and what he'd like
to see in there. I ask him whether he looked
into his own eyes today.

**THE VISITOR**

I tell him about the mirrors in my house. What I use them for.
I tell him what I'm looking for when I use a mirror. I tell him
what I want to see in my own eyes, what I saw in them today.

## 03.  PROJECTION TALK

*AVATAR 1*

When the shaded lamp in front of the projection screen is turned off, I invite the visitor to
follow me behind the screen. We sit down on
chairs, facing the screen. I switch the shaded
lamp back on to indicate the booth is occupied.
The projection is visible on both sides, so we're
watching footage of the next visitor in the waiting room. I start the 'projection talk'. The purpose is to make the visitor invent a life for the
person on the screen, just by observing him or
her. I ask questions, but this is mainly to stimulate the visitor's imagination. I start by telling
the visitor that we're going to play a game. This
is to take away the pressure and to surpress the
idea that it's all about judging people.

It's important to be patient with the visitors. Not everybody has a vivid imagination.
I try to find the right way to stimulate them, e.g.
by offering multiple choices, leaving a pause,
repeating previous answers to get them back on
track. I try to avoid yes-or-no-questions. In a
way, talking about other people is a relief after
the self-scrutiny of the previous rooms.

I start the questions:

*What do you see?*
*Do you know this person?*

**NOTE**
If they know the person, I
ask them to imagine they've
never seen him or her before.
This is hard, especially with
family members or close
friends, but then I try to
make them imagine an 'ideal
life' for the person. To avoid
this situation, we ask the
usher to separate people who
know each other and put a
stranger in between. We also
disencourage the visitors to
chat before they enter.

*How does she look?*
*Why would you say that?*
*Is she happy with the way she looks?*
*Is it important for her?*
*Is she attractive?*
*Who could she be?*
*What could she do for a living?*
*Is she good at it?*
*Is this what she always wanted to do?*
*What did she want to become when*
*    she was a child?*
*Does she earn a lot of money?*
*Do her colleagues like her? Why?*

*Is she like that in private?*
*What about her personal life...*
*First of all, what could be her name?*
*Does she have a partner?*
*Is it a new relationship or have*
*they been together for a while?*
*Are they in love?*
*Are they faithful? Are you?*
*Do they live together?*
*Does she have children?*
*What 's her house like?*
*Would you like to live there?*
*If you sat on her couch, would you*
*be comfortable?*
*Does she have pets? A cat, a dog?*
*Does she spend a lot of time there?*
*Does she have a lot of friends?*
*Is she a good friend?*
*Where does she hang out with them?*
*Does she drink? What is she like*
*when she drinks?*
*Does she dance or talk?*

**All of these questions can be altered or rephrased to suit the purpose: getting the visitor to create a character that reflects parts of himself. My task is to figure out which parts of the visitor's creation are a projection of his own life and which parts reveal his desires, ideals, worries or dislikes. Most**

of the time, the principle works, confirming the notion that it's hard to talk about others without talking about yourself.

**THE VISITOR**
I answer an endless series of questions about a person I don't know. It's like sitting on a terrace in a busy street and discussing passers-by, trying to guess what their lives look like. The more answers I come up with, the more 'real' the person becomes, as if there's some internal logic to the elements that constitute her life, and I just need to follow it. Some things I'm certain of, others make me hesitate, but my companion keeps pulling me through. I just hope the person on the screen can't hear me.

*AVATAR 1*
**My final questions explicitly turn the focus back to the visitor:**

*What could you have in common*
*with her?*
*Is there something you're envious of?*
*What would she think of you?*
*How would the first encounter be?*

**THE VISITOR**
Now I have to imagine a connection with the person I just invented. My companion hints at a possible encounter. I tell

him how I think that would be. I guess the person I've just made up would still be on my mind, even if she'd turn out to be totally different in reality.

> *AVATAR 1*
> When the image of the person is gone, I pull back the red curtain on my right side and reveal a pitch-dark corridor. I tell the visitor to walk through it, towards the other side. I close the curtain, switch the shaded lamp off to signal that the next avatar and visitor can come in, then I walk around the set to the next room.

## 04.   RED ROOM

**THE VISITOR**
I'm walking through a dark corridor. I don't know where I'm
going. I've been told to go straight on, so I'm just following
instructions.

> *AVATAR 1*
> I'm behind the room at the end of the corridor.
> I ran, to make sure I was here before the
> visitor. I turn on the shaded lamp in the room
> using a dimmer.

**THE VISITOR**
There's light at the end of the corridor. I walk towards it, into
another room. It has the same design as the previous rooms,
but this time the atmosphere is darker. The wall I'm facing
is painted black and the mirror is an opaque glass surface,
vaguely reflecting me. I take a seat. On the table in front of
me there's a phone. It starts ringing. I answer the call.

> *AVATAR 1*
> The phone conversation I'm about to have is
> very concentrated and complex. I will call my
> visitor as the character he just created. I've had
> very little time to prepare what I'm going to
> say, so I will need to improvise a lot and make
> quick decisions, based on the information I got
> out of the projection talk. I start by introducing
> myself with the name he gave to the woman in
> the projection. I thank him for it. I mention:

*You never choose your own name...*

I give a quick summary of my life: my profession, my relationship status, some details that mark my personality. I ask him to fill in the gaps, to tell me things I don't know about myself.

**THE VISITOR**
I'm having a conversation with the woman I've just created. She has a man's voice, but I get it's all about the game, so I don't mind. She asks me to tell her more about herself. I ask her what she wants to know.

*AVATAR 1*
I ask him why he made me the way I am, to motivate his choices. For instance, if he made me a single woman, I ask him why he didn't give me a partner. If he gave me a traditional, uneventful life, I ask him why he made me so average. If he made me an incompetent person, I ask him why he didn't give me more skills.

If the visitor only mentioned positive aspects, I ask if there is a dark side to me, if I hide secrets. I try to figure out what I'm trying to hide. I ask him if he could change something for me. I ask him for advice.

If he objects, I use the stock line:

*You've created me. I can't decide*
*for myself.*

**THE VISITOR**
**I'm forced to think about the way I look at other people. I know this woman isn't real, but she has a point in asking me why I've made all these assumptions about her. Even if I try to argue that I've been tricked into commenting on her, the essence is still that we all pass some kind of judgment on each other, on a daily base. I'm tempted to avoid the confrontation by telling her she 'simply looked like that', but that would be a poor argument. She asks me to change something about her present condition. I give her some suggestions. Inevitably, I fall back on my own life. The advice I give her, is advice I could give to myself or people I know. The more we talk, the more I realize that this character reflects me. I tell her about myself, we compare our lives. Strangely enough, I feel I can be totally honest with her.**

**In the end, she tells me she has to go. Before she puts down the phone, she wonders if this conversation was about her or about me. She says we'll figure it out.**

*AVATAR 1*
**The conversation has to stop at the 3'00" signal.**
**I put down the phone and turn off the light.**

**THE VISITOR**
**The voice is gone. I'm in the dark again.**

## 05.   DUNGEON MASTER

*USHER*
**When the light is out in the Red Room, I fetch the visitor and take him into the central space of the set.**

*DUNGEON MASTER*
**I offer the visitor a chair next to me.**

**THE VISITOR**
**The usher takes me into an open space. There's a woman behind a laptop. She beckons me and offers me a chair. I sit next to her. On the screen of her laptop, I can follow how she makes films of people sitting in the waiting room, projects footage on the projection screen and meanwhile records the conversations behind the screen. This looks like the nerve centre of the performance. She lets me hear my comments about the woman on the screen. I listen to my voice inventing a life for her. After the telephone conversation in the previous room, I listen to it differently. Then a CD is ejected from the laptop. The woman takes the CD and writes on it: 'ABOUT YOU' She puts it in paper sleeve and hands it over to me.**

*DUNGEON MASTER*
**I gave the visitor a CD with the recording of another visitor inventing a life for him.**

### USHER
I open the entry to the space behind the mirror
of the waiting room. I let the visitor sit down
and tell him to put the headphones on.

## THE VISITOR
Just as I thought the performance was over, the usher takes
me into another space, a small booth behind a two-way mirror.
I put the headphones on and watch.

### AVATAR 1
While my visitor is with the dungeon master,
I prepare the monologue in the back space.
I've got about three minutes, so I need to work
efficiently. First, I adjust my clothes to my visitor's style. I can put on a shirt or a T-shirt to
look more formal or casual. There are glasses,
scarves, bags in case we need accessories.
Sometimes we do funny things like fabricating
jewellery from paperclips or wrapping a hoody
around our heads to imitate a turban. Then
I reiterate the journey I made with my visitor.
The order of the monologue largely follows
the order of the rooms, so I start by repeating
the postures and gestures I remember from
the waiting room. I think of the things my
visitor said about the mirror, his appearance
and the way he feels about his looks. I make
a selection of remarkable quotes. I collect the
information I got from the red room: his job,
his relationship status, the way he relates to

other people, at which point in life he thinks
he is. There are other things I can use, if I got
the data: how he feels about waiting, if he likes
to judge people or not, if he has any specific
interests or passions, what happened during
his day before he came here. Colourful details
are always useful to make the monologue more
lively. Finally, I think of the impression my
visitor made on me. Is he happy? Is he satisfied
with his life? What's his main concern, what
are the things that truly define him? I think of
a statement I can make about him. It doesn't
have to be spot on, but plausible in view of the
information I gathered. The statement should
be daring, perhaps provocative. I do not need
to respect the visitor's view of himself, I'm
allowed to present my own intuition about him
as a sudden insight. I quickly rehearse my key
points and then I'm ready.

## 06.   THE MONOLOGUE

**THE VISITOR**
I see a woman waiting on the other side of the mirror. Next
to me, there is a woman observing her and copying her movements. I realize I'm behind the mirror of the waiting room, the
first room I entered. The woman on the other side of the mirror is a visitor, the woman next to me a performer preparing to
impersonate her.

  The man who accompanied me through the different
stages of the show must've been observing me here behind this
mirror while I was waiting, some twenty minutes ago.

*AVATAR 1*
At 1'20", counting from the moment the new
visitor came in, the usher lets me into the waiting room. I'm ready to deliver my monologue.

**THE VISITOR**
Then another person comes in, just like it happened with me.
But I recognize this one. It's the man who was with me all the
time, who mimicked me, asked me questions, made me talk
about the woman in the projection.

  He takes a seat. I immediately recognize the posture: it's
mine. He starts talking. Everything he says sounds familiar. He
talks about how he feels in the room: my words. How he feels
about the mirror: I told him this. He tells the new visitor about
the flaws in his face, what he would like to change about his
appearance what he sees when he looks into his own eyes.

  Meanwhile, he's looking into my eyes through the mirror,
as if 'I' am talking to myself.

I witness how my insecurities, inner thoughts, my philosophy of life are all laid out in front of me, behind this mirror, and I'm unable to interfere.

I can only watch this man being me. A version of me I could never come up with. It's not how I'd present myself and yet there's truth in it.

He introduces himself to the new visitor using my name. Now I figure out the woman in the beginning was impersonating a man watching her behind the mirror. She was playing a character, but the real person was there as a spectator. I see how the system works: it's a circle and this is the closure. I've become a character performed by an actor.

The man makes a statement about me. Not a literal repetition of things I've said. It sounds more like a summary, a conclusion. Something he has read between the lines on my journey through this labyrinth. It's me, it's not me. My acceptance of his view on me decides which one it is.

When he finishes, he sends the new visitor away into the corridor. He looks at me for a second, acknowledging my presence behind the mirror. The usher comes and fetches me. He takes me to the exit. I leave.

When I'm out, the CD is burning in my pocket. I want to listen to it as quickly as possible. I wonder what's on it. I've seen myself in the mirror and on a video. I've seen a version of myself performed by an actor. I've created a character which turned out to reflect a lot of me. I've discussed another person and…another person must've discussed me.

I put the CD on. I think I'm ready to hear what other people think of me •

p.160 'A Game of You'

# TEENAGE TRILOGY

ONCE AND FOR ALL
WE'RE GONNA TELL YOU
WHO WE ARE
SO SHUT UP AND LISTEN

A celebration of raw teenage energy.

Performer ONE
Performer TWO
Performer THREE
Performer FOUR
Performer FIVE
Performer SIX
Performer SEVEN
Performer EIGHT
Performer NINE
Performer TEN
Performer ELEVEN
Performer TWELVE
Performer THIRTEEN

Visitor Visitor Visitor Visitor
Visitor Visitor Visitor
Visitor Visitor Visitor Visitor
Visitor Visitor Visitor
Visitor Visitor Visitor Visitor
Visitor Visitor Visitor
Visitor Visitor Visitor Visitor
Visitor Visitor Visitor
Visitor Visitor Visitor Visitor
Visitor Visitor Visitor
Visitor Visitor Visitor Visitor

# OUTLINE

'Once And For All We're
Gonna Tell You Who We
Are So Shut Up And Listen'
is essentially: teenagers
play teenagers who play
teenagers. Fourteen young
performers act out all the
clichés attached to puberty
with an awareness locked
between indifferent cool and
soaring self-consciousness.
It's a kicking, playful, wild,
life-affirming, crazy, cheeky,
ribald, sensuous, intoxicat-
ing, funny and knockabout
celebration of all those
aspects of adolescence that
adults sweat over.

'Once And For All We're
Gonna Tell You Who We
Are So Shut Up And Lis-
ten' is the first part of the
Teenage Trilogy

· Thirteen teenagers between
  11 and 18 years old.
· Time.
· A rehearsal room that can
  act as a free space for the
  cast.
· A longing to celebrate
  teenage destruction.
· A disbelief in imposed
  rules as received truths.
· Thirteen different chairs.
· Nine rebellious songs of
  different eras.
· A collection of props
  bought together with the
  performers in a second
  hand shop.
  We used:
loads of plastic cups, rope,
lipstick, big garbage bags,
two pairs of roller skates,
a digital camera, bal-
loons, plastic waterbottles,
cigarettes, chalk, eyeliner,
sheets, a skateboard, over-
sized undies, Barbie dolls,
make up-remover, cheer-
leader pompoms, ribbon
twirlers, a little quad bike,
buckets, plastic clothes-
lines, a ramp, rags for
mopping, brooms, boxing
gloves, sunglasses, post-
its, fake blood, handbags,
feather dusters, broken
mobile phones, cush-
ions, a mannequin head,
sunglasses.
  Inevitably, the props you
choose will lead to different actions than the ones
described on pp. 174–177.

## CREDITS

Created by
  Alexander Devriendt
  (director)
In collaboration with
  Joeri Smet
And
  Aaron De Keyzer
  Barbara Lefebure
  Charlotte De Bruyne
  Christophe De Poorter
  Dina Dooreman
  Edith De Bruyne
  Edouard Devriendt
  Elies Van Renterghem
  Febe De Geest
  Helena Gheeraert
  Ian Ghysels
  Koba Ryckewaert
  Nathalie Verbeke
  (the cast)

First performed
  April 25th, 2008
  Kopergietery, Gent, BE

Originally produced by
  Ontroerend Goed
  Kopergietery
  Richard Jordan
    Productions Ltd.
With the support of the
  Flemish Community
  Province of East-Flanders
  City of Ghent

# CREATION

The first goal is to create a 'mother sequence': a collection of different actions you create together with the cast. Mainly what you should get is five minutes of messy horseplay. Make sure that all the actions they perform are things they really want to do. The whole performance will be built around this sequence. Each act in the play is a variation on this mother sequence.

The first step to create this mother sequence is to put the chairs in a row. They act as a structure the teenagers try to challenge but on the other hand also use as something to hold on to. The chairs also reflect the seating of the audience. Tell the cast to sit on the chairs and then tell them they can do anything they want. Play music. If nothing happens, go to a second hand shop and tell them they can buy anything they want. Try the exercise again, with the props. Watch and enjoy. Tape everything. Select each action you want to include in the play based on your own preference. Pay attention to the interaction between the cast members, that is the most important thing. Allow chaos. Try to make them forget about your presence. Only intervene when you are really needed. (In our rehearsals only one mirror broke.) Install one rule: 'Don't hurt anybody who doesn't want to be hurt.' Take at least 96 hours of rehearsal time to create this act.

When you've chosen a collection of actions, compose the sequence, so the cast can repeat it exactly. Give each player a different trajectory. The scene must start with the cast entering and sitting on the chairs and evolve more and more into a wild and free environment. Creating tableaus based on famous paintings/images is optional, but it helps to bring structure into the seeming randomness of the act. 'The Last Supper' by da Vinci and Delacroix's 'The Raft of the Medusa' were very useful to us.

When you have created the mother sequence, rehearse it, and try variations on it. The sequence acts as a basic structure to create each new scene, where each action reflects the 'mother' action. It's less important that the variation is close to the original, as long as the audience can see the resemblance.

During the creation of the mother sequence, use note cards to label every action so that you will be able to organize the whole process. The following is an overview of all our note cards and can help as an inspiration for creating the mother sequence.

Swap chairs
  Suffer the complaints
    Do whatever the girls ask
      Connect two others with a rope
        Crawl into a garbage bag
          Look at pictures on camera
            Pretend to be killed by someone
              Put a plastic cup in your mouth
            Airplane with someone
          Don't know what to do
          Mess around with someone
        Write with crayon on the floor
          Pretend to see your ex in the audience
      Copy the image of the Last Supper
    Smoke a cigarette in the sides
Gurgle
Make a fountain with your mouth
  Walk around in wetlook
    Have a wellness moment
      Play doggy
        Clean and mop
          Work to death
            Flip flop in oversized undies
              Pretend to kill someone
                Joyride with motorcycle toy
              Hang upside down
              Lean back on chairs
                Tumble backwards
            Pretend pain
              French kiss with someone
          Chill a little
            Crawl under a white sheet
        Burp words
      Blow up a balloon
        Empty balloon with hooting sound
    Make a balloonwilly
    Compliment someone's balloon willy
  Give slap/Get slapped

Pose for a photo shoot
   Play the Balloonwrestlegame
      Win it
         Lose it
            Strip someone naked
               Say 'dick' too many times
                  Confuse someone
                     Push away skateboard
                        Skate on someone's back
                     Stuff someone's mouth
                  Get nervous with someone
                     Separate whoever's together violently
               Let someone run over you
            Lie dead
         Fight with someone
      Be sarcastically sweet to someone
Pull back a chair
   Run away
      Limbodancing
         Say 'hello' to someone
            Destroy something
               Say 'I'm gonna beat my mother'
                  Hit someone with a handbag
                     Wander around
                        Get lost in yourself
                           Intervene in fight
                              Hurt someone by accident
                           Put some food in my mouth
                        Be hungry for someone
                     Spit on the floor
                  Get what you want
               Draw someone's attention
            Give someone a loving massage
         Have my picture taken by someone
      Bite the dust
   Strip for someone
Complain to someone
   Rollerskate around

Be a cheerleader
Write 'dick' on someone's forehead with lipstick
Remove make-up
Hug someone
Stand on chair
Be styled by someone
Sneeze
Be turned on by someone
Show my naked torso
Wave with top
Assemble and destroy a Barbie
Be helpful to someone
Make myself invisible
Something with a stuffed camel
Be invisible
Do some yoga
Build a pyramid with cups
Kick pyramid of plastic cups
Put a post-it message one someone's back
Make a parachute for Barbie
Ask for attention from the audience
Tumble on purpose
Hang on to someone
Check out the boys
Draw someone in
Make a washing line
Be beaten by someone
Get massage
Be angry at someone
Take a picture of the audience
Call someone a sissy
Fuck up photo shoot
Pinch someone
Fail a high five
Greet sarcastically
Instigate someone
Bite tits and thighs
Stir up a fight

Lie down
  Pretend to clean up
    Make faces
      Make eyes at someone
        Feel excluded
          Grope someone with pompoms
        Rant at someone
      Put lipstick on an audience member's face
    Draw someone out of his world

# SCRIPT

The following script is conceived as an instruction manual. We address the reader as the future director of a teenage performance based on how we made 'Once And For All We're Gonna Tell You Who We Are So Shut up And Listen.' Feel free to adjust the order of variations on the mother sequence according to your own insight and the material you created during rehearsals. Props can also vary. On the other hand, the atmosphere of total loss and bursting energy is compulsory.

## 00.   AUDIENCE ENTERS

From the moment the audience enters the theatre, allow the cast to scream, chat and cheer and make as much noise as possible from behind the curtains. They shouldn't be visible.

The only thing the audience sees on stage are thirteen different chairs, lined up in a neat row, facing the audience's seats. One skateboard is subtly visible with the gray grid side facing the audience.

When the audience is seated, the lights fade. The first of the cast to notice this screams out for silence. The cast waits until everybody shuts up.

## 01.   WELCOME TEXT

**An actor/actress enters the stage, alone.**
**To create this text, make a collection of all the prejudices the audience will feel when watching a play about teenagers. Present these clichés as truths. Make several parts incomprehensible. Let the actress/actor tease the audience. End with a collection of swear words.**
**For example:**

*Goodevening,*
*Welcome*
*We are…adolescents.*
*I mind being called like that*
*I don't mind being called like that*
*Whatever's in my mind it's a cliché*
*but tonight,* ~~kiteyou befrangeling~~*,*
*  trussonly see clichés*
*that we are free as birds*
*nothing* ~~faligefos~~
*that everything is still possible for*
*  us*
~~thaiwogeet~~ *rebel against the system*
~~toudart labeeu~~*rage,*
*do you understand what I'm*
*  saying?*
*(exaggerated)* ~~toudart labeeu~~*rage,*
~~eastromititainp~~ *and thormones*

*fantsickamits emotionally stuck*
  *and a danger to ourselves*
*and by looking at us*
*you have to start feeling old*
*or to see your romantic ~~miriadun~~*
  *~~els~~see confirmed*
*long back for your ~~frolick~~*
*or to envy us, that we are able to*
  *start over again*
*but actually,*
*we ~~calacerish~~ start over again as*
  *little as you*
*and ~~movialithayoucubdoingripst~~*
  *~~richaaaaaaaa~~*
*but fuckitsucksyoukississy*
  *shiddeshuddup'nmepee*


**She/he exits the stage.**

## 02.   BASIC VERSION/MOTHER SEQUENCE

| MUSIC | OPTIONAL SONG |
|---|---|
| A song from the teenage years of the main core of your audience, around five minutes long, a live version of the song will support the free and live atmosphere on stage. | The Velvet Underground, 'I'm Waiting for the Man' (Live at Max's Kansas City version) |

The music starts.

One by one the actors casually enter the stage and take a seat on one of the chairs.

Present your mother sequence.

End the mother sequence with the sound of a beeping alarm sound. Everybody immediately cleans up the stage and exits behind the curtains. At the end of every countdown let one actor or actress count down the last three beeps.

*Three,*
 *Two,*
  *One*

There is a moment of silence, during which the stage is exactly the same as before they entered.

## 03.   BASIC VERSION TWO

**SONG**
Same as previous (with a
short break in the song).

**The same music starts again and all the actions they performed in the previous scene are repeated exactly and with the same intention.**

**Even the mistakes they made, the reactions that differed from the 'ideal' version have to be copied exactly.**

**The chaos of the mother sequence is revealed to be a carefully choreographed piece of theatre.**

**NOTE**
The purpose of this duplicated version is to show the paradoxical experience of being a teenager. On the one hand, they seem to have great freedom but on the other hand they're becoming overly self-conscious. The prejudice against teenagers as chaotic and irresponsible creatures is countered by the discipline they show in meticulously copying the first act.

Another benefit of the repetition is that the fast-paced profusion of actions in the opening scene can be seen twice. By offering a second viewing, the actions are imprinted in the mind of the audience, which will then be able to identify the variations later on in the play.

**The only difference is this: after two minutes the music stops and you hear a drum sound ticking in the soundtrack. At that moment they freeze and look straight into the audience, trying to spot everybody who is watching them.**

**COMMENT**
This to accentuate the
self-consciousness and the
presence of the seemingly
neglected audience.

After that they continue their copy of the
mother sequence. Then suddenly the beeping
alarm bell sounds and everybody cleans up
the stage; even the cleaning up is a copy of
the previous clean-up. There is a moment of
silence, during which the stage is exactly the
same as before they entered.

## 04.   BALLET VERSION

**MUSIC**
Just a short classical song
you love, preferably lyrical or
opera, with a dramatic climax
to give a boost to the cast.

**OPTIONAL SONG**
Delibes Lakmé, 'Flower Song'

**The classical music starts and the cast perform their previous actions but this time as a ballet piece. The girls show off their ballet skills, the boys give it their best try. Everybody has to be deadly serious. The variation ends around the middle of the mother sequence.**

**COMMENT**
Most of the girls will have
some ballet- or dance-school-
training they can use, and
the boys won't.
    Embrace this cliché.

## 05.  JUMP VERSION

| MUSIC | OPTIONAL SONG |
|---|---|
| Any hardcore track is possible as long as it provides the opportunity to go crazy and dance without restrain. | Donkey Rollers, 'Revolutions' (hardbass) |

In the middle of the Ballet variation, the music switches to the heavy beats with a clear build-up towards a climax. The variation of the mother sequence is now reproduced as if they were on a party, but during the song the variation principle is fading and becomes a collective party moment. When the music erupts, they dance wildly, until somebody counts down and they all simultaneously perform the same choreography towards the audience. (We used the jumpstyle, which was the hype then in Belgium. Don't choose a silly dance; it works best if it is deadly serious.)

Then suddenly the alarm bell sounds. This time it's faster and everybody cleans up the stage.
      No countdown. There is only one person who doesn't exit the stage, because he sneakily wants to say something to the audience.

## 06. TEXT: I'M AFRAID

**He/she walks towards the front of the stage and addresses the audience directly.**
**Let him walk over the boundaries of the stage, maybe in front of the lights, as if he needs to escape the playground in order to talk to you.**

*I'm afraid*
*I'm afraid that I will do the same*
*like everybody before me,*
*that I will become like my parents*
*I want to do things differently but*
*somehow, I find that I can't*
*It's like I'm afraid that I'll be*
*forced to do the same –*

**NOTE**
The basic principle of this text is to explain the teenagers' fear of being ordinary and following the same life pattern as everybody before them. This text gives the audience a key to look at the play as a prison, from which the actors try to break free by performing different variations on the same set of actions. For this text, we chose a cast member who was an adopted child; he didn't know his real parents, and he once said that 'he didn't want to become like his foster parents.'

## 07. WORDS/ACTIONS VERSION

The speaker is interrupted by the other actors. In this scene, the actors copy the position of the mother sequence, but instead of performing the actions they only name them, always looking straight at the audience, robot-like, as if they are merely vessels for the actions they've performed.

For this scene you use the note cards of the mother sequence as text for the actors. Allow weird descriptions that only make sense to the cast. (See list on pp. 174–177)

The actor who was speaking to the audience tries to continue his text, but when he notices it's impossible he steps backward and names his action of the moment: 'Say your lines.'

This scene ends with some of the cast saying 'clean up' while they exit the stage.

The last one to exit should be the one who always cleans up the least in the rehearsal room. He says: 'pretend to clean up.'

No beeping alarm sound, but let the one responsible for counting down during clean-up say: 'Count down until it starts again.'

## 08. LOVE VERSION

**MUSIC**
A heartfelt love song, preferably with just a voice and a
guitar or piano.

**OPTIONAL SONG**
Jose Gonzalez, 'Heartbeats'

**The version in which everybody performs
all actions, but seductively, romantically
involved and walking on air. Allow the difference between the more innocent variations
the younger ones will perform and the more
'experienced' actions of the older ones. This
variation is interrupted way too soon.**

## 09.   RESISTANCE & BOYS-ONLY VERSION

In the middle of the love version the music stops. When the actors notice this, they drop their actions and turn towards the audience and the tech cabin. They protest and ask the technicians if they could do this variation all over again. After a long silence one of the boys ask if they can continue without the music.

Exit girls, calling the boys 'perverts', 'unromantic', 'losers' and other names. The boys are left behind and look awkwardly at the audience.

**COMMENT**

For this variation only the boys remain on stage. In a group of young performers, males will usually be in the minority. Make your selection of the cast to reflect this.

For this scene, the performers' over-awareness of the audience is important.

With more than half of the cast offstage, those who remain are no longer protected by the group. At the same time, keeping only the male performers is a great opportunity to show the awkwardness of teenage-boy interaction.

Choose two actions from the mother sequence for them to reenact. Each of the actions should require a girl, so at least one boy has to stand in for a girl. This will bring up machismo and latent homosexuality/-phobia.

One by one the boys sneak out, leaving just one of them on stage. When this boy becomes aware that he's left all alone, he runs away offstage muttering swear words.

## 10.   EMPTY STAGE VERSION

**SONG**
Peggy Lee, 'Is That All
There Is'

**NOTE**
Don't choose a different song
for this. It enriches this variation perfectly.

**This is the version in which the performers
remain offstage and throw the props onstage
chronologically, mirroring the mother sequence
but without the actors.**

**NOTE**
This version can be the most
poetic of the whole play, and
it creates breathing space in
the performance. The chrono-
logical order will allow the
audience to relive the mother
sequence in their minds.

## 11.   TEXT: THE SILENT GIRL'S EXPERIENCE

One girl enters the stage with all the props.
She grabs her chair and brings it in front of the
stage. She – it could also be a boy – recounts
the mother sequence from her point of view,
commenting on other performers and inter-
preting their actions, the way they relate to each
other. By this, she reveals that she is a careful
observer. Let her reflect about her position in
the group.

**NOTE**
Choose the performer who
is maybe the most silent
of them all and among the
youngest, but most impor-
tantly who possesses a racing
mind and sees everything.

One girl enters the stage to recollect a prop
(preferably a little quad bike that makes noise).
In doing so she interrupts the silent girl's
monologue.

**NOTE**
Choose the wildest girl of
your cast. Make her seem
unaware of what the speaker
is doing. She leaves the stage
noisily and remains audible
even behind the curtains.

When the noise stops, the girl continues,
slightly annoyed, and finishes her story.

## 12. DRUG VERSION

**MUSIC**
Psychedelic song with a dark edge and a feel of an ongoing intense trip.

**OPTIONAL SONG**
Monster Magnet, 'Cyclops Revolution'

**This is the version in which the cast performs a variation of the mother sequence as if they're under the influence. It is a variation where all the actions don't seem to work out, are left unfinished, unfocused. It should be the longest variation of all. Use smoke and dimmed lights.**

**COMMENT**
During rehearsals the younger ones will enact a more energetic, joyful variation whereas the older ones will enact more languid and weary actions. Make sure this version reflects these two different experiences, which depend highly on what they know or don't know.

During the creation you will come across darker fantasies of the older group of the cast. Allow them to share those in this scene.

## 13.   DOWN VERSION

| MUSIC | OPTIONAL SONG |
|---|---|
| A modern, slightly depressing song, perfect for a hangover. | (Part of) Radiohead, 'Videotape' |

**Together with the music, the previous version fades into 'the morning after'. Make the stage brighter. During the whole song only two or three actions are repeated, completely lacking willpower or enthusiasm. In the end the performers no longer do anything.**

## 14.   TEXT: BACK OFF

**When the music stops, one performer walks to the front of the stage, and looks at the audience.**
**In this text the purpose is to make the audience scream 'back off' and after that 'fart'.**
**Try to reach the moment where both the performer and the audience are screaming at each other to back off.**

NOTE
Choose the girl/boy with the most anger inside her/him so he/she can use this scene to find a release for that – or just the one with the loudest voice. For the one who makes the audience scream 'fart', choose the funniest or most mischievous one.

*I'm gonna count to three*
*and then you're all gonna shout*
*'Back off'*

*Okay, get ready,*
*no holding back*
*no waiting for the person next to*
*    you*

*At three, you will shout*
*'Back off'*

*One,*
*Two,*
*Three*

*[*

*...*
*]*

*No, seriously, this is really not*
*enough,*
*think about it,*
*When was the last time that you*
*shouted in public?*
*Go for it*
*Shout until you're hoarse*

*One,*
*Two,*
*Three*

*[*

*...*
*]*

*(some text depending on the audi-*
*ence's reaction)*
*I see some people thinking*
*'Ow, I won't do it, it's so weird, it's*
*so embarrassing'*
*Come on, it feels so good not to care*
*about that*

*Just let yourself go*
*Shout it*

*One,*
   *Two,*
      *Three*

*[*

   *...*
         *]*


*Come on scream it.*
*(screams)*

*One,*
   *Two,*
      *Threeeee*

*[*

   *...*
         *]*


**One actor jumps next to her.**


*No, no*
*I got a better idea*
*On three you're all gonna shout*

*'Fart.'*
*Okay?*

*One,*
   *Two,*
      *Three*

*[*

   *...*

      *]*

*Yeaaaah...*

**Music starts and with renewed energy they
clean up the stage.**

| MUSIC | OPTIONAL SONG |
|---|---|
| Short 20 second part of an uplifting song. | Shout Out Louds, 'Hurry Up' |

## 15.   SCHOOLPLAY VERSION

This scene is a variation of the mother sequence but everything is played as a simple-minded schoolplay.

Overacting is the key principle and all the things they remember from playing old-fashioned theatre. They pretend to be one happy family: mother, father and all their children say hello every time someone enters the stage.

When the cast is seated, everybody starts to do their actions from the mother sequence but in the style of a cliché schoolplay, acting childishly, like caricatures. Everybody acts happy, but trying to be inventive in playfully hurting each other is a nice extra. Gradually the actions become a little bit more aggressive, but always with a smile. When an actor asks his companion for advice everybody is silent. They still act as if they are members of one happy, well-mannered family.

*Actor 1:*
  *Brother, can I ask you some-thing manly?*

*Actress 1:*
  *Something manly!*

[

*Silence*

]

*Actress 2:*
   *Girls*
   *Something manly?*
   *Please close your ears!*
   *[Urges the other girls to put their*
   *fingers in their ears]*

*Actor 1:*
   *Well, lately, I'm getting tiny bits*
   *of hair around my doodle*

*Actor 2:*
   *Don't worry, I've been having*
   *that for years*

*Actor 1:*
   *Do I need to brush them?*

*Actor 2:*
   *No, they curl by themselves*

*Actor 1:*
   *Thank you brother*
   *I can always count on you…*

*Actor 1 & 2:*
   *Mum, it's okay!*

*Actress 2:*
*Girls...*
*[She indicates that the girls can*
*uncover their ears again]*

**Everybody continues with their actions. The playful agression will build up more and more to show their frustration of the prison they're in. The scene ends with one actress announcing that she wants to hit her 'mother'. She hits the actress playing the mother. She then asks the others if she's allowed to hit her again. Everybody consents. All family members start hitting one another.**

## 16.   OUTBREAK

**MUSIC**
Any climax of a wild electronic song will do.

**OPTIONAL SONG**
(Part of) Armand Van
Helden, 'Nympho'

**All the actors start fighting, the wildest girl in the group starts trashing the chair, until all the chairs are, for the first time in the play, scattered all over the stage.**

**This burst of violence should only take about twenty seconds.**

## 17.  TEXT: LET ME BE

**The music stops. Everybody is on the ground except for the girl who trashed the chairs. She doesn't come forward, and starts looking at the audience. Give this text to the wildest girl, the one you could barely control during rehearsals.**

*Let me be*
*Please*
*Let me be*
*You can ask all sorts of things from me*
*You can tell me what to do and*
    *what not to do*
*At what time I have to be home*
*You can do all that, I don't care*
*…*
*But I will be home late*
*whatever hour you give me*
*I will pass that limit*
*and I will be piss drunk*
*and I will not be ashamed of myself*
*I have no choice, you see?*
*I have to go too far…*
*The moment that some of you are*
    *thinking:*
*'Does she have to?'*
*'Does she really have to do what*
    *she's doing?'*

*Yes, I do,*
*Okay?*
*Because I need to go further, a lot*
*    further,*
*until I don't know what to do*
*    anymore*
*and it's not because you've been*
*    there and done that*
*that I shouldn't go there and do*
*    that*
*because everything has been done*
*    before*
*but not by me*
*not now*

## 18.   EXAGGERATED VERSION

**MUSIC**
Choose a post-rock song, uplifting and melancholic at the same time, with a nice build-up and a joyful climax.

**OPTIONAL SONG**
Explosions In The Sky, 'First Breath After Coma'

On the first notes of the song, everybody starts to clean up, eagerly but not rushed. One actor/actress is behind the curtains and asks every single cast member, by name, if they're ready. They answer 'yes' or 'almost', depending on where they are with their preparations for the final scene. When everybody's name is called out, and the stage is clean, the chairs and the skateboard back in place, like at the beginning of the play, he/she asks if everybody is ready. When they all shout 'yes', this last variation starts.

They enter the stage, mirroring the mother sequence, but the props they're carrying are bigger versions of the first ones. For instance: the plastic motorcycle in the first variation is replaced by a quad, a little plastic cup is a huge transparent bucket... When everybody is sitting on the chairs, they stare into the audience, like a silence before a nice storm.

After that they start to perform their actions from the mother sequence but multiplied, inflated, magnified and tenfold.

NOTE
In this scene you can also use props that were not used in the mother sequence. For instance, we used body paint and party spray to make a nice big mess. Whichever extra props you choose, always end with a giant heap of bodies and the messiest stage you have ever seen.

**Fade to black-out. Lights on. Actors bow for the audience.**

## 19. CLEANING UP

**MUSIC**
Also a post-rock song, preferably of the same band as the previous act, but maybe a little bit more nostalgic.

**OPTIONAL SONG**
Explosions In The Sky, 'Remember Me As A Time Of Day'

When the applause fades away, the music starts, and all the actors clean up the stage until it's finished. The doors are open so the audience can decide to leave or stay and watch.

**NO END ·**

# TEENAGE RIOT

A performance about the (im)possibility to rebel:

Performer ONE
Performer TWO
Performer THREE
Performer FOUR
Performer FIVE
Performer SIX
Performer SEVEN
Performer EIGHT

Visitor Visitor Visitor Visitor
Visitor Visitor Visitor
Visitor Visitor Visitor Visitor
Visitor Visitor Visitor
Visitor Visitor Visitor Visitor
Visitor Visitor Visitor
Visitor Visitor Visitor Visitor
Visitor Visitor Visitor
Visitor Visitor Visitor Visitor
Visitor Visitor Visitor
Visitor Visitor Visitor Visitor
Visitor Visitor Visitor
Visitor Visitor Visitor Visitor

# OUTLINE

'Teenage Riot' asks the question whether it's still possible to revolt, through eight teenagers who shut themselves away from the outside world in a shed on stage, communicating with the audience mainly through a camera. The performance explores the right to riot without providing solutions or a reasonable cause and reflects the chaos inside a teenager's mind. It's both for adults who forgot what it means to rebel and those who still feel the teenager inside them.

'Teenage Riot'
is the second part of the
Teenage Trilogy

- Eight teenagers between 13 and 17 years old.
- Time (approximately nine months, at a rate of two rehearsals a week).
- A wooden shed, blank so the teenagers can create their personal dream place inside.
- Objects that are usually kept out of reach of teenagers, e.g. cigarette vending machines, alcohol dispensers...
- A film camera.
- Energizing, inflammatory music.
- Arts-and-crafts material.
- A rehearsal space that can be turned into a mess.

## CREDITS

**Created by**
  Alexander Devriendt
    (director)
**In collaboration with**
  Joeri Smet
**And**
  Jorge De Geest
  Edouard Devriendt
  Alice Dooreman
  Ian Ghysels
  Marthe Hoet
  Nanouk Lemmerling
  Koba Ryckewaert
  Verona Verbakel
    (the cast)

**First performed**
  May 7th, 2010
  Kopergietery, Gent, BE

**Originally produced by**
  Ontroerend Goed
  Kopergietery
  Theatre Royal Plymouth
  Richard Jordan
    Productions Ltd.
**With the support of the**
  Plymouth City Council
  Arts Council England
  Flemish Community
  Province of East-Flanders
  City of Ghent

# CREATION

Like 'Once And For All We're Gonna Tell You Who We Are So Shut Up And Listen', 'Teenage Riot' is a reflection on puberty, as a life phase in which you can strongly disagree on everything, without the obligation to give an alternative. The former took the form of a celebration, the latter confronts us with teenage rebellion, revolt and resistance. 'Teenage Riot' explores the right to riot without proposing solutions or even providing a reasonable cause. The performance also reflects the chaos inside a teenager's mind: the bewildering range of options that life seems to offer when you're fourteen, the feeling of being lost in this abundance, the tangle of contradictions that comes with having too much choice, the loss of knowing who you are and what to do and the unmanageable anger that overpowers you.

'Teenage Riot' is set in a free space, created to give way to aimless anger and mindless provocation. The space takes the form of a shed in the middle of the stage. It's closed on all sides, its surface painted white – the audience can only guess how it looks on the inside. In this shed, eight teenagers shut themselves away from the outside world. They only come out for short moments, by accident, as a punishment or with a brief message for the people watching them.

Inside the shed, they do whatever they want. The rules of the outside world don't apply, there is no logic except their own. Communication with the audience runs on their terms, through a camera, displaying only what they are willing to show. Paradoxically, they shut themselves in but they constantly crave the attention of the audience – they want to be seen. The often extreme footage of gang bangs, pimps and whores, drinking, teenage pregnancy, torturing insects, etc. is projected onto the front wall of the shed.

Are they real or manipulated? The audience speculates, the performers know. In the end, they leave the shed and face the audience, only to confront them with their rage, their view on the current state of the world and their ambitions for the future.

Although performed by teenage performers, 'Teenage Riot' is not a performance for young people. It is addressed both at the adults who forgot what it means to rebel and those who still feel the teenager inside them. 'Teenage Riot' toured all over Europe and in Australia for several years and was described as 'a shock for adults' and 'a 50-minute onslaught' that leaves the audience discomfited by its frankness and exuberance.

### Cast: smaller than 'Once And For All'

There are several reasons:

· The stories in this show are more personal: more time and room for individual challenge is needed.
· The pedagogic side of the process demands the performers to develop deeply felt opinions and concerns about society, which might take a while before they grow.
· The selection of personalities is quite specific: choose kids who show a hint of rage, who are edgy, worked-up, likely to pass boundaries, curious, alert and eager to learn and understand what is going on in the world.

There are several steps, all of them crucial to the development of dramatic material and of the 'spirit of total freedom and riot' at the heart of the performance. We worked around different topics and media to achieve our goal.

1.   YouTube:

Watch YouTube clips posted by young people, preferably containing display of emotions, awkward confessions, weird behavior, aggression, exhibitionism or bullying. Look for those clips that push the boundaries and provoke extreme reactions. Ask the performers to consider whether the images are real or if they could be faked for maximum shock effect.

Using the clips for inspiration, let them record their own videos, individually and in small groups. Let them think of ideas that could work as a YouTube clip. Whether weird, outrageous, dangerous, violent or sexual, the clips should never be apologizing or explain their motives.

Four stories to give examples of how we generated material:

·   A fifteen-year old boy came up with the idea to create a series of sex instruction clips. In them, he tells the viewers in coarse and misogynistic language how to finger a girl properly, how to persuade a 'slut' to have anal sex or how to fake a male orgasm.

·   Two girls brought a jar of insects to the rehearsals, after a discussion about the largest size of animal they were able to kill without feeling guilty. They produced a video in which they cut up worms and centipedes into tiny pieces on a table cloth.

·   Two girls who were frequently accused of being obsessed with losing weight looked up the most extreme and damaging dietary tips on the

internet. They used them to make a video 'manual' for turning yourself into a bag of bones.
.     One boy filmed an endless string of everyday
objects, one by one, and let them introduce themselves to the point of exasperation. This series
became the opening scene.

NOTE
To give an idea of the objects series, they used: a fluted glass, a rack, a bottle of Tabasco, a bag of rosehip tea, a piece of string, UHU glue, a sock, a little plastic cat, a cube of detergent, a hideous magnet, a post-it, a tampon, a pencil, a Speedo bathing cap, a piece of chalk, a box of cacao, a drawing pin, a tooth pick, a tiara, a pot-holder, small change, needle and thread, a diaper, an ugly plastic midget, a plastic bag, a piece of cheese (brie), a picture of a presumed pedo-phile (found on the internet), a slutty cigarette, a cork-screw, a lighter, a picture of a tiny Chinese girl, a low fat stock cube, a picture of a dog, an Artline 70N pen, make up, a roll of wallpaper...

NOTE
Using the clips in the per-formance is a very important contributor to the perform-ers' sense of ownership over the show. It also proves to them that their work in rehearsals was relevant.

Another series of clips orginated from an assignment.
Each performer was asked to make three private confessions in front of the camera. The rule was: at least
one of the confessions had to be true, they didn't need
to tell which. Disturbing revelations were encouraged.
     When the performers feel comfortable with
each other and the group is tight and supportive, you
can ask them to push the boundaries. At one point,
during winter rehearsals, there was a thick layer of
snow. The group wanted to go out and have a snowball fight. To make it relevant for the show, they
came up with the idea to target one of them and go
as far as they could in bullying that kid. This 'fight'
would be filmed. They agreed on which person
would be the victim – in the end, they took turns.
Of course there was an agreement not to cause inju-
ries or continue when the victim really couldn't handle it anymore. It was also important to have some

aftercare, since the bashing became quite violent and sadistic. Every session was ended with a group hug.

Another series of videos was recorded in public spaces. It started with performing pranks or behaving in a disturbing way in the middle of the street. In the end, the performers were eager to get out and act as spastics in a public park. They got so carried away that some of them jumped into the pond, others scared bystanders and chased them through the park. Part of the footage was used in the performance.

2.   Bonding:

To create the 'spirit of freedom and riot', you need the group to stick together and feel confident to let themselves go in each other's presence. There are many ways of achieving this, but here are a few steps we took.

· Put loud music on. Ask the performers to (inter-) act as they would on a very wild party. Tell them they can do whatever they want, anything they ever dreamt of but didn't dare to do. Allow weird- ness. If they are reluctant, feel ashamed or shy, allow them to pull a plastic bag over their head. Their actions will be all the freer. Let them dis- cover and cross their boundaries. There is only one limit: they all have to consent to every action.

NOTE
We often rehearsed on 'Surf Solar' by Fuck Buttons, 'Thunderbeats' by Donkey Rollers and 'Sound Guard- ians' by Lightning Bolt.

· 'Lend' your house to the performers for one night, on the condition that they leave it as tidy as they entered it. They should also film what happens throughout the night. Therefore, each of the performers has to learn how to handle a camera. This is not only an exercise in responsibility, it also gets the cast accustomed to spending time together in an enclosed space, unsupervised.

**NOTE**
The camera is a very important device in the performance. It will be the performers' only means of communication with the audience. In front of a camera, there are less restrictions, there is less censorship of their own as well as the others' actions.

· Lock up your performers for a longer period in a tiny room, preferably so crammed that they have to give up their personal space. We used a lavatory. After a while, shove some snacks under the door. See what happens. In case this sounds cruel and inhumane: our performers begged to stay a bit longer.

3.   Ownership:

The performance benefits greatly from having the performers create much of the material themselves. This includes the scenery, but also the camera work. This is how we helped them to make it 'their' show.
· Build a shed in any suitable material. We used wood, painted white. Make sure the shed is completely closed. No windows. Only two doors that can be locked from the inside. Even if the performers didn't construct the shed themselves, it's totally theirs to personalize.
· Let them furnish and design the interior of the shed. Provide materials they can't bring in themselves. They wanted a car seat and a drinks

dispenser with cans of beer installed in the shed.
Cover the walls, e.g. with collages of magazine
pictures and plenty of graffiti. They wrote about
a hundred 'FUCKs' and 'WANKs' on the inside of
one door.

· Let them experiment with the camera to learn
how to mislead the audience. For instance, a
gang-bang or group sex can be suggested by filming bare skin of innocent body parts. Suffocation
can be simulated by pulling a plastic bag over
your head and tightening it around your face.
'Cutting' wrists with ketchup on knives also
proved very convincing. Remind them that they
are masters of the camera. They decide what they
want the audience to see.

NOTE
During the performance, all
the footage will be projected
on the front wall of the shed.
To give your performers an
idea of these projections,
let each of them look at the
images they produce from the
seating area. They need to
be aware that whatever they
film, inside or outside the
shed, will be magnified on the
screen, so precision is essential. Every shaky movement
can make the audience dizzy,
which is not the purpose.

4.    Dreams & Fantasies:

Once they turned the shed into a room of their own,
focus on their inner life. Ask them about their secret
dreams and invite them to 'stage' those dreams in
front of the camera. One boy dreamt of being a pimp,
although he cared less about the girls pampering
him than about the boys performing humiliating
actions on his order. Another boy felt the desire to be

worshipped as a rock star; one girl had a fantasy of time standing still and another one dreamt of a secret hatchway, hidden under the floor of the shed.


5.    Criticism & Resistance:

Have lengthy talks with your performers. Gauge their criticism and their comments on society. Ask them questions such as: What's wrong with the world? What do you disagree with? What are you confronted with, personally? Is life a lot harsher for your generation compared to the generation before you? Do you have more responsibilities, or less? Where's your riot, your rebellion? What makes you angry? What do you criticize? How do adults criticize young people? What's your criticism of adults, in particular of your parents? How do you express your criticism? How does an ideal world look to you? How do you see your future? Who do you want to be in 20 years? Who will you be?

Two videos were essential as a guideline for these discussions. As a positive answer to the anger teenagers feel towards adults, we watched Severn Suzuki's address to the United Nations. As a negative one, we watched the video of 'Stress' by Justice.

NOTE
Some performers may not have the slightest idea of what you are talking about. Perhaps because they're too young to consider such questions, but sometimes they don't care. Don't let this lack of response disencourage you. They probably haven't yet found the words to express their opinions, if they have developed any at all. Listen to the most alert and responsible ones and observe the behaviour of the others. If they can't put into words what they think and feel, let them make drawings of their riots.

- **Improvisation: 'Self-criticism'**
Let them describe themselves as their most critical enemy would describe them. Let them state
this description in front of the camera.
- **Improvisation: 'Parents'**
Let them play their parents criticizing them.
A variation on this theme: make one performer
the 'target' and let the others imitate adult members of his/her family throwing remarks at him/
her. A close-up of the 'target' is fascinating to
observe. Spot the frustration, the anger, the irrita-
tion, the embarrassment on their faces.

NOTE
Our performers improvised
over more than an hour and
a half, and still they couldn't
get enough of it. Apparently
they were boiling with frustration, which benefited the
performance. Let them also
criticize you. 'You are old,
you don't understand us'
was a much heard sentence.
Allow them to forbid you
entrance to their shed.

- **Improvisation: 'Whining'**
Let them whine like spoiled brats.
- Ask the performers if they would be able to
burn pictures of their family, to signal that they're
ready to stand on their own two feet. Don't push
anybody. In our group, only one out of seven performers refused. Burning the pictures was a collective moment and a cause to come out of the
shed for the first time.
- Give them the opportunity to demonstrate un-
compromised anger in a playful way. We used the
camera to create an image of the audience, in particular of the older spectators, which could then
be attacked without causing physical damage. We
chose tomatoes to bombard the close-ups on the

front wall of the shed, referring to 'Aktie Tomaat', a historical riot from the sixties, which took place in a theatre in Amsterdam.

· When the shed has come 'alive' – when the performers have invested it with meaning and made it their mental home – discuss about its function. Point out that, unlike the real world, this is a place where they are allowed to criticize society without the pressure to offer an alternative. Tell them this is the prerogative of their age. Ask them, when time comes to make a choice, if they'd want to stay in or step out. Let them motivate their choice. Respect their individual decisions and see to it that they are reflected in the performance.

· When dealing with criticism, challenge the performers to phrase their thoughts and feelings as bluntly and provocatively as possible, let them express themselves beyond fear or good manners, uncompromisingly. Help them to make their case and to find the right words.

# SCRIPT

This script is less a manual than an example of how all the material can be poured into a structure. Because of the barrier between the performers and the audience, embodied by the shed on stage, we will present the performance from two points of view. The supposed 'adults' in the seating area and the adolescent performers in the shed.

As a future creator, it's completely up to you how to organize the bits and pieces. Consider every text/scene as the stones of a mosaic. The most important thing is to create and support a provocative spirit of freedom, riot and fun. Challenge your performers, trigger them, exclude yourself and let them be. Good luck.

## 00.   INTRO

'HELLO, I AM ...'

*THE TEENAGERS INSIDE THE SHED*
**We have a collection of stupid objects to present to the audience. While they're entering, we hold them in front of the camera, one by one, and let them say 'hello' to the people. Some are props that we will use in the performance. The ones that make us crack up the most are:**

*Hello. I am*
*UHU glue.*

*Hello. I am*
*a hideous magnet.*

*Hello. I am*
*a slutty cigarette.*

**and of course:**

*Hello. I am*
*a pedophile.*

**But they're all pretty hilarious if you pronounce their names very articulately.**

**THE ADULTS IN THE HOUSE**
**When we enter the theatre, we hear a rough voice saying 'hello' over and over again. As we move to our seats, we see a cube; the front side is used as a projection screen. On the projection, objects are displayed one after the other. They're ordinary, everyday items: gadgets and food, tools and luxury products. The voice is introducing the objects as if they're speaking to us. This goes on until we're all seated.**

**THE TEENAGERS INSIDE THE SHED**
**We get the signal to start.**

*WANK WANK WANK WANK WANK WANK WANK WANK WANK*
*WANK WANK WANK WANK WANK WANK WANK WANK WANK*
*WANK WANK WANK WANK WANK WANK WANK WANK WANK*
*WANK WANK WANK WANK WANK WANK WANK WANK WANK*
*WANK WANK WANK WANK WANK WANK WANK WANK WANK*
*WANK WANK WANK WANK WANK WANK WANK WANK WANK*

01.  PART I

'WANK X 381'
'THE FOREST'
'FUCKED UP WORLD DRAWING'

### THE TEENAGERS INSIDE THE SHED
We point the camera at the WANKs written
on the interior wall of the shed and move over
them slowly. There are hundreds of WANKs so
we can take our time. The image is projected
on the front wall, magnified, and every shaky
movement will make the audience dizzy. Meanwhile, those of us who weren't in yet cross the
stage and enter the shed.

## THE ADULTS IN THE HOUSE
We see an endless series of WANKs projected on the cube
and we get to read them all. The words are written in alcohol
marker, so we can assume they're on the wall, somewhere
inside the cube, and someone is filming them. We also hear
the amplified scratching sound of a marker on wood.

The performers enter the stage one by one and get inside
the cube, or rather: the shed, through a door on the side.
Some glance at us briefly before they go in.

FUCK FUCK FUCK FUCK FUCK FUCK FUCK FUCK FUCK
FUCK FUCK FUCK FUCK FUCK FUCK FUCK FUCK FUCK
FUCK FUCK FUCK FUCK FUCK FUCK FUCK FUCK FUCK
FUCK FUCK FUCK FUCK FUCK FUCK FUCK FUCK FUCK
FUCK FUCK FUCK FUCK FUCK FUCK FUCK FUCK FUCK
FUCK FUCK FUCK FUCK FUCK FUCK FUCK FUCK FUCK

*THE TEENAGERS INSIDE THE SHED*
When all eight of us are in, we start filming FUCKs instead of WANKs. We film the hand writing those FUCKs. Then we move the camera to a picture of a forest. It's time for a little piece of puppet theatre. We're all in to help realizing it, handing out the props and producing sounds that accompany the story. We start with sounds of birds, owls, insects and rustling leaves. We move a cardboard picture of a Chinese girl in front of the camera.

THE ADULTS IN THE HOUSE
We see a Chinese girl taking a walk in the forest. Suddenly, she sees a piece of cheese, pulled on a thread. She follows the cheese and runs into a middle-aged man wearing a diaper. He rapes her. They disappear off camera. Next, there's a dog sniffing around. He finds the girl's blood-stained dress and he howls. End of the story.

*THE TEENAGERS INSIDE THE SHED*
Of course they don't really get the deeper meaning of the story. It's based on the game 'Mousehunt' on Facebook. In the game, you need 'superbrie' to catch mice. It's quite expensive, but you can donate it to other players. One of us sucked up to an older guy who gave him the cheese in return for some attention. The pedophile in our story is a picture of that guy. We don't really know who he is, but we don't care. He lures kids with cheese, that's it.

*WANK WANK WANK WANK WANK WANK WANK WANK WANK*
*WANK WANK WANK WANK WANK WANK WANK WANK WANK*
*WANK WANK WANK WANK WANK WANK WANK WANK WANK*
*WANK WANK WANK WANK WANK WANK WANK WANK WANK*
*WANK WANK WANK WANK WANK WANK WANK WANK WANK*
*WANK WANK WANK WANK WANK WANK WANK WANK WANK*

Now we move the camera to one of our drawings. It depicts what's going on in the world nowadays.

**THE ADULTS IN THE HOUSE**
We see a close-up of a cartoonish drawing. It's a sequence of war scenes, demonstrations, traffic jams, animals slaughtered by a butcher, skinny women…accompanied by feigned sounds of sirens, helicopters and machine guns and a commentator's voice growling, mumbling and stuttering words. In a way, it's funny, but the subject matter isn't. It's like a little kid reenacting the news to come to terms with it.

02.    **PART II: WE DO WHAT WE WANT AND
WE WON'T EXPLAIN**

~~'THE RULES'~~
~~'ALL ON EDDY'~~
~~'GANG BANG'~~
~~'PLASTIC BAG'~~
~~'SKIN'~~
~~'VIRGINITY'~~
~~'THE EYE'~~
~~'BEER'~~
~~'SPASTICS IN THE PARK'~~
~~'RAPE'~~
~~'CAUTION: SUFFOCATION'~~
~~'MONOLOGUE'~~
~~'BLOODBROTHERS'~~

*THE TEENAGERS INSIDE THE SHED*
**The music has started: 'Surf Solar' by the
Fuck Buttons. We cover the camera with our
hand and move it back and forth, so they get
glimpses of us doing stuff. We handle the
camera in such a way that the image goes from
sharp to blurry. We all take turns in shouting
what we want and don't want:**

*I don't wanna go home. I want you to see us.*

**Actually, we're screaming what we will do in the performance. They're the rules for the shed.**

*We're not gonna explain anything. We're gonna have a shitload of fun. Everything should be possible in here.*

**Then we all jump on one of us and pretend to smack the shit out of him.**

**THE ADULTS IN THE HOUSE**
**The next part is a bit of a mess. Sometimes, the screen goes black. Then the image is blurry. The music is loud and noisy. We hear the performers shout statements about what they want and what they're going to do. Then we see them ganging up on one kid and beating him up. The kid pushes his assaulters away so hard, that one of the girls is kicked out of the shed. We see her getting back on her feet and hurrying in again. She did look at us for a brief moment. All of this happens in a split second.**

*THE TEENAGERS INSIDE THE SHED*
While one of us is pushed out of the shed –
this is choreographed, of course, just like
the fight – we start a gangbang. One of us is
filming. There's no nudity involved, it's all
suggestion. Two of our girls move in front of
the camera with a sleazy look on their face
and start taking off their top. Just as they're
about to reveal something, we cover the
lens. One of us shouts:

*I'm not gonna show you, I'm not
gonna show you.
'Cause I don't have to do shit,
I don't have to do shit!!!*

## THE ADULTS IN THE HOUSE

The mess goes on inside. We see the kids having sex, two
underage girls strip for us, but we're not allowed to see the
whole act. It's their private party. They even scream that they
won't show us. On top of that, they make it clear, in their
language, that they're not obliged to do anything.

*THE TEENAGERS INSIDE THE SHED*
We all uncover one part of our body – fingers,
backs, bellies, shoulders, arms, thighs – and lie
down in a row. One of us moves the camera

along the naked skin, careful not to show any clothes. We all rub against each other.

**THE ADULTS IN THE HOUSE**
Now we get to see them fondling each other, naked. We don't see their faces, but from their throbbing bodies, we can tell there's some sort of orgy going on.

*THE TEENAGERS INSIDE THE SHED*
When we've filmed every body part, one of us licks the lens with a really wet tongue, so the image on the screen is dripping with saliva. We take off one of the girls' T-shirts, push her out on stage and throw the shirt behind her. Before she goes out, she grabs a plastic bag and puts it over her head. The wet lens and the moment of distraction outside the shed gives us some time to prepare the next scene. When the girl is back in, she uses her T-shirt to clean the lens.

**THE ADULTS IN THE HOUSE**
Again, one girl is kicked out, still partly undressed. She's wearing a plastic bag over her head and she's looking for her T-shirt on stage. She obviously doesn't want us to see her face. They seem to be hiding from us.

*THE TEENAGERS INSIDE THE SHED*
We point the camera at one of our girls, who shouts:

*Who wants to lose their virginity*
*in the shed?*

**We all raise our fingers. We take a close-up of**
**an eye. One of our boys shouts:**

*We do whatever we want here,*
*get that? Do you get that?*

**THE ADULTS IN THE HOUSE**
**They all declare they want to have their first sexual experience**
**in the shed. Again, they rub our noses in the fact that they're**
**totally free inside their hideout. One of their eyes is looking at**
**us on the screen. It's as if they're allowed to watch us, but we**
**can't look at them. They decide what we get to see.**

*THE TEENAGERS INSIDE THE SHED*
**Now we take a general shot of the whole gang.**
**We all have our positions: sitting, standing,**
**hanging in the used car seat that we installed**
**in the shed. We make it look random, but we**
**need to be very precise. A prerecorded film of**
**us, in the same position, will be mixed into the**
**projection and the images have to overlap. Next**
**to the seat is an old vending machine. It's out**

of function, but we fabricated a system to drop cans of beer from it. We all wave at the camera as if we're saying hello to the audience. Small detail: we act like spastics, with our tongues out, cross-eyed and our faces in a cramp. While the live stream cross-fades with the recorded footage, we all take cans of beer and crack them producing as much foam as we can.

**THE ADULTS IN THE HOUSE**
**They wave at us. But not kindly. They act like spastics, twitching and sticking their tongues out. The projection shifts to a scene in the park, where they do the same thing in public. They're near a pond, and in the fervour of the game, one of them tumbles into the water and splashes around in hysterical laughter.**

*THE TEENAGERS INSIDE THE SHED*
We throw one can out of the shed. One of our girls gets out to fetch it. This gives us some time to prepare the rape scene and the plastic bag.

**THE ADULTS IN THE HOUSE**
**Another girl comes out. She's turned towards us but her face is dark. We know she's looking at us.**

*THE TEENAGERS INSIDE THE SHED*
One of our girls lies down on her back and one of our boys gets on top of her. He makes thrusting movements with his hips. Another boy fondles her. First we film the whole scene, then we take a close-up of the girl's frightened face.

**THE ADULTS IN THE HOUSE**
On the screen we see a girl getting 'raped'.

*THE TEENAGERS INSIDE THE SHED*
One of our girls pulls a Marks & Spencer's bag
over her head and sucks in the air until the
plastic sticks to her face. We take a close-up of
the warning on the bag:

WARNING: TO AVOID DANGER OF SUFFOCATION KEEP THIS BAG AWAY FROM BABIES & CHILDREN. THIS BAG IS NOT A TOY.

**THE ADULTS IN THE HOUSE**
Someone deliberately ignores the warning on a plastic bag
that there's danger of suffocation.

*THE TEENAGERS INSIDE THE SHED*
It's time for us to show clearly that we're just
pretending. The boy and the girl who just acted
out the rape, smirk at the camera and wave at
the audience. We end our first sequence of wild
behavior with a monologue, our first spoken
message to the audience.

## 03. MONOLOGUE

~~**'YOU'RE WRONG...'**~~
~~**'YOU'RE SO OFTEN WRONG'**~~

*THE TEENAGERS INSIDE THE SHED*
**One of our boys takes over the camera and gets out on stage. With his back to the audience, he takes a close-up of his face, which is projected on the shed next to him. He starts talking into the camera:**

*I want to try and say something,
    but I don't want to look at you.*

*Because, when I'm speaking to you
    and I see you looking at me,
It's really hard to find the right
    words.*

*In my mind it makes perfect sense,
    but what comes out of my mouth
    never seems to be what I really
    think, you know?*

*And then I look at you.*
*And I see in your eyes.*
*That you think I'm a bit dumb*
     *or even worse...*
*Cute.*

*It makes me so angry.*
*So I say more and then it becomes*
     *about that.*
*And then things make even less*
     *sense, and your voices are*
     *always louder anyway and you*
     *know more.*
*NO.*
*You know more words and more*
     *people who agree with you when*
     *you're talking,*
*But you don't listen, or not really,*
     *otherwise you'd hear it, don't*
     *you see that?*

*Because you're wrong.*
     *You're so often wrong.*

### THE TEENAGERS INSIDE THE SHED
**Our boy comes back in and we're performing a
ritual. We use fake blood and the blunt side of
a knife to pretend we're cutting our fingertips.
We film this in close-up. We put our bloody**

fingers together to seal the bond, again in front
of the camera. One of us shouts:

*WHO WANTS EVERYTHING
TO BE POSSIBLE HERE?*

We all reply:

*ME.*

04.   PART III: PORTRAITS & FANTASIES

'ADORATION'
'P.I.M.P.'
'TIME STANDS STILL'
'TEENAGE PREGNANCY'
'I JUST FEEL ALONE'

### THE TEENAGERS INSIDE THE SHED
Now that we've announced everything should
be possible in the shed, it's time to act out our
dreams and fantasies. One of our boys wishes
to be adored and idolized. We all raise our
hands to produce the image of a hysterical
crowd at a concert. We grope and touch him
and when he hits the floor, we move into the
camera frame so he can slip away. He climbs
up a ladder behind the shed and stands on the
roof, his arms stretched out. We all look up and
scream in front of the camera. A prerecorded
message is mixed into the live stream.

## THE ADULTS IN THE HOUSE
On the projection, we see the kids change into a bunch of
ecstatic groupies. One of the boys plays an idol who's literally devoured by his audience. One second later, we see him
standing on the roof of the shed, bright lights from the back,

producing the silhouette of an unattainable rockstar. On the screen, his adoring fans desperately try to reach out to him. The song that accompanies the scene has very appropriate lyrics:

I GET (ALMOST) ANYTHING I WANT

The projection shifts to a close-up of the boy's face, telling us that, in this world:

*You need to be perfect,*
*Know a lot of people,*
*Have a pretty girlfriend and*
*  get ahead.*
*If you're ever going to mean*
*  something.*
*I hate that pressure, but you've got no*
*  choice. Otherwise you're a nobody.*

**THE TEENAGERS INSIDE THE SHED**
During the recorded message, we change the
setting in the shed. A rap song is played: Lil
Wayne's 'A Milli'. One of our boys, who fanta-
sizes about being the 'king' and getting all
the girls takes central position in the frame.
Our girls gather around him and stroke his
arms, chest, face and hair. The boy says to the
camera:

*I'M A P.I.M.P., WELCOME TO
MY PLAYBOY MANSION.*

He looks up and commands the boy on the roof
to slap himself in the face and say out loud:

*I'M A SPASTIC.*

To get a good view of the humiliation, he orders
the boy to show his face upside down through
a window hole in the shed. The 'pimp' also asks
another boy to lick his feet. Then he pretends
to doze off while the girls are still cuddling him.

**THE ADULTS IN THE HOUSE**
The attention shifts from the boy on the roof to another boy,
inside the shed. Everything is centered around his desires.
Then the camera moves to one of the girls.

> ### *THE TEENAGERS INSIDE THE SHED*
> We all freeze, except for one girl. Again, we
> need to be very exact, since we prerecorded
> the scene and the images have to crossfade
> seamlessly. We take a close-up of the girl,
> who smiles mischievously. This is the cue for
> the crossfade.

**THE ADULTS IN THE HOUSE**
The scene comes to a halt. Nobody moves, as if time stood still.
The girl smiles at us on the projection. There's a slight shift in
the quality of the image, but then we see the girl grabbing two
pies with loads of whipped cream. She takes advantage of the
situation and smashes them into the face of the pimp and of
the superstar on the roof. Then she walks out, clearly excited,
grabs her crotch, yells at us and sneaks back in. We see her
entering the shed on the projection. Again, the camera moves
to another person.

> ### *THE TEENAGERS INSIDE THE SHED*
> During the projection of the footage, we
> changed settings again. One of our girls
> is now performing a slutty dance in front
> of the camera. This image is mixed with
> a prerecorded message.

**THE ADULTS IN THE HOUSE**
We see a girl dancing provocatively. The image crossfades with a close-up of the same girl's face. She tells us a story about a relationship she had when she was fourteen. At the end she confesses that she was pregnant and got an abortion.

> ### *THE TEENAGERS INSIDE THE SHED*
> We're all pretending to party and be very, very drunk. One of us moves the camera around and stops at one of our girls, who fakes a break-down. One of our boys is comforting her. She looks up and we zoom in on her eye.

**THE ADULTS IN THE HOUSE**
We see a close-up of an eye. The music stops, the camera zooms out. The girl is alone. She looks at us. She starts talking.

## 05. MONOLOGUE

### ~~'I JUST FEEL ALONE'~~

*You're a long way away from me.*
*I see you doing jobs that you have*
*  to do that you don't wanna do.*
*And you whine about it all the time,*
*  but you don't do anything.*
*Day in, day out you drive around*
*  in your cars telling other people*
*  what to do.*
*You make such a big deal of*
*  everything.*
*I see you laughing – when you've*
*  bought something new or in the*
*  evening at dinner, when you've*
*  been drinking.*
*With people you supposedly don't*
*  see often enough.*
*You're happy when you go to other*
*  places and take a load of pictures.*
*It's so different there and so great,*
*  because it has to be.*
*Not because it really is.*
*You always go back home anyway.*
*Everything you do is so far away.*

*It's as if I'm in a cage*
  *and I look at you.*
*Or actually, the other way round.*
*You are in a cage.*
*And I don't understand that you*
  *don't want to get out.*

*I could be jealous,*
  *that I'm not part of it.*
*I could want it too*
  *and climb into it.*

*Or I could feel special*
  *because I'm different.*
*And you're just animals I could*
  *shoot if I wanted to.*

*But I don't feel that way*
  *I just feel alone.*

06.   PART IV: ABOUT MYSELF

~~'WHINING'~~
~~'MAKE-UP'~~
~~'CUTTING WORMS'~~
~~'SNOWBALL FIGHT'~~
~~'TIPS FOR LOSING WEIGHT'~~

**THE ADULTS IN THE HOUSE**
**We hear a voice whining:**

*I am so alone.*

> ### *THE TEENAGERS INSIDE THE SHED*
> **We zoom in on the collage on the wall and**
> **move the camera over it. Meanwhile, we start**
> **our whining-session, making fun of our self-pity.**
> **Anything is good enough to complain about.**

**THE ADULTS IN THE HOUSE**
**On the screen we see bizarre, disturbing, sad, violent and**
**hilarious images of people, animals and nonexistent places.**
**We hear the kids saying, in a mock-lamenting tone:**

*I feel so alone.*
*Nobody reads my poems.*
*Why do I want to buy so much*
    *stuff?*
*I'm too creative for this world.*
*Why does the government never*
    *listen to us?*
*God is dead.*
*Belgium should be for Belgians.*
*Why is my birthday on*
    *September 11?*
*My wrists are completely cut open.*
*My only friend is my diary.*
*Who am I in the universe?*
*My pension is at risk.*
*I don't have ADHD.*
*The charity shop smells.*
*When I wear a condom I don't feel*
    *anything.*
*I want a record contract.*
*My shrink doesn't understand me.*
*I don't have enough friends on*
    *Facebook.*
*No, I haven't shagged yet, back off.*
*I have a bad self-image.*
*Let me be.*
*I'm starting to get love handles.*
*I don't get how the stock market*
    *works.*
*Nobody talks about the children*
    *in Africa anymore.*

*All my followers on twitter are
    pedophiles.
Immigrants are taking all our jobs.
My favourite animal went extinct.
Fairtrade chocolate spread tastes
    bad.*

### THE TEENAGERS INSIDE THE SHED
We take a close-up of one of our girls putting on make-up. She's using a black crayon around her eyes. It's totally overdone. There's another series of prerecorded clips.

### THE ADULTS IN THE HOUSE
A girl is painting her eyes black in emo-style. We see worms on a table cloth getting cut up into pieces with a kitchen knife. Two girls are commenting on it, at times grossed out but also shrieking with laughter. The image shifts to a video portrait of a girl telling us:

*I'm an attention-seeking fat frump
    who can't take alcohol or criticism.
I use other people's secrets to make
    myself more interesting.
I cry when I don't get my way.
My friends aren't allowed to have
    a good time without me.*

*I keep talking so people won't look
at my blubbery body.
I'm intolerant, racist and
conservative.*

**Another one informs us she is:**

*A pale-skinned bitch, a slut.
Who gets off with guys for my
image.
But actually I'm still a virgin.
I fake anxiety attacks to get
attention.
I cultivate depression and I walk
the streets half naked to work
through my problems.
I'm definitely the kind of girl who
cries herself to sleep.*

**And a third one describes herself as:**

*Apparently good-looking.
But if you look properly…*

*There's nothing beautiful about me.*
*You'll just see the career bitch I'm*
*bound to become.*
*I always agree with my parents*
*because I don't have any opin-*
*ions of my own.*
*I'm doing this play to get the*
*attention,*
*but I don't really understand a*
*word of what I'm saying here.*
*If my reputation was ruined,*
*I'd kill myself.*

The image shifts to a video clip of the kids having a snowball fight. One girl is singled out and brought to her knees under a relentless, violent shower of snowballs.

### THE TEENAGERS INSIDE THE SHED
Meanwhile two girls have climbed the roof of the shed. They sit on the edge and share a cigarette. They take turns in giving tips to lose weight.

## THE ADULTS IN THE HOUSE
Two girls address us from the top of the roof. They're smoking. They teach us how to stay thin and become even thinner. Their tips include vomiting, chain smoking, swallowing chewing gum or drinking broth to suppress hunger, staring at fat people or at your own fat wobbling in the mirror to invoke disgust. They even take it as far as hurting themselves to associate food

with pain, using drugs to avoid the fattening effect of alcohol, or swallowing pills that make them shit the fat out. If all this causes your nails to change colour or your hair to fall out, they recommend hiding the side-effects under nail polish or a cap. They wish us good luck.

> *THE TEENAGERS INSIDE THE SHED*
> One of our boys now tells us and the audience how to finger a girl properly. We take a close-up of his face and let him talk.

**THE ADULTS IN THE HOUSE**
Now we get a lesson in how to finger a girl. Proud of his sexual expertise, one of the boys takes us through the steps, from collecting the necessary ingredients ('a clean finger and a slutty girl'), the general approach ('you need to build it up because women are emotional and have feelings and stuff'), over the foreplay ('a big but common mistake is to go in straight away on the first date'), the signal to move on ('you stroke, not with the intention of "I want to finger you" but with the intention of "I want to know you better"'), to the actual finale including techniques like 'the worm', 'the tornado' and, for more advanced practitioners, 'the twizzler'.

> *THE TEENAGERS INSIDE THE SHED*
> We interrupt the class by asking our boy about his skin problem. We point out his spots and zoom in on them with the camera. We start giving him advice in a patronizing tone. This leads to the next part, in which we impersonate our parents.

**THE ADULTS IN THE HOUSE**
**We see how the boy is put in his place by the others. The camera is on him all the time, so we can observe the emotions on his face.**

### 07. PART V: IMITATING OUR PARENTS

*THE TEENAGERS INSIDE THE SHED*
We start a rant, using all the typical phrases we get to hear from our parents, educators, teachers, family members, adults in general. We chose the ones that irritate us most, especially remarks about us in the third person, as if we weren't there or had no opinion. Three of us take turns to serve as targets to fire the parental shit at. The rest of us just revel in imitating the 'worried', self-righteous or just stupid tones of voice that surround us all the time.

## THE ADULTS IN THE HOUSE
The voices commenting on the faces we see are not their real voices. They're imitating what they hear. These are a few quotes and snippets of conversations we get thrown at our faces:

*They have a lot of issues…from*
*fourteen to eighteen you know…*
*no love life.*
*Hey, we walked around in weird*
*clothes once, didn't we?*
*It's a phase, she'll grow out of it.*
*What do they call it? in our day*
*it was goth, but now it's called*
*something else…'emo'.*
*Yeah, that's it, an 'emo'…*

*I read about it.*
*Are you unhappy, maybe?*
*That music they listen to nowa-*
*days, I'd be depressed too.*
*Does she eat properly?*
*Are you still studying Latin? Is she*
*still studying Latin?*
*Don't you love us, is that it?*
*Come, give me one more hug…*
*She's in love, isn't she… I can tell,*
*it's in the eyes…*
*If I was your age, you could have*
*me… you definitely could have me.*
*Be careful with strange men, will*
*you? – No really, sometimes*
*I'm worried about her.*
*She always calls – Don't you*
*darling? – We always know*
*where she is.*
*Let her take the pill.*
*We know you're having a hard*
*time but you need to listen to me.*
*Could you stay over somewhere*
*tonight?*
*Sorry, I'm a bit plastered, sorry, it*
*won't happen again.*
*Mum and dad are going through*
*a difficult patch…and dad is*
*going to live on his own for*
*a while, but it won't change*
*anything for you… I promise.*

*I'm trying really hard to be on
time, didn't you have a key?
Auntie Mary and I, we like each
other, and sometimes, we like
to hold each other tight but
don't go and tell your mum, ok?
It's our little secret.
Please don't look so sad, I can't
take it…
Your girlfriend, she's gonna break
your heart, mark my words.*

**THE TEENAGERS INSIDE THE SHED**
**We all start squeezing the last 'target' boy's**
**face, first gently, then more and more violently.**

**THE ADULTS IN THE HOUSE**
**Looking at the boy in close-up, we are forced to see things**
**from his perspective. Hands move into the frame, stroking and**
**pinching his cheeks. However kind these gestures seem, they**
**get an annoying, even suffocating quality. Music swells, the**
**hands become increasingly rough and aggressive, to the point**
**of slapping the boy.**

**THE TEENAGERS INSIDE THE SHED**
**We take out our family pictures, showing our**
**moms and dads, and hold them next to our**
**faces in front of the camera. We put plastic**
**bags over our heads and leave the shed.**

08.  **PART VI: THE WORLD OUTSIDE SOMETIMES SUCKS**

~~'BURNING PICTURES'~~
~~'TOMATOES'~~
~~'MANHUNT'~~
~~'WARNING, NOT EXAMPLE'~~
~~'STAY OR LEAVE'~~
~~'I'LL BE RIGHT BEHIND YOU'~~

**THE ADULTS IN THE HOUSE**
The kids come out of the shed, wearing plastic bags over their heads. It's the first time we get to see all of them in the flesh. They hold their family pictures, come to the front of the stage in a line-up and start burning them. When the pictures are turned to ashes on the floor, they remove the plastic bags and look us straight in the face. They bring on a bag of tomatoes. One of them climbs the shed and points the camera at us, taking close-ups of our faces. The others direct him towards 'old' or 'grumpy' people. They all start throwing tomatoes onto the projection of our faces.

> *THE TEENAGERS INSIDE THE SHED*
> As we get excited throwing tomatoes at the screen, we start a mock fight among ourselves. Apart from the tomatoes, we also use the plastic bags as weapons.

**THE ADULTS IN THE HOUSE**
**While they're at it, a good old food fight starts. On the screen,**
**we see a projection of a very violent video game, involving**
**neck breaking, cutting off limbs and blood splashing all over**
**the place. As the others have stopped, two boys are still fight-**
**ing. They take a break and watch the video. Then one of them**
**addresses us.**

## 09.  MONOLOGUE

### ~~'YOU'RE NOT AN EXAMPLE,~~ ~~YOU'RE A WARNING'~~

*Amazing game, isn't it?*
*I like to play it.*
*So fucking, yeah…you know?*
*I've got another one on the internet*
*where you can torture someone.*
*By putting him in a bath of acid*
*or grate off his skin with a*
*cheesegrater.*
*Awesome shit. It's hilarious.*
*I think it's funny you complain*
*whenever I play it.*
*Because apparently I'm going to get*
*de-sensitized to violence.*
*Hey, I didn't create this game.*
*The guy who did, he's the one*
*I don't get.*

*You know, all the girls in this play*
*are skinny as a rake.*
*Except Nanouk, but okay.*
*She says every week she's going on*
*a diet.*

*But the other four, their mothers go on*
*    and on that they don't eat enough.*
*But those mothers are always on a*
*    diet themselves.*
*Buying stupid magazines full of*
*    fucking diet tips and pictures of*
*    ugly skinny chicks.*

*Sometimes, I pity you.*
*Because you have so little grasp on*
*    the world. And it's all so very,*
*    very complicated.*
*But honestly, I think that's a fucked*
*    up explanation.*

*You just gave up.*
*And I think I can understand that.*
*Because what do you care that in so*
*    many years this, and in so many*
*    years that.*
*It's not your problem.*

*You know, it's mine.*
*So do something about it.*

*For me. You're not an example,*
*    you're a warning.*

**A girl on the roof starts talking.**

## 10.   MONOLOGUE

### ~~'I'LL BE RIGHT BEHIND YOU'~~

*If you stopped forgetting to pick me*
*up at one o'clock in the morning.*
*Maybe that would be a start…*
*And if you love me uncondition-*
*ally…whatever I do…*
*That would be good.*
*If you could solve at least a few prob-*
*lems before you dump them on my*
*plate, actually that's quite urgent.*
*And if occasionally, instead of*
*giving up, you'd make a fuss and*
*try and do something different.*
*I wouldn't think you were ridiculous.*
*I'd think it was brilliant.*

*For example, if I saw you on TV.*
*Being blasted apart by a water*
*cannon at a demonstration, which*
*is not a pretty sight…*
*I'd be proud of you.*
*And if things don't always work out,*
*If you sometimes have a hard time,*
*I'll be right behind you.*

## THE ADULTS IN THE HOUSE

One girl stands up, as if she's about to speak. She announce she wants to go back into the shed. The boy who just talked to us joins her, as well as the girl on the roof. There are four of them left on stage, two boys and two girls. They watch how the others retreat into the shed. They look at each other. Slowly their gazes turns towards us. One of the boys leaves the stage and takes a seat in the audience, among us. One of the girls follows his example.

## 11.   PART VII: THE END

~~'ANGRY AS A FOURTEEN YEAR OLD'~~
~~'I'M NOT GONNA STAY'~~
~~'THE HATCH'~~

**THE ADULTS IN THE HOUSE**
**The girl who's left on stage addresses us:**

> *I do want to be like you. I'm up for it.*
> *Earn good money. Preferably a little*
>     *bit more than most of you.*
> *A car, a nice house, children, but wait*
>     *long enough before I have them.*
> *I want two.*
> *And they can do theatre too.*
> *I'll be concerned about the world as*
>     *much as I can.*
> *As much as you are.*
> *I'll be sorting, donating, discussing,*
>     *taking offence, voting, following*
>     *the topics of the day and learning*
>     *to live with them.*
> *And like you, I will always be a left-*
>     *wing intellectual.*

*And I'll go to the theatre*
*including plays about teenagers.*
*And I'll watch them being angry*
*    and unable to change anything.*
*But... I will continue to care.*
*I promise. I'm never going to accept*
*    things. I'll always be angry about*
*    everything that's not right.*
*And if someone meets me when I'm*
*    eighty or something...*
*– Not you, you'll be dead –*
*And they say: 'So? Did you actu-*
*    ally do anything? You see, you're*
*    just like the rest of us. You haven't*
*    changed anything.'*
*Then I'll say: 'I am still as angry as*
*    a fourteen-year old.'*

**The girl chooses to sit with us. Now there's only one boy left. He comes down from the roof and stands in front of the shed, into the projection. He catches the face of one of the girls on his shirt. Then he talks to her.**

*THE TEENAGERS INSIDE THE SHED*
**The dialogue we perform now, is a goodbye scene between one of us who chose to stay and one of us who will move to the other side. We chose not to resent those who want to leave, but accept their decision.**

> Boy:    *Could you stand still?*
> Girl:   *Why?*
> Boy:    *You fit exactly on my T-shirt...*
>             *(brief silence)*
>         *I'm not gonna stay.*
> Girl:   *I got that.*
> Boy:    *Do you mind?*
> Girl:   *No, I understand.*

**THE ADULTS IN THE HOUSE**
**The boy gently carresses the face on his shirt, then takes a seat on the first row.**

> ### *THE TEENAGERS INSIDE THE SHED*
> **In the shed, we move stuff to the side to clear the floor. As we remove the vinyl carpet, the live footage shifts to a prerecorded clip.**

**THE ADULTS IN THE HOUSE**
**We now see the ones left in the shed on the projection screen. Music starts: a melancholy indie song.**

> ### *THE TEENAGERS INSIDE THE SHED*
> **The song playing is 'Spanish Sahara' by Foals.**

**THE ADULTS IN THE HOUSE**
**We see one of the girls pick up the floor covering, revealing a shutter. She lifts it. We see a ladder, leading down to a large, worn-down space, like a deserted factory or country house.**

It's daytime, the sun shines through the broken, overgrown windows. All the kids go down the ladder, except for one, who stays. The camera takes a brief close-up of her. Then we see the others roaming around in the space underneath the shed. They're clearly excited. Very soon, they each go their own way and we lose track of them. We only follow one girl who opens a door into the open air. As she's making her way into a garden, the lyrics of the song resonate:

**LEAVE THE HORROR HERE**

**FORGET THE HORROR HERE**

**IT'S FUTURE RUST**

**LEAVE IT ALL DOWN HERE**

**AND IT'S FUTURE DUST**

She heads for the bushes and struggles to find a way in. Again the lyrics accompany her escape:

**I'M THE FURY IN YOUR HEAD**  **I'M THE FURY IN YOUR BED**

**I'M THE GHOST IN THE BACK OF YOUR HEAD**

Before she finally disappears, she grabs the cable of the camera, holds it up to us and disconnects it. The image distorts, then the screen goes black.

It's the end of the performance, but even more than that: they stopped communicating with us. At least the ones who stayed in the shed. They found their way out and it's no longer our business. After the applause, we are invited to take a look inside the shed on stage. Both entry doors are opened and we get to pass through it. We are surprised how small it is, but we recognize all the images they used to project on the screen. Our short visit to the shed is perhaps the only moment of the show we truly feel welcome. When we go out of the shed, they're there, to talk to us. If we want to.

p. 279   'Teenage Riot'

**THE END** ·

# ALL THAT IS WRONG

A performance about the power of the written word:

Visitor Visitor
Visitor Visitor
Visitor Visitor
Visitor Visitor
Visitor Visitor
Visitor Visitor
Visitor Visitor
Visitor Visitor
Visito isitor
Vis itor
V r

Performer ONE
Performer TWO

Visitor Visitor Visitor Visitor
Visitor Visitor Visitor
Visitor Visitor Visitor Visitor
Visitor Visitor Visitor
Visitor Visitor Visitor Visitor
Visitor Visitor Visitor
Visitor Visitor Visitor Visitor
Visitor Visitor Visitor
Visitor Visitor Visitor Visitor
Visitor Visitor Visitor
Visitor Visitor Visitor Visitor
Visitor Visitor Visitor
Visitor Visitor Visitor Visitor

# OUTLINE

'All That Is Wrong' is an installation/performance of a young girl attempting to write down all the wrongs in the world, in order to get an overview and see what she can do about it – if she can do anything about it. It's a performance through and about writing, the power and impotence of words and an 18-year-old's answer to that.

'All That Is Wrong' is the third part of the Teenage Trilogy

## REQUIREMENTS

- One young person, preferably between 18 and 20 years old, with a sharp eye, good brains, a talent for free association and a passion for words.
- Another young person of the opposite sex, willing to assist and encourage her, morally, intellectually as well as technically.
- A camera.
- A flat theatre floor coated with black chalkboard paint.
- Lots of crayon.
- A screen.
- Two overhead projectors.
- A slide projector.
- A laptop.
- A printer.
- Images of written messages/publicity, brought together in a slideshow of a few minutes.
- Optional: moulded iron letters, size 10 x 10 cm; quantity: as in Scrabble.

## CREDITS

Text by
  Koba Ryckewaert
Created by
  Alexander Devriendt
    (director)
In collaboration with
  Joeri Smet
  Zach Hatch

First performed
  July 27th, 2012
  Theatre Royal Plymouth,
    UK

Originally produced by
  Ontroerend Goed
  Laika
  Theatre Royal Plymouth
  Richard Jordan
    Productions Ltd.
With the support of the
  Flemish Community
  Province of East-Flanders
  City of Ghent

# CREATION

First off: your choice of performer is crucial. The girl we worked with also performed in 'Once And For All' and 'Teenage Riot'; she was used to our way of developing plays and open to invest personally in the process. We knew that she loved writing and considered words a means to get a hold on reality. If you have more than one option, choose someone with similar qualities: curious to learn what's happening in the world, sensitive to injustice and ambitious to do something about it. 'Shy and smart' is a good combo: the shyness adds integrity to the performance, the intelligence assures relevance in content.

It's also important that you choose a young person, but not an adolescent at the height of puberty. The performance captures a moment in life where you have to start positioning yourself in the world and take up responsibility. Most adults have found a way to deal with world issues, they've made up their minds, even if they've chosen to ignore the problems altogether. The credibility of the performance depends highly on the sincere effort of your performer to make a conscious decision of how to enter the world.

Before you take to the rehearsal space, have long talks with the performer of your choice. Discuss his or her life and the problems he or she encounters, especially the ones that cannot be solved easily. Shift the conversations to world issues. Shower your performer with literature and movies, documentaries, interviews, YouTube clips and other media concerning global problems, then encourage the urge to write down thoughts and feelings. To keep things going, a mail correspondence between creator and performer is very useful. In our case, one of our performer's mails was read out loud in the performance. It was never intended as a performance text, but the letter expressed a point of confusion she had reached that put the essence of the show into words.

Once your performer's mind is racing, you can start working in the rehearsal space. Cover the floor with black chalkboard paint and provide crayons. Tell your performer to write down all that is wrong in the world, in keywords, beginning from his or her direct surroundings. Start with 'I'. From there, let your performer explore his or her train of thoughts. Tell him or her to be exhaustive. If it takes hours to complete the task, that's fine. Make sure you film the whole effort. This first, spontaneous attempt serves as a blueprint for further development. Pay special attention to the rhythm and dynamics of the writing: breaks, hesitations, looks of doubt and confusion, sudden eruptions of inspiration are of great value for the final performance. These moments will be reproduced to create the impression that it's all happening here and now, for the first time. In a way, the performance will be a compressed, edited version – a 're-enactment' – of this first rehearsal.

Before you start, make sure your performer doesn't feel pressured. Give him or her time to choose the right words. Allow deletions, corrections, underlines and punctuation marks. Let him or her explore different ways to describe certain topics, through quotes, symbols, dotted arrows, lists and so on. Let him or her highlight words and add or remove letters and words to change the meaning. It's important that the meanderings of your

performer's thinking become visible. Discourage
rationalization and chronology, don't let correctness
become an inhibiting factor. Stimulate free association. Music can be helpful to encourage the stream
of consciousness.

You will need a second performer. He or she will
ensure the visibility of the writing process and
act as an assistant and a companion to your main
performer. Choose a young person with a minimum
of technical talent, who is able to handle a camera
with precision, but also someone who cares about
world issues and shares the critical attitude at the
heart of the performance. His or her task includes
filming the words written on the floor, which will
then be projected on the back wall, bringing on
crayons, boards, a cloth to wipe out words, putting
on music and soundbites, adjusting the light,
suggesting topics when the main performer is at a
loss and reading out the e-mail at the end of the
performance. The two of them should form a tight
team, if not become friends.

Repeat the writing sessions and tape each of
them, to select the most poignant sequences. Bring
structure in the words, slowly fix the order of topics
and create different levels, e.g. the 'personal' in
the centre, surrounding the 'I', and more peripher-
ally the 'big issues' marked by keywords such as
'WAR', 'RELIGION', 'MONEY' and so on. This will
help your performer to build a system, which will
then enable him or her to perform chaos without
losing control.

Keep in mind that your performer's ownership
over the content is essential for the performance.
Resist forcing your own opinion or ideas upon him
or her, however subtly or cunningly. The value of
'All That Is Wrong' strongly depends on the authen-
ticity of the communication. The audience needs to

feel the performer's personal need to convey his or her message. Anything that interferes with that, will diminish the power of the show. Consider yourself an assistant or a guide, rather than a director.

'All That Is Wrong' is mainly a silent performance. However close to an installation or word art, we consider it a radical way of staging a theatre monologue. The virtual absence of voices carries meaning in itself, in that it avoids the fleetingness of spoken words and uses silence as a sign of resistance. The statements made in the performance are there to be remembered. In order to add some kind of secondary articulation, we paid close attention to the dynamics of the writing process. Speeding up and slowing down became means to convey emotions. The camera also plays an important role in magnifying the words and increasing their impact.

# SCRIPT

'All That Is Wrong' consists essentially of one idea or pitch: a young person writes down everything that's wrong with the world. The play follows the structure of a classical tragedy, with a catharsis at the end. We will use this structure as a guideline.

## 00.   PROLOGUE: POINT OF ENTRANCE

As the audience enters the theatre space, the performers await them, sitting on a blackboard centre stage. In front of them is their equipment: an old-fashioned slide projector, two overhead projectors, a laptop, speakers and a printer.

When everybody's seated, the main performer gets up and nods at the technician, who turns the light down.

Dark.

The second performer turns on the slide projector. We watch a slide show of written messages, from various contexts and media: protest banners, advertisements, art works, magazine covers.

All the messages are more or less self-conscious about the use of words. 'Language is not transparent' is one example, and the last one is also clear: a woman holding up a protest sign that says 'We cannot remain silent.'

The second performer directs the light of the slide projector onto the floor. The main performer steps forward, stands in front of the empty blackboard and looks at it.

01.   EXPOSITION: 'I'

The main performer writes down:

# I

This is the starting point. Around this word, the centre of her universe, she writes her coordinates, like an identity card:

# GIRL

# 18

# BELGIAN

She connects the words to the 'I' and elaborates. First she writes about her family situation, then her characteristics, both self-acclaimed and attributed by others, her physical appearance, education, friends, habits, prejudices, prospects.

Sometimes she uses quotes of other people to describe how the outside world approaches her:

# SKINNY
# I WANT YOUR LEGS

Sometimes a detail reveals a whole situation:

# FATHER
# (SUNDAYS 2PM – 7PM)

Gradually, she moves towards her inner life. We get to know that she doesn't sleep very well, that she thinks too much and that she's frustrated. At one point, she gets confused. We can notice, because she crosses out words or wipes them, rewrites sentences, gets caught up in paradoxes ('I like being alone'/'I like being with people') or takes a long time to think.

FOR NOW
I DO WHAT IS
EXPECTED

LATER ON
I'M GONNA DO
MY THING

SOMETIMES
I DON'T SEE 'NOW'
AS PART OF MY LIFE

. . .

To overcome the block, she eliminates words until only 'Now, I'm gonna' is left. She adds three dots. She's clearly considering which action to take.

EXPOSITION: THE WORLD

By now, all the boards are on the floor, lit by
the overhead projectors, and there's music. All
of this is the work of the second performer.
     The next sentence the main performer
writes is:

# I
# WANT TO
## UNDERSTAND
### EVERYTHING

This is the starting point for exploring the world.
First she writes down bigger issues such as
CRISIS, POLITICS, BANKS, ENVIRONMENT,
WAR – and connects them to her personal
cluster of words. The pace is going up, we can
see how she's getting into a flow of associations.
One issue leads to another, specific examples
alternate with more general, abstract notions:

WALL STREE
1%
GREEC
WALL STREET
MARKET
JOBS
MULTINATIONALS
ANIMALS
PEOPLE DON'T LIKE
VEGETARIANS
ENVY

She turns to the internet for inspiration. On her laptop, she plays YouTube clips of a financial trader welcoming the crisis, a corporate businessman defending sweatshops, a member of congress explaining the harmlessness of $CO_2$. The soundbites provide more words – more issues – to write down, literally, like a dictation, but also indirectly, to comment on. For instance, while the trader is talking, she writes down 'ASSHOLES' or changes 'GREECE' into 'GREED'.

The second performer, who has been busy adding boards, adjusting the light, handing out a wet cloth, now installs a camera to enhance visibility. The image of the words in close-up is projected on the backdrop behind the boards. The second performer also puts on music and increases the number of soundbites.

The chaos of voices becomes too much for the main performer. She can't keep up with the pace. Running from one side of the stage to the other, she asks the second performer to play one soundbite at a time. As she dives into issues of old age, illness and loneliness, the mood turns bleak. We hear a torture victim describing what happened to him. When the voice starts crying, the performer stops writing. It looks as if she can't handle it alone.

## 02.   RISING ACTION

Facing the camera, and us, through the projection on the backdrop, the performer breaks a crayon in two and holds it up, as if she's asking us to join in. The second performer takes the crayon, puts on an energizing song and starts writing with her.

It's an invigorating moment. The music conveys a sense of protest and activism. We hear a rap song by Death Grips and a punk song by Crass, interspersed with more soundbites. The two performers are writing like maniacs, united in their cause. The writing looks more like a carefully crafted choreography.

In their joint effort, the performers have filled the whole stage with words in no time. They reach a saturation point and inspiration seems to have dried up. The main performer looks at the complex web of words, takes a moment to let it sink in, then starts marking. She wants to create order, separating main issues from details, causes from effects. The second performer offers to help and carries out instructions.

They start highlighting the big words in chalk. The second performer offers to help by using metal letters instead of chalk to foreground the important issues.

03. CRISIS

With the clanking sound of the metal letters in the background, the main performer turns to the overhead projectors to continue writing. She writes on slides and projects them on the side walls.

First she goes on summing up the wrongs of the world, but gradually the tone changes. She starts reflecting on the impossible task she has set out for herself.

# WHO DECIDES WHAT'S IMPORTANT?
# I DON'T KNOW SHIT
# I STILL
# HAVE BLIND SPOTS
# INDIFFERENCE
# APATHY
# DENIAL

# 'S NEVER ENOUGH

She seems to have reached a point of deficiency.
Knowledge is insufficient and always will be,
commitment is faltering. The writing on the wall
disempowers her.
    In this moment of crisis, she turns back
to the floor. The second performer is still highlighting. We see…

WAR
  HUNGER
    DEATH
      PAIN
        POWER
          POLITICS
        LOVE
          FEAR
          SEX
            RELIGION
           HATE
              ENVIRONMENT
            MONEY
              VIOLENCE

...emerging as the main sources of evil in the world. The girl pays little attention to it, ignores the suggestions of the second performer, who is still eager to complete the scheme. She picks up the metal letters E, V, I and L and puts EVIL on the floor. This brings the whole effort to a halt.

The second performer pauses and looks at the main performer. He turns off the music.


Silence.

04.   FALLING ACTION

The main performer turns off the slide projectors one by one and last, the camera. She pulls
down the backdrop, picks up a metal hook
from the floor and attaches it to the boards.
The hook is connected to a rope and a pulley.
With the help of the second performer, she
pulls the whole board up.
　　The metal letters fall down on the floor,
producing a thundering avalanche of clanking
metal. The main performer takes a look at the
board. This is her overview. She kneels down
and writes a new 'I' on the floor.
　　Instead of elaborating and describing the
issues of the world, she now takes note of her
own personal resolutions. She uses the board
as a guide, the floor as a notepad to make a
selection.

I WANT TO STOP
WANTING TO BE
PERFECT

**DONATED 30€ ONCE**
**DON'T WANT TO CARE**
**ABOUT MONEY**

**HAVE THE LUXURY**
**NOT TO DO SO**
          **CAN GIVE MORE**

**WILL TRY**
**NOT TO BUY**

She turns to the board and marks the multinationals she will avoid in the future. Nike, Shell,
Coca-Cola, McDonald's and Starbucks are
crossed out. Apple gets a question mark.
      She writes down: 'So they'll go bankrupt',
but she doesn't believe in it. Her body language
suggests resignation. She drops the crayon. Her
project has come to an end.

## 05.   CATHARSIS

The second performer picks up on the resignation and offers some help. He asks the main
performer if she remembers the mail he sent
her. She nods. He suggests she read it out loud,
she doesn't want to. She allows him to read it
for her.

*For now, I'll pretend this is a mail*
  *because, writing over Facebook*
  *seems perverted, in a way*
*because on Facebook, you have to*
  *be happy and cheerful,*
*but I'm still a lazy bum and*
  *I haven't fixed my e-mail*
  *address yet*
*So…subject*
*About the things I cannot solve*
*About everything basically*

*I have a friend and she has a*
  *mother who has a brain tumor.*
*And every time she opens her front*
  *door*
*she's afraid to find her mother dead,*
*she also signs inheritance docu-*
  *ments and deals with funeral*
  *shit.*

*She has already lost her mother*
*    because her character has*
*    changed so much*
*that she makes everyone's life*
*    miserable*
*threatens with suicide*
*and is in a messy divorce*
*My friend can do nothing,*
*I can do nothing*
*I can buy her coffees and ask*
*    stupid questions.*

*I like to resolve things and before*
*    recently, I thought everything*
*    could be resolved.*
*Silly me.*
*Maybe I wouldn't have cared so*
*    much if the girl wasn't goodness*
*    itself.*
*If she didn't look sincerely disap-*
*    pointed when I tell her someone*
*    gave me too much change and*
*    I didn't tell.*
*Or when I leave my can somewhere*
*    (not on the floor, but not in the*
*    bin either),*
*that's how we are right?*
*So I cannot resolve everything.*

*I've already forgotten the whole*
*    point of mailing you*

*(yes-no not-mailing, I know)*
*Maybe because by tomorrow*
*    I won't remember how*
*    I felt today*
*And that in connection with the*
*    performance,*
*I've always thought:*
*Later on, I'm gonna solve things.*
*Not hunger in Africa, I got that far.*
*But something anyway.*
*And now I'm not so sure if that's*
*    gonna work out.*

*And I feel that making certain*
*    choices (putting my can in*
*    the bin)*
*is not enough.*
*If you're going to live in a cabin in*
*    the woods*
*yelling you're not causing any*
*    problems anymore*
*you're not fixing them either right?*

*There it is. Voila. Or not.*

*I also wanted to say that it feels*
*    good that we do this together*
*and I'm proud of you because you*
*    do something.*

*x*

They look at each other. The main performer
regains courage, gets up and grabs a camera.
She takes a picture of the board and asks the
second performer to print it.
    While he is uploading the photo into the
laptop, she wets the cloth in a bucket.
    The water is her new ink. She starts
wiping the board, writing the letters:

She repeats the message, like a mantra. Meanwhile we hear the sound of the printer spurting
copies of the picture.
    When she's at her third line, she turns to
the technician and nods.

Blackout.

p.315   'All That Is Wrong'

When the audience leaves, they each get a copy of the picture.

**THE END** ·

p. 317 'All That Is Wrong'

DICTATORSHIP
OPPRESSION
GANGS
CORRUPTION   FRAUD
VOTERS

TERRORISM   GUANTANAMO
LIES
TORTURE
RACISM   SY
WRITTEN THING
BITCHING   L
ABOUT
BURQAS   MISC
WRITING   GI
MORE CONTRO
WILL   ST

→LOBBY   POPULARITY
(COM) PROMISES ← CAMPAIGN
SPIN DOCTORS   FLEMISH
1ST   SELFISHNESS
2ND   SUPERFICIALITY
3RD WORLD   PLASTIC - BOTOX
4TH   LITTLE   SURGERY   ASSHOLES
MISS
AMERICA   GREED
SWEATSHOPS PROFIT $ €
CAPITALISM   CRISIS
CHILD LABOUR   BANKS

BALDNESS
BEAUTY
YOUTH   18
SKINNY
GIRL
NOT
ANOREXIC
NOT A LOT   SING
OF MONEY   M
AWESOME - SI

£2/DAY
NEOLIBERALS   JOBS
ADVERTICL   GOLD
'I DON'T   STOCK
FEEL IT   MARKET
   CRASH
NUCLEAR
WASTE   L
MEDIA   MULTINATIONALS   OIL
×NIKE×STARBUCKS
CARS
×SHELL ?APPLE
×COCA-COLA ×M
GLOBAL
WARMING
CO₂

GENOCIDE

GODS

ABUSE

CHILD RAPE

URAN BIBLE
SHARIA

BATMAN SHOOTING

SOLDIERS

KONY

SIN

HOMOPHOBIA PORN

MUNICATION
E FACEBOOK

POPE

DAMENTALISM
ANGUAGE

CONDOMS

NO

PHYSICAL

K TOO MUCH

PAIN

LGIAN?

MENTAL ILLNESS
WILL

NTROVERT

CRUELTY
DO

ON'T SLEEP WEL

MADNESS

SICK

INHUMANE

EPENDENT

WANT TO UNDERSTAND

FATHER
SUNDAYS
(2PM-7PM)

EVERYTHING
LIKE BEING WITH PEOPLE
(BUT NOT ALL OF THEM).

OLD AGE

LE DON'T
EGETARIANS

ACCIDENTS HOMES BLINDNESS
PARKINSON DEMENTIA

DO I WANT
CHILDREN?

LONELINESS LOSS DRUGS

NIMALS

UNHAPPINESS PILLS

TOO MANY
PEOPLE

I TRUST DOCTORS
CANCE

SUICIDE

MURDE

p.323 'All That Is Wrong'

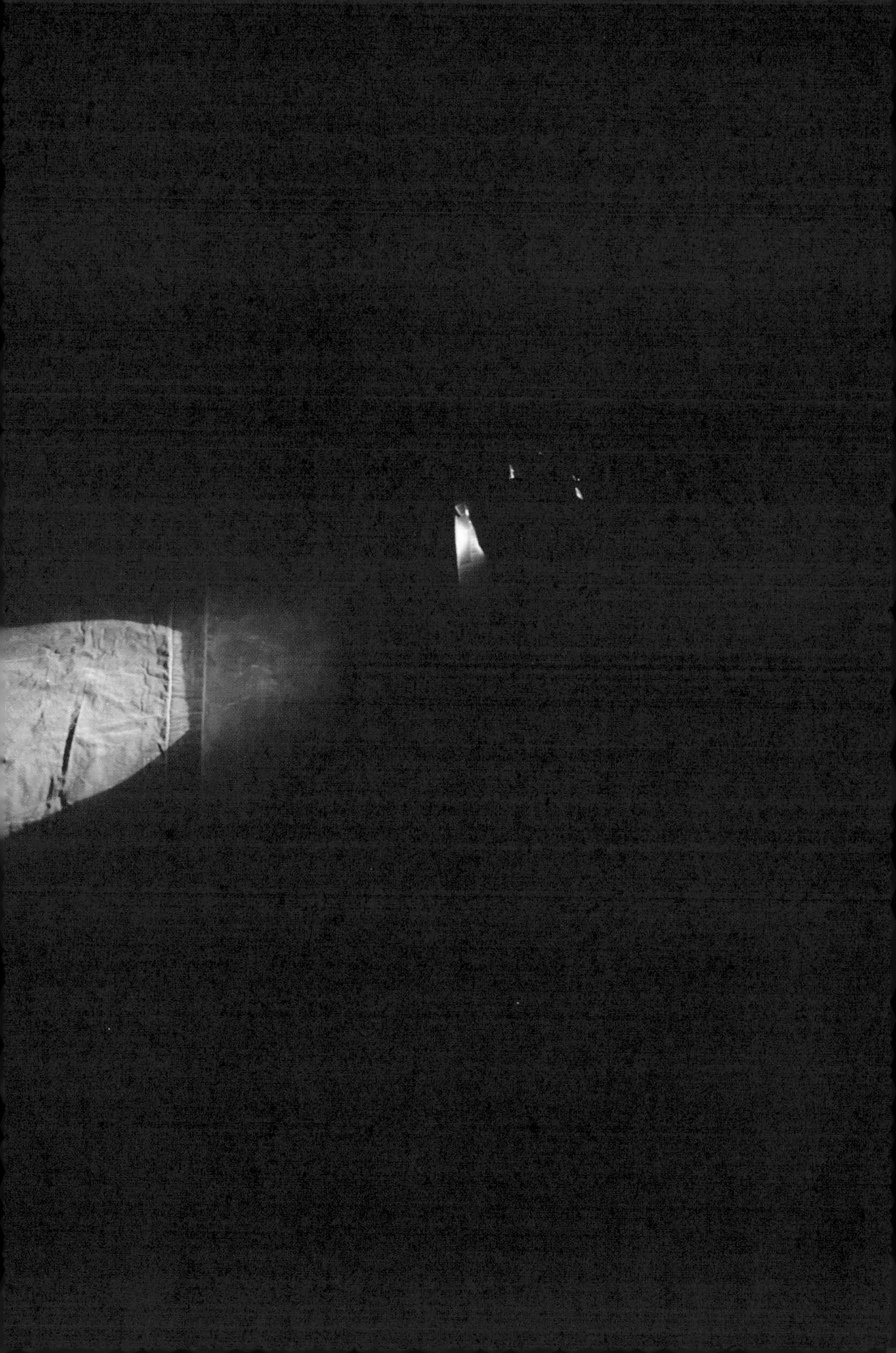

**p. 325 'All That Is Wrong'**

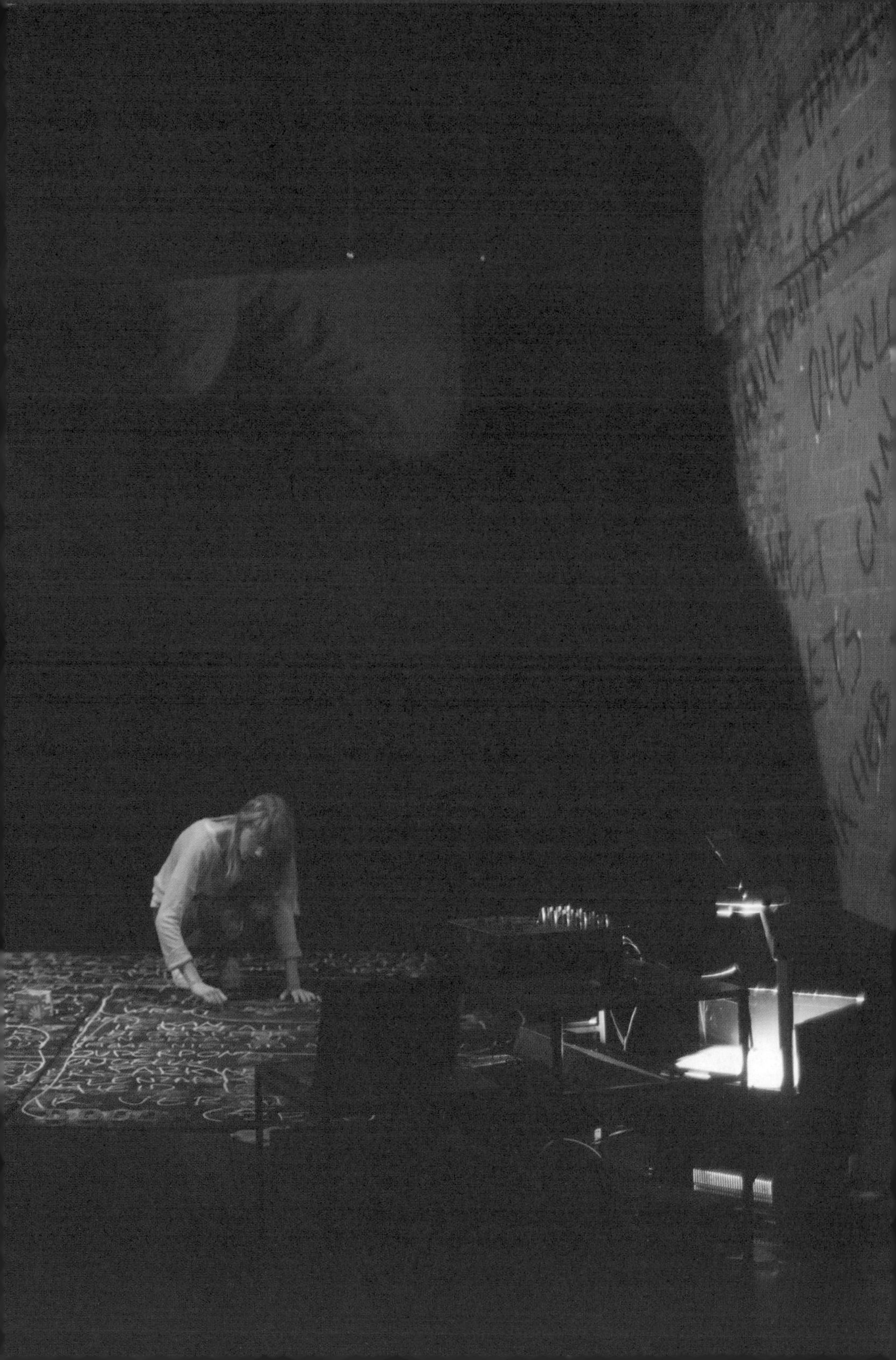

# A HISTORY OF EVERYTHING

A performance about how insignificant we humans are and how everything means a lot:

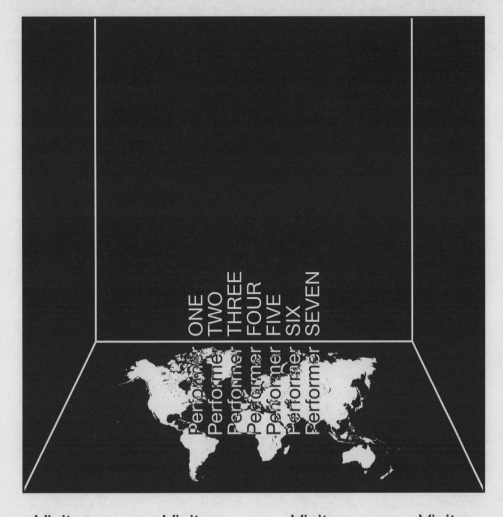

ONE TWO THREE FOUR FIVE SIX SEVEN
Performer Performer Performer Performer Performer Performer Performer

Visitor       Visitor       Visitor       Visitor
   Visitor       Visitor       Visitor
Visitor       Visitor       Visitor       Visitor
   Visitor       Visitor       Visitor
Visitor       Visitor       Visitor       Visitor
   Visitor       Visitor       Visitor
Visitor       Visitor       Visitor       Visitor
   Visitor       Visitor       Visitor
Visitor       Visitor       Visitor       Visitor
   Visitor       Visitor       Visitor
Visitor       Visitor       Visitor       Visitor

## OUTLINE

'A History of Everything' squeezes 13.8 billion years of history into an hour and a half of theatre. It puts human existence into perspective, by having seven performers try to tell the story of the universe, moving back in time until the Big Bang. With the help of a cardboard world map, heaps of props and a projected countdown, the performance delivers an homage to life, evolution and the dazzling vastness of infinite space.

## REQUIREMENTS

- A world map the size of the stage and solid enough to survive seven actors running, crawling and spraying over it repeatedly.
- A projector and a black backdrop.
- Uniform costumes with loads of pockets to contain small and medium-size props.
- Pointed KKK hood, top hat, Indian feathered tiara, Andy Warhol wig, seven bronze crowns, bunny-ears-tiara, Louis XIV masks, laurel wreath, Hellenic helmet, Napoleon hat, two burqas, cowboy hat, three black Abu Ghraib headcovers, US army helmet, crown of thorns, chain mail caps, furred Mongolian helmet, Chinese hat, bowler hat, yellow cloth, red cloth, protest cloth sprayed with slogans, blue velvet cloth, black fabric bag to dispose of the world, black cloth to cover the world, Michael Jackson glasses, Sarah Palin glasses, Ghandi glasses, P Diddy glasses, Harry Potter glasses, Andy Warhol glasses, miniature Twin Towers, clay blocks, miniature oil tank, factory, houses, space rocket, cars, cannons, boats (one large, one tiny), planes, tanks, volcano, spray can, pressurized air can, a chain, white lace collars, a ruff, white wrist, two white bras, two white corsets, a pimp chain, white Michael Jackson glove, two flat caps, a pipe, whips, Soviet badge, USA badge, star of David badges, swastika badge, black fake beard, baseball cap, silver nipple star, two nuclear signs, WAR signs, French, Italian, Spanish, Portuguese, Belgian, Dutch and British flags, EU flag, UN flag, Currency signs (£, ¥, €, $), a miniature guillotine, a rifle releasing a BANG flag when fired, a gun of the same kind, foldable wooden crosses, a noose, miniature nuclear clouds, a funnel, fake iPod, iPad and iPhone, fake Gameboy, miniature telescope and microscope, a transparent tube with a thick red thread for blood transfusion, a prism, a throwaway camera, two plates of slate, miniature wheel, abacus, block of gold, miniature cows, sheep, goats, lamas, kangaroos, penguins, horses, pigs, deer, brontosaurs, stegosaurs, and triceratops, three black skulls, small container, tea bags, hammer and sickle, rugsack, pink balloons, flowers, golden frame, miniature tree, a shoe, a Bible, a ring, magic wand, white linen pieces of cloth for foot binding, marbles for planets, cotton wool for galaxies and meteors, inflatable globe, snow confetti, sunflower seeds, white chalk, milk cups, sparklers, an apple, walnuts, fuel paste, lighters, talcum powder, snow bags, Facebook sign, Nike sign, McDonald's sign, Coca-Cola sign, World of Warcraft sign, End of the World sign.

## CREDITS

Created by:
  Alexander Devriendt
  (director)
In collaboration with:
  Charlotte De Bruyne
  Nathalie Verbeke
  Tahki Saul
  Cameron Goodall
  Zindzi Okenyo
  Joeri Smet
  (the cast)

First performed
  January 13th, 2012
  Sydney Theatre Company,
  Sydney, AU

Originally produced by
  Ontroerend Goed
  Sydney Theatre Company
  Stadsschouwburg
  Amsterdam
  Theatre Royal Plymouth
  Richard Jordan
  Productions Ltd.
  Art Happens
With the support of the
  Flemish Community
  Province of East-Flanders
  City of Ghent

# CREATION

If you were to write your own history of everything, what would you include? Man walking
on the moon or the sinking of the Titanic? The
death of Alexander the Great or birth of the
first IVF baby? Would you favour the inven-
tion of cuneiform script over the development
of the contraceptive pill? And what about the
first stirrings of biological life in the primordial
oceans? Or the formation of our galaxy?

These questions were part of the challenge
we set ourselves to create a play in the grand
environment of Sydney Theatre Company. We
always had these crazy ideas about making
something that has never been seen before. We
were reading about evolution and cosmos theory
and found it fascinating and baffling. People
read about the history of the world or the history
of human civilisation but they've never seen it
set on stage, so we figured we'd give it a try. It
was a big idea but it also needed to be personal.
The play is driven by questions of identity,
memory and significance. Do our memories
decide who we are? We know we believe in
human rights and we believe in love but those
ideas are not ours, they are passed on from all
these other people throughout time. We didn't
want to make a play that merely points out our
insignificance; instead, we wanted our audiences
to feel treasured *because* of that insignificance.

From the start, our idea was to begin
the performance in the present and let the

narrative run backwards in time. In this way mankind would not be presented as an end-point. With
the timer going back exponentially – slow at the
start, in bigger leaps at the end – we could spend
more time on human history and evolution, which
would enable the 'human' audience to identify with
the actions. The further back in time, the slower
changes would happen.

By showing history in reverse, the audience
could see how things disintegrate or disappear, rather
then come into existence. The 'first' use of fire is presented as an extinguishing flame, the first prototype
of an eye will make the actors blind and the moment
when there's no more life on earth, the performers
turn into faceless puppeteers, covered in black.

With a title like 'A History of Everything', we
also felt the play should reflect on how we conceive
history. We distinguished different phases, that
structure the progression of the performance. At
first, we adopt an egocentric point of view, in which
our own memories, the stories of our parents and
direct ancestors connect us with the past. Then
there's the eurocentric view, when direct memories
don't matter anymore and the historical account
of the culture we live in dominates. Because we're
humans, the logical frame of perceiving our evolution from animals is antropocentric, but when all life
disappears, the geocentric view of the world seems
the only one left to us. Modern science confronts us
with the existence of other universes, which again
limits our concept of history to a cosmocentric view.

The way we deal with this constant shift of
world views is relevant to the question why we're
here, the seemingly purposeless presence of our lives.
By showing the vast and enormous timeline that
precedes us (and will succeed us), the play wants to
give the viewer the opportunity to treasure this tiny
fragment of life in the history of everything.

# SCRIPT

Since every attempt at recounting history is a highly subjective, personal interpretation of lived and recorded events, we feel this show represents our – the cast and director's – version of history. Anyone who feels tempted to reproduce the performance, should select their own facts and storylines. The possibilities are endless. Therefore we didn't want to print a complete copy of the script, but rather an impression of the enormous collection of quotes, images, ideas, factual data and other information we processed to create the show. Since 'A History of Everything' is also a very visual performance, we included the images that helped us convey the story.

00.

## 01.   FIRST MONOLOGUE

NOTE

Based on 'Reversal' from the collection 'SUM. Tales of the Afterlife' by David Eagleman.

*Some people say that since the big
   bang our universe is expanding.
And in the beginning its speed was
   enormous, but it's slowing down
   day by day.
And one day that expansion will
   stop, and the universe will start to
   shrink.
And at that moment, time will reverse.
Everything that has happened on
   the way out will happen again,
   but backwards.
And on that journey backwards I'll
   live again.
It will start like this.
The wind will bring my ashes
   together, because I think I want to
   be cremated,
So there will be fire and when the
   fire goes out, my coffin will appear.
From the ceremony I'm taken to the
   hospital, where, surrounded by
   doctors, I'll open my eyes for the
   first time.*

*In daily life, rain goes up into the
     sky, my skin grows tighter and
     fresher, day by day.
I always leave the shower sweaty and
     dirty. Sleep makes me feel tired.
Only being stuck in traffic is still
     pretty much the same experience.
I don't lose my parents, I witness how
     they are born again from the grave,
And I finally get a chance to tell
     them everything I couldn't tell
     them before they died,
Or maybe I can't change what
     happened.
Maybe I can only relive it. I relive
     each memory that I have, every
     memory that makes me who I am.
For instance that one day, when
     my father forgot to pick me up
     at school,
I remember I wasn't crying, but
     I decided at that moment only to
     depend on myself.
And it won't be a memory of a
     memory anymore, I'll relive
     that moment,
Fully, and feel and see what really
     happened.
And with each memory I relive,
     I become less and less who
     I am now.*

*Near the end, I lose my teeth and
  become a baby again.
I experience what it's like to be
  totally, utterly dependent on
  someone, and not to feel frightened about that,
At the very end of my life, I climb
  back into the womb of my mother,
  and she will live her youth again
Until she climbs back into her
  mother's womb, and so on, like
  those Russian dolls.*

*Every life will live again.
Everybody will get a chance to see
  what made them who they are,
But also every tree will become a
  seed again, every stone part of
  a mountain…
Until there is no life and just
  a big bang.*

02.

The black cloth covering the stage is removed, revealing a map of the world. One performer adjusts accidentally folded parts of continents and straightens crinkles, then exits.

Empty stage, blank world map. Performer enters. Projected on the backdrop:

# TODAY'S DATE:
# THE ACTUAL DATE ON WHICH
# THE SHOW IS PERFORMED.

03.   **PART I**

Performers enter the stage one by one and recite events. They use the world map and the time indication on the backdrop as a reference, enabling the audience to situate the information in time and space. Sometimes props are used to illustrate the facts. Sometimes the performers impersonate a historical character through quotes, adopting an accent. Sometimes they work together to produce images.

To give an impression of the speedy, over-straining succession of facts in part one, we will present the lines, actions and images without tabs or line spacing, like a stream of consciousness. Bear in mind that this is acted out by seven performers, so the audience might feel like they're watching a tennis match, moving their heads from left to right depending on the focus.

**KEY:**

*'Quotes are set in italics, between quotation marks. These are lines in the performance. They are preceded by the name of the quoted character, which is not spoken in the perform-ance.'* REPORTED FACTS ARE SET IN CAPITALS. THESE ARE ALSO LINES IN THE PERFORMANCE. Actions are high-lighted in yellow. These are often stage directions. ⌐⌐ Images are between symbols.

These are choreographed movements and stills performed by the actors in order to create an impression of a painting, picture or movie scene. The words in between indicate the image we used for inspiration. ⌐⌐ (Slots are between parentheses. These are filled in differently every performance. Between parentheses is the description of the type of information that is needed on that spot.) **DATES ARE HIGHLIGHTED IN BLACK. THESE ARE PROJECTED ON THE BACKDROP.** ~~Cities, countries and continents are struck through. They indicate the performer's position on the map/stage while delivering their lines.~~

NOTE
The script is updated every performance. This is the version of November 2013.

(~~country where the performance takes place~~) TODAY IS THE FUNERAL OF (local newspaper obituary: name), LEAVES BEHIND (names of widow/widower, offspring), AT (name of the deceased)'S REQUEST: (specifics about the funeral ceremony, e.g. 'no flowers' or 'wear colourful clothes'). THE HUMAN POPULATION OF THE WORLD TODAY IS AROUND (number of people on earth at the moment of the performance). (~~countries at war~~) Performer puts cards that say 'war' on the map and continues until every country at war is covered. TODAY'S SPORT RESULTS (local sports news, typically concerning a highly popular national sport and eagerly anticipated game or match; if results are known, the performer quotes them). ~~New York~~ DOW JONES (stock price at the time of the performance). Performer puts a Dollar sign on the map. ~~London~~ FTSE (stock price at the time of the performance) The performer puts Pound sign on the map. ~~Germany~~ DAX (stock price at the time of the performance) Performer puts a Euro sign on the map. Performer puts cards with brand names on the map. (~~country where the performance takes place~~) TODAY (local news, typically a trivial story delivered as the talk of town or the gossip of the day by two performers). ~~Japan~~ NIKKEI (stock price at the time of the performance)

Performer puts a Yen sign on the map. (country where the reported event took place) TODAY (global news event delivered as a headline or brief summary). (country where the reported event took place) Today (another global news event delivered as a headline or brief summary). TODAY IS THE BIRTHDAY OF (name of a has-been celebrity who's still alive, e.g. Rick Astley, Jason Donovan, MC Hammer, etc.). (name of the last country in the list of countries at war). Performers look at the date on the backdrop. The date changes. YESTERDAY'S DATE (country where the reported event took place) YESTERDAY (global news event delivered as a headline or brief summary). YESTERDAY (name performer) TOLD ME THE FULL STORY OF A MOVIE SO I CAN'T GO AND SEE IT ANYMORE. (country where the reported event took place) YES-TERDAY (global news event delivered as a headline or brief summary). (country where the reported event took place) YESTERDAY (weird or funny fact of little importance reported in the world media). DATES OF TWO TO THREE DAYS AGO (country where the reported event took place) THE PAST FEW DAYS (ongoing news item). DATES OF FOUR TO FIVE DAYS AGO (country where the reported event took place) (headline of four to five days ago). DATES OF SIX TO SEVEN DAYS AGO (country where the reported event took place) ABOUT A WEEK AGO (ongoing news of six to seven days ago). DATES OF TWO WEEKS AGO (country where the reported event took place) TWO WEEKS AGO (ongoing news of two weeks ago). DATES OF TWO AND A HALF WEEKS AGO (country where the reported event took place) (ongoing news of two and a half weeks ago). DATES OF THREE WEEKS AGO (country where the reported event took place) THREE WEEKS AGO (ongoing news of three weeks ago). DATES OF FOUR WEEKS AGO (country where the reported event took place) (headline from 20 to 24 days ago). DATES OF FOUR TO FIVE WEEKS AGO China IN CHINA, THE FOL-LOWING WORDS ARE BANNED FROM BEING USED ON FOOD PACKAGING: SEX, GOD, MAGICAL RESULTS AND ETERNAL LIFE. 8 OCTOBER 2013 Belgium BELGIUM'S PROFESSOR ENGLERT WINS NOBEL PRIZE IN PHYSICS. 7 OCTOBER 2013 Brazil RIOTS IN RIO DE JANEIRO. 3 OCTOBER 2013 Mediterranean Sea SHIPWRECK IN LAMPEDUSA, ITALY, 274 DIED. 25 SEPTEMBER 2013 Mexican Gulf TROPICAL STORM MANUEL AND TORNADO INGRID HIT MEXICO. Performer sprays water on the map with spray can. 10 SEPTEMBER 2013 California MILEY CYRUS BREAKS A RECORD: 19.3 MIL-LION VIEWS IN A SINGLE DAY ON YOUTUBE. Female performer twerks. 28 AUGUST 2013 New York Joe Biden: 'There is no doubt that Syria's government was responsible for chemical attacks in Damascus.' London David Cameron: 'The world should not stand by and watch.' Moscow Vladimir Putin: 'There is no proof.' Syria SYRIA Performer puts war card on the map. 13 AUGUST 2013 Belgium Performer: 'My son is born, his name is Gaston.' Performer shows picture of her new-born baby. 12 AUGUST 2013 Europe AFTER 18 MONTHS OF RECESSION, THE EUROZONE IS FINALLY GROWING AGAIN. Question from another performer: BY HOW MUCH EXACTLY? Answer of the first performer: 0.3%. 21 JULY 2013 Belgium Vive le roi! 3 JULY 2013 Egypt PRESIDENT MOHAMED MORSI IS DEPOSED IN A MILITARY COUP, LEADING TO WIDESPREAD VIOLENCE. 13 JUNE 2013 USA Performer lifts 'Facebook'-sign. FROM NOW ON HASHTAGS WILL BE CLICKABLE! Another performer comments ironically: WOW. 2 JUNE 2013 Central Europe EXTREME FLOODS HIT AUSTRIA, CZECH REPUBLIC, SWIT-ZERLAND AND GERMANY. Performer uses spray can. 31 MAY 2013 Turkey PROTEST IN TURKEY AGAINST... Performer holds 'Twitter'-sign. Erdogan: 'There is now a menace in Turkey which is called Twitter. Social media is a threat to our society.' 14 MAY 2013 Los Angeles ANGE-LINA JOLIE HAS BOTH HER BREASTS AMPUTATED TO AVOID BREAST CANCER. 30 APRIL 2013 The Netherlands QUEEN BEATRIX ABDICATES IN FAVOUR OF HER SON WILLEM-ALEXANDER. 15 APRIL 2013 Boston BOSTON MARATHON BOMBINGS: THREE PEOPLE KILLED. 8 APRIL 2013 London MARGARET THATCHER DIES OF A STROKE AT THE AGE OF 87. Opponents of Margaret Thatcher: 'The witch is dead.' 3 APRIL 2013 Argentina ARGENTINA FLOODS: 80 PEOPLE KILLED. Performer uses spray can. 12 FEBRUARY 2013 Rome FOR THE FIRST TIME IN 600 YEARS, THE POPE RESIGNS. Performer holds slightly crooked wooden cross with shaking hands. Benedict XVI: 'In view of the rapidly changing world... I lack the strength...' Other performer adjusts the cross. 27 JANUARY 2013 Denver DENVER UNIVERSITY ESTIMATES THERE WILL BE AS MANY WOMEN AS MEN IN TOP JOBS WORLDWIDE...BY 2085. 18 JANUARY 2013 USA Oprah Winfrey: 'Mister Armstrong, yes or no: did you ever use EPO?' Lance Armstrong: 'Yes, Oprah, I truly believed I was invincible.' 22 DECEM-BER 2012 New Delhi PROTESTS AFTER GANG RAPE ON A BUS IN NEW DELHI. Female *protester: 'Don't tell us how to dress, tell them not to rape.'* 8 DECEMBER 2012 ~~Doha~~ DOHA: 195 COUNTRIES TRY TO TAKE EXTRA MEASURES AGAINST GLOBAL WARMING. Performers spread all over the map. *Worldwide response: 'I'll sign, I'll sign, I'm not sure, I'm not sure – then let's just prolong the Kyoto protocol.'* 14 NOVEMBER 2012 ~~Israel~~ ISRAEL AND PALESTINE ON THE BRINK OF DECLARING WAR. *Representative of Israel: 'You launched a hundred rockets.' Representative of Palestine: 'Yes, but you launched 1500 rockets.'* 6 NOVEMBER 2012 ~~Washington~~ *Barack Obama: 'We know in our hearts that for the United States of America the best is yet to come!' Democrat supporter: 'Four more years!'* 29 OCTOBER 2012 ~~Mexican Gulf~~ TORNADO SANDY. Performer uses spray can. 14 OCTOBER 2012 ~~Belgium~~ *Kenji Minogue: 'Aje nie kun kommen, a kom gie tan nie.'* 14 OCTOBER 2012 ~~Belgium~~ *Bart De Wever: 'In vredesnaam…zet die ploat af.'* SEPTEMBER 2012 ~~Switzerland~~ SCIENTISTS AT THE LARGE HADRON COLLIDER DISCOVER A NEW PARTICLE: THE HIGGS-BOSON. 5 JUNE 2012 ~~United Kingdom~~ THE DIAMOND JUBILEE OF ELIZABETH II… 5 JUNE 2012 ~~South Korea~~ *PSY: 'Wop…wop wop wop-wop woppah Gangnam Style!'* Performers worldwide do the Gangnam-Style jump. 5 JUNE 2012 ~~United Kingdom~~ *Queen Elizabeth II: 'It has touched me deeply to see so many thousands celebrating together in such a happy atmosphere.'* Other performer reports: UK ECONOMY PLUNGES INTO RECESSION. 13 MARCH 2012 ~~Switzerland~~ A BELGIAN BUS CRASHES IN SWITZERLAND, KILLING 28 PEOPLE, MOST OF THEM ARE CHILDREN. 4 MARCH 2012 ~~Moscow~~ PUTIN WINS THE PRESIDENTIAL ELECTIONS DESPITE ALLEGATIONS OF VOTER FRAUD. Performer uses spray can to wet his eyes. *Vladimir Putin: 'I'm not crying it's just windy.'* 4 MARCH 2012 ~~Moscow~~ *Protesters: 'Pussy Riot!'* 2 MARCH 2012 ~~Europe~~ 26 MEMBERS OF THE EU SIGN A NEW FISCAL COMPACT. *European leaders: 'I'll sign.' David Cameron: 'I'm not signing.'* FEBRUARY 2012 ~~Central Europe~~ BECAUSE OF EXTREMELY COLD WEATHER 600 PEOPLE DIE IN EUROPE. Performer scatters white confetti to suggest snow. MINUS 40 DEGREES IN THE CZECH REPUBLIC. 11 FEBRUARY 2012 ~~Los Angeles~~ Performer holds shrine with a picture of Whitney Houston. *Whitney Houston: 'And I will always love you…'* 14 JANUARY 2012 ~~Bejing~~ JIEU IS THE NEW PRESIDENT OF CHINA. Other performer responds: I DON'T KNOW. First performer throws back: NO, THAT'S HIS NAME. 13 JANUARY 2012 ~~Italy~~ CRUISE SHIP CONCORDIA SINKS. 28 DECEMBER 2011 ~~North Korea~~ ⌐⌐ Weeping North Korean women in the snow ⌐⌐ Performer scatters white confetti while two others kneel down, spray their eyes and weep. *Representative of the communist regime: 'North Korea announces to the world: Our beloved leader, Kim Jong-Il, the sun of the communist future, the inventor of the hamburger has died.'* 21 DECEMBER 2011 ~~Washington~~ *Barack Obama: 'After nine years, America's war in Iraq will be over. The tide of war is receding.'* 11 DECEMBER 2011 ~~South Africa~~ DURBAN: 194 COUNTRIES TRY TO FIND A SOLUTION FOR GLOBAL WARMING. *World leaders: 'I'll sign. I'll sign. I'll sign. I'll sign. Barack Obama: I might sign.' ~~Canada~~ World leader: 'Then I'm not signing anymore.'* 8 DECEMBER 2011 ~~Europe~~ 5,2% 3 DECEMBER 2011 ~~Middle East~~ WITCH BURNINGS ON THE INCREASE IN SAUDI ARABIA. 5 DECEMBER 2011 ~~Belgium~~ AFTER 541 DAYS, BELGIUM FINALLY HAS A GOVERNMENT. 29 NOVEMBER 2011 ~~Europe~~ 5.5% 7 NOVEMBER 2011 ~~Italy~~ SILVIO BERLUSCONI STEPS DOWN… ~~Europe~~ 5.7%. ~~Southeast Asia~~ THAILAND FLOODS. Performer uses spray can. ~~Italy~~ *Silvio Berlusconi: 'The life in Italy is a life of wealthy people. Our restaurants are full.'* ~~Europe~~ 5.9% 31 OCTOBER 2011 ~~(Unspecified)~~ HUMAN POPULATION IS NOW 7 BILLION. ~~Europe~~ 6.1% 23 OCTOBER 2011 ~~Turkey~~ EARTHQUAKE IN TURKEY, 582 DEAD. Performer shakes Turkey. ~~Europe~~ 6,5% EUROPEAN INTEREST RATES INCREASE. 20 OCTOBER 2011 ~~Libya~~ *Libyan rebel: 'We announce to the world that Gaddafi has died in custody of the revolution.'* ~~Iran~~ NUCLEAR WEAPONS CONFIRMED IN IRAN. Performer holds up nuclear sign. ~~Libya~~ *Muammar Gaddafi: 'I am not such a dictator that I would ban Facebook. I would merely imprison anyone who used it.'* ~~Antarctica~~ Performer holds miniature penguin. GLACIAL MELTING AT AN ALL TIME HIGH. 18 OCTOBER 2011 ~~Israel~~ ISRAEL AND PALESTINE: PRISONER SWAP. *Representative of Israel: 'I will give you 1,027 prisoners. Representative of Palestine: 'I will give you 1.'* ~~USA~~ Performer holds sign that says 'the end of the world.' *Harold Camping: 'God has left all these proofs and keys for us to find in the bible…'* ~~Israel~~ DEAL Performers in Israel shake hands. ~~USA~~ *'There can be no question, judgment day will come, the world will end in October 2011.'* 5 OCTOBER 2011 ~~Los Angeles~~ *Spokesperson of Apple: 'Every once in a while a person comes along who changes everything…'* ~~USA East Coast~~ HURRICANE IRENE Performer uses compressed air can to blow away miniature houses. ~~Los Angeles~~ *'Apple and the world say goodbye to Steve Jobs. He was…'*

31 OCTOBER 2011 ~~Moscow~~ Putin and Medvedev switch jobs again. ~~Los Angeles~~ *'Amazing. Amazing.'* 17 SEPTEMBER 2011 ~~New York~~ Performers hold the protest cloth sprayed with slogans and symbols. *Protesters: 'We are the 99%.'* 6 AUGUST 2011 ~~Belgium~~ FIVE PEOPLE DIED AT THE PUKKELPOP FESTIVAL. ~~London~~ THE START OF THE LONDON RIOTS. Performers move protest cloth from New York to London. *Protester: 'We deserve more.' Other protester: 'You know what I mean?' Third protester: 'Yeah.'* 23 JULY 2011 ~~London~~ Performer holds shrine with picture of Amy Winehouse. THEY TRIED TO MAKE HER GO TO REHAB, BUT SHE SAID NO, NO, NO. 22 JULY 2011 ~~Norway~~ ANDERS BREIVIK KILLED 77 PEOPLE. MOST OF THEM WERE TEENAGERS. *Survivor of the Utøya massacre: 'I was lying in between my shot friends. I was pretending to be dead myself.'* ~~Wall Street~~ AA PLUS RATING. 4 JUNE 2011 ~~Chile~~ Performer brings on miniature volcano. PUYEHUE VOLCANO ERUPTS IN CHILE, DISRUPTS AIRPORTS FROM SOUTH AMERICA ALL THE WAY TO AUSTRALIA Performers land miniature planes in Chile and Australia. 16 MAY 2011 ~~Portugal~~ PORTUGAL BAILED OUT FOR 78 BILLION EURO. 1 MAY 2011 ~~Washington/Afghanistan~~ ⌐ 'Situation Room Picture' with Hillary Clinton, Barack Obama and White House officials ¬ BIN LADEN CAPTURED AND SHOT *Barack Obama: 'Finally... We got Osama.'* 29 APRIL 2011 ~~Los Angeles~~ *Charlie Sheen: 'Yeah, I'm on a drug. It's called Charlie Sheen. It's not available.'* ~~London~~ Two performers impersonate Kate Middleton, with cardboard face mask, and Prince William waving at the crowds. ~~(Unspecified)~~ *Tweeter: 'Tweet. Cate's wedding gown looks stunning.' Other tweeter: 'Tweet. Yeah. But did u c Peepa's butt?'* ~~Libya~~ UPRISING IN LIBYA Performer puts down war sign in Libya. ~~Belgium~~ Performer holds the cross. *Bishop Roger Vangheluwe: 'I don't have the impression I am a pedophile... It was just a little relationship.'* 23 MARCH 2011 ~~Los Angeles~~ Performer holds the shrine with a picture of Elizabeth Taylor. ELIZABETH TAYLOR DIES. 11 MARCH 2011 ~~Japan~~ TSUNAMI IN JAPAN Performer holds up nuclear sign and pours water on the stage. 15 MARCH 2011 ~~Egypt~~ Performer holds the protest cloth. *Protester: 'Ash-shab yurid isqat an-nizam.' Translator: 'The people want to bring down the regime.'* 26 FEBRUARY 2011 ~~Japan~~ NINTENDO 3DS LAUNCHED IN JAPAN. 15 FEBRUARY 2011 ~~Libya~~ Performers hold the protest cloth. *Protester: 'Let's hope and pray that Gaddafi's regime will break soon...'* ~~Mexican Gulf~~ *'There is a shark...here.'* ~~Libya~~ *'... It's now or never.'* ~~Russia~~ SCIENTISTS ATTEMPT TO CLONE A WOOLY MAMMOTH IN RUSSIA. 25 JANUARY 2011 ~~Egypt~~ *protester: 'I'm going back to the Tahrir square. They cannot trick us...'* ~~Los Angeles~~ *Rebecca Black: 'Friday. Friday.'* ~~Egypt~~ *'... We want the fall of that whole regime, not only the head of Mubarak.'* ~~Los Angeles~~ *Arnold Schwarzenegger: 'I'm going to start acting again.'* 14 JANUARY 2011 ~~Tunisia~~ A TUNISIAN STREET VENDOR SETS HIMSELF ON FIRE. THIS MARKS THE BEGINNING OF THE ARAB SPRING. 11 JANUARY 2011 ~~Brazil~~ MUDSLIDE IN RIO DE JANEIRO Performer uses spray can and passes it on to another performer in Australia. 21 DECEMBER 2010 ~~(Unspecified)~~ HUBBLE TELESCOPE TAKES PHOTOS OF A YOUNGER UNIVERSE. THE LIGHT WE SEE IN THE PHOTOGRAPHS IS 13.2 BILLION YEARS OLD. ~~Australia~~ QUEENSLAND FLOODS Performer uses spray can. ~~(Unspecified)~~ WIKILEAKS All performers move away from their spot playing dumb. 26 JULY 2010 ~~Pakistan~~ PAKISTAN MONSOON. 22 NOVEMBER 2010 ~~New Zealand~~ NEW ZEALAND MINERS. 14 OCTOBER 2010 ~~Chile~~ THE CHILEAN MINERS. 11 JULY 2010 ~~South Africa~~ *Spanish football supporter: 'España!'* 25 JUNE 2010 ~~China~~ CHINA MUDSLIDE Performer uses spray can. 24 JUNE 2010 ~~London~~ Two performers, wearing caps, mimic a tennis match. *Umpire: 'Wimbledon. 56-56 tie...'* ~~Australia~~ *Julia Guillard: 'My values and my beliefs...'* 1 MAY 2010 ~~Greece~~ GREECE Performer shows empty pockets. ~~Australia~~ *'...have driven me to step forward...'* 20 APRIL 2010 ~~Mexican Gulf~~ THE MEXICAN GULF Performer suggest oil spill. ~~Australia~~ *'...to take this position as a Prime Minister.'* ~~London~~ *'...70-68.'* LONGEST TENNIS MATCH EVER. 21 MARCH 2010 ~~Iceland~~ Performer brings on the miniature volcano. EYIAFJALLAJOKULL Performer lands planes near the volcano. ~~Los Angeles~~ Performer holds fake iPad. *Steve Jobs: 'Every once in a while, a new product comes along that changes everything. Apple is proud to present the iPad. It's amazing. Amazing.'* 19 FEBRUARY 2010 ~~Los Angeles~~ *Tiger Woods: 'I ran straight through the boundaries that a married couple should live by...'* ~~(Unspecified)~~ Performer puts on protective mouth mask and points at the countries she lists. SWINE FLU BREAKS OUT IN NEW ZEALAND...AUSTRALIA... ~~Los Angeles~~ *'... I was wrong, I was foolish...'* ~~Thailand~~ THAILAND... ~~Los Angeles~~ *'... I do plan to return to golf one day...'* ~~Turkey~~ TURKEY... 12 JANUARY 2010 ~~Haiti~~ EARTHQUAKE IN HAITI. 14 DECEMBER 2009 ~~Canada~~ CANADA... ~~Mexico~~ MEXICO... 1 DECEMBER 2009 ~~London~~ *Nigel Farage: 'Mister Van*

*Rompuy... Who are you? Nobody in Europe has ever heard of you.'* **9 DECEMBER 2009** ~~Sweden~~ SWEDEN...NOBEL PRIZE FOR BARACK OBAMA **Performer hands other performer a copper cup.** ~~Brussels~~ HERMAN VAN ROMPUY BECOMES THE FIRST PRESIDENT OF THE EUROPEAN UNION. ~~Greece~~ GREECE... ~~Bulgaria~~ BULGARIA... ~~United Kingdom~~ UNITED KINGDOM... ~~London~~ *Nigel Farage: 'You come from Belgium...'* ~~Belgium~~ BELGIUM... ~~London~~ *'...which, of course is pretty much a non-country.'* ~~France~~ FRANCE... **18 OCTOBER 2009** Performer moves miniature sailing boat over the South Indian Ocean, two other performers are in Australia. ~~Australia~~ *Jessica Simpson's mother: 'Oh Jessica we are so proud of you for circumnavigating the globe solo.'* ~~Ireland~~ IRELAND... ~~Australia~~ *Jessica Simpson's father: 'You're not using all your fresh water on your hair are you?'* ~~Indian Ocean~~ *Jessica Simpson: 'Oh mom, just let me get back to sailing alright.'* ~~Iraq~~ AMERICA'S PRESIDENT GEORGE BUSH VISITS IRAQ **Performer throws shoe at other performer.** ~~USA~~ UNITED STATES... ~~Iraq~~ *George W. Bush: 'So what if the guy threw a shoe at me?'* **23 SEPTEMBER 2009** ~~Sydney~~ A RED DUST STORM DESCENDS ON SYDNEY. ~~Sydney~~ *Performer: 'And my daughter is born, she has red hair.'* ~~Haiti~~ HAITI... **9 SEPTEMBER 2009** ~~Washington~~ *Barack Obama: 'We came here to build a future. So tonight, I return to speak to all of you about an issue that is central to that future...and that is the issue of health care.'* ~~Brazil~~ BRAZIL...AND SOME 83 OTHER COUNTRIES. **JULY 2009** ~~Afghanistan~~ BEHEADINGS IN AFGHANISTAN **Performer pulls a black bag over the head of another performer, who falls down.** **25 JUNE 2009** ~~USA~~ **Performer puts on sunglasses, gold chain and cap.** *P Diddy: 'Michael Jackson showed me that you can actually see the beat.'* **Performer holds shrine with picture of Michael Jackson, wearing sunglasses and one white glove.** *Michael Jackson: 'What about sunrise? What about rain?'* **Performers worldwide wipe away tears, which have been sprayed in their faces during the Swine Flue listing.** **26 JANUARY 2009** ~~Iceland~~ ICELAND **Performer shows empty pockets.** ~~Belgium~~ I AM DATING TWO GUYS AT THE SAME TIME. **Other performer comments: WOW.** ~~USA~~ THE GLOBAL FINANCIAL CRISIS. **Performers worldwide show empty pockets.** **4 NOVEMBER 2008** ~~Washington~~ *Barack Obama: 'Man touched down on the moon, a wall came down in Berlin, a world was connected by our own science and imagination. YES WE CAN.'* **31 OCTOBER 2008** ~~Tibet~~ WORST SNOWSTORM EVER IN TIBET. MINUS 60 DEGREES. **11 SEPTEMBER 2008** ~~Alaska~~ *Interviewer: 'What insight into the Russian actions does the proximity of the state give you?'* **10 SEPTEMBER 2008** ~~Switzerland~~ HADRON COLLIDER SMASHES PROTONS. ~~Alaska~~ *Sarah Palin: 'Well, they are nextdoor neighbours and you can actually see Russia from land here in Alaska.'* **21 JULY 2008** ~~Serbia~~ **One performer plays Radovan Karadzic while another performer 'discovers' him.** RADOVAN?...RADOVAN KARADZIC, IS THAT YOU? **A third performer interferes.** (name performer who plays Radovan) NOBODY REMEMBERS. **26 APRIL 2008** ~~Austria~~ *Josef Fritzl: 'Hallo, ich bin Josef Fritzl aber ich muss mich nicht vorstellen. Ich bin weltberühmt.'* *Translator: 'Hello. I am Josef Fritzl but I don't have to introduce myself. I am world famous.'* **12 FEBRUARY 2008** ~~Australia~~ *Kevin Rudd: 'For the pain, suffering and hurt of the Aboriginal people of Australia...'* **22 JANUARY 2008** ~~New York~~ **Performer holds shrine with picture of Heath Ledger.** HEATH LEDGER DIES. **27 DECEMBER 2007** ~~Pakistan~~ BENAZIR BHUTTO **Performer 'shoots' other female performer.** ~~Australia~~ *'...we say sorry.'* **10 DECEMBER 2007** ~~Sweden~~ NOBEL PRIZE FOR AL GORE. AN INCONVENIENT TRUTH. **17 OCTOBER 2007** ~~Washington~~ *Dalai Lama: 'Of course I love President Bush. Wonderful person...'* **6 SEPTEMBER 2007** ~~Italy~~ **Performer holds shrine with picture of Luciano Pavarotti.** *Luciano Pavarotti: 'Nessun Dorma.'* ~~Washington~~ *'... I love you but some of your policies I have grave reservations.'* *George W. Bush: 'You know it just goes to show that God is universal and God is love and no state, man or woman should fear the influence of religion.'* ~~North Africa~~ WAIT...DID WE SKIP SOMETHING IN AFRICA? **Other performer responds: I DON'T THINK SO. Third performer adds: I NEED TO PUT SOME WAR CARDS THERE. Performer puts war cards on the map.** **10 SEPTEMBER 2007** ~~Tennessee~~ *Chris Crocker: 'And how fucking dare anyone out there make fun of Britney. She made the song Give Me More because all you people want is MORE MORE MORE!'* **9 JUNE 2007** ~~Los Angeles~~ **Performer presents fake iPhone.** *Steve Jobs: 'Every once in a while a new product comes along that changes everything... Apple is proud to present the iPhone. It's amazing. Amazing.'* **3 MAY 2007** ~~Portugal~~ **Performer holds picture of Madeleine McCann.** *Kate McCann: 'Please, please give us our Madeleine back.'* **30 DECEMBER 2006** ~~Iraq~~ **Performer puts noose around her neck.** *Saddam Hussein: 'No, I am a militant and I have no fear for myself. I have spent my whole life fighting in jihad.'* *Iraqi citizen: 'Saddam Hussein, go to hell!'* *Saddam Hussein: 'The hell that is Iraq?'* **20 APRIL 2007** ~~Rome~~ THE CHURCH STATES: UNBAPTISED BABIES

WHO DIE NO LONGER GO TO LIMBO. IN FACT, LIMBO NEVER EXISTED. 24 AUGUST 2006 (Unspecified) *young kid: 'Dear Mr. Scientist, why do you think Pluto is no longer planet? I miss my friend.* 14 AUGUST 2006 Israel/Lebanon ISRAEL. HEZBOLLAH. STOP FIGHTING. *Representative of Israel: 'You started it.' Representative of Lebanon: 'You started it.'* 14 FEBRUARY 2005 San Bruno YOUTUBE IS FOUNDED IN SAN BRUNO. 27 OCTOBER 2005 Paris RIOTS IN THE OUTSKIRTS OF PARIS. *Nicolas Sarkozy: 'Moi, j'en ai marre…de cette racaille!'* 29 AUGUST 2005 Florida HURRICANE KATRINA. 7 JULY 2005 London LONDON METRO BOMBINGS. *Terrorist: 'Allahu Akbar!' Translator: 'God is great!'* Los Angeles *Tom Cruise: 'You know I think it's a privilege to be a scientologist and its something that you have to earn. And when I read about it I just went, poof! This is it. This is exactly it.'* 19 APRIL 2005 Rome *Church official: 'Habemus Papam.' Translator: 'We have a pope!'* USA WORLD OF WARCRAFT IS FOUNDED. Southeast Asia TSUNAMI IN SOUTHEAST ASIA Performer pours water on the map. (Unspecified) STILL FLYING AFTER TWENTY-EIGHT YEARS: THE VOYAGER 1 SPACECRAFT REACHES THE BOUNDS OF OUR SOLAR SYSTEM. THIS IS THE PLACE WHERE OUR SUN'S INFLUENCE ENDS. 29 APRIL 2004 ⌐ Picture of American militaries abusing Iraqi prisoners ⌐ ABU GHRAIB. 11 MARCH 2004 Spain MADRID TRAIN BOMBINGS *Terrorist: 'Allahu Akbar!' Translator: 'God is great!'* 4 FEBRUARY 2004 Massachusetts FACEBOOK IS FOUNDED AT HARVARD UNIVERSITY. 1 FEBRUARY 2004 Texas *Justin Timberlake: 'Have you naked by the end of this song.'* ⌐ Janet Jackson's nipplegate ⌐ 29 FEBRUARY 2004 New Zealand Performers impersonate characters from Lord of the Rings. *Frodo: 'Come on, Sam.'* A ring is dropped on stage. *Gollem: 'My own, my precious. Tricksy little hobbits.'* One performer follows the ring as it rolls away. MARCH 2003 Washington *George W. Bush: 'The war on terror involves Saddam Hussein because of the nature of Saddam Hussein and his willingness to terrorise himself.'* Iraq Performer lights a sparkler attached to a war card and puts it on the map. 28 AUGUST 2003 Los Angeles *Madonna: 'Everybody comes to Hollywood.'* Two female performers impersonate Madonna and Britney Spears kissing. MARCH 2003 Washington *George W. Bush: 'I am honored to shake the hand of a brave Iraqi citizen who had his hand cut off by Saddam Hussein.'* 15 FEBRUARY 2003 (Unspecified) GLOBAL PROTEST OVER THE WAR IN IRAQ. Australia *Protester: 'Smart weapons, dumb president.'* Germany *Protester: 'Kein Blut fur Öl.'* Europe *Protester: 'Let's bomb Texas, they have oil too!'* 16 NOVEMBER 2001 London Performer puts on glasses and holds a magic wand. *Harry Potter: 'Wingardium Leviosa!'* Europe THE EURO IS INTRODUCED Performer removes the Euro sign. Israel Performer uses clay blocks to build a miniature wall. *Representative of Palestine: 'Israel, is it really necessary to build that wall?' Representative of Israel: 'Yes it is.' Representative of Palestine: 'No it isn't.' Representative of Israel: 'Yes it is.' Representative of Palestine: 'No it isn't.'* 23 OCTOBER 2001 Los Angeles Performer holds fake iPod. *Steve Jobs: 'Every once in a while a new product comes along that changes everything. Apple is proud to present the iPod. It's amazing, amazing.'* 7 OCTOBER 2001 Afghanistan Performer lights sparkler attached to war card. OPERATION ENDURING FREEDOM BEGINS. 11 SEPTEMBER 2001 New York *George W. Bush: 'Today our nation saw evil. Americans have many questions tonight. Americans are asking 'What is expected of us?' I ask you to live your lives and hug your children.'* Two performers use wooden miniature planes to topple a miniature version of the Twin Towers. 1 APRIL 2001 The Netherlands SAME SEX MARRIAGE IS FINALLY LEGALIZED IN THE NETHERLANDS. Two male performers kiss. Israel ISRAEL AND PALESTINE, FAILED PEACE TREATY. *Representative of Israel: 'It's not my fault. It is your fault.' Representative of Palestine: 'It is your fault.'* They go on quarrelling until the next line. 10 MARCH 2000 (Unspecified) INTERNET BUBBLE BURSTS. DECEMBER 1999 (Unspecified) MILLENNIUM BUG. Dark. Lights back on. (Unspecified) THE HUMAN POPULATION IS NOW 6 BILLION. France Female performer uses two pink balloons to impersonate Lolo Ferrari. LOLO FERRARI, THE WOMAN WITH THE BIGGEST BREASTS IN THE WORLD, DIES OF SUFFOCATION. EACH BREAST WEIGHED THREE KILOS. The Netherlands *Big Brother interviewer's voice: 'So guys, what have you been up to today?' Big Brother participant: 'Nothing.' Other participant: 'Not much really.' Interviewer's voice: 'This is Big Brother.'* APRIL 1999 Colorado Performer wears rucksack, cap and holds a gun. COLUMBINE MASSACRE. AUGUST 1998 Congo/Ruanda THE GREAT WAR OF AFRICA. AN EAST CONGOLESE BROADCAST STATES THAT… DECEMBER 1998 Atlantic Ocean ⌐ Kate Winslet and Leonardo Di Caprio in Titanic ⌐ *Leonardo Di Caprio: 'I'm the king of the world.'* Congo/Ruanda *Radio Mille Collines: 'Bring a machete, a spear, electric irons, barbed wire, stones…'* Washington Performer impersonates Monica Lewinsky giving the president a blowjob. *Bill Clinton: 'I did not have sexual relations with that woman.'* ~~Congo/Ruanda~~ *'...an arrow, a hoe, spades, rakes, nails, truncheons...'* ~~Sydney~~ *Performer: 'I pay $650 to stay in the same hotel as the Spice Girls.'* SEPTEMBER 1998 ~~Congo/Ruanda~~ *'...anything, dear listeners, in order to kill the Ruandan Tutsis.'* ~~Los Angeles~~ GOOGLE WAS FOUNDED. Performer removes the Google-sign. DECEMBER 1997 ~~Japan~~ KYOTO. 170 COUNTRIES TRY TO REDUCE GREENHOUSE GASES BY 5%. *World leaders: 'I'll sign.' US president: 'I'm signing, but it's not official.' Australian leader: 'I'll sign later.'* AUGUST 1997 ~~Paris~~ Performer holds shrine with picture of Princess Diana Princess. DIANA DIES. JULY 1997 ~~China~~ HONG KONG IS RETURNED TO CHINA. Performer puts English flag on the map to mark that Hong Kong is now English territory. FEBRUARY 1997 ~~United Kingdom~~ THE FIRST EVER CLONING IS OF A SHEEP. Two performers, preferably those who also play Israel and Palestine, play Dolly and her clone. *Cloned sheep: 'I'm Dolly. No, I'm Dolly. No, I'm Dolly. No, I'm Dolly.'* AUGUST 1996 ~~Belgium~~ TWO GIRLS, LAETITIA AND SABINE, AGED 13 AND 15, SURVIVE IMPRISONMENT IN MARC DUTROUX'S BASEMENT. FOUR OTHER GIRLS DIDN'T. JULY 1995 ~~Bosnia-Herzegovina~~ SREBRENICA. 30,000 BOSNIANS ARE KILLED. UN PEACEKEEPING TROOPS WERE ORDERED NOT TO INTERVENE. Three performers line up and kneel down one by one to symbolize the massacre. ~~Ruanda~~ GENOCIDE IN RUANDA. 800,000 PEOPLE WERE KILLED OVER 100 DAYS. IN ONE INCIDENT, 1,500 PEOPLE WERE CRAMMED INTO A CHURCH, WHICH WAS THEN BULLDOZED. Here too, three performers line up and kneel down one by one. ~~Israel~~ ISRAEL AND PALESTINE, SUCCESSFUL PEACE TREATY. *Bill Clinton: 'Thanks to me.'* A fourth performer takes a picture of the handshake. *Representative of Israel: 'No, thanks to me.' Representative of Palestine: 'No, thanks to me.'* They quarrel till the next line. APRIL 1994 ~~Seattle~~ Performer holds shrine with picture of Kurt Cobain. KURT COBAIN DIES. ~~Los Angeles~~ L.A. RIOTS. *Rioter: 'For Rodney King!'* OCTOBER 1993 ~~Los Angeles~~ Performer holds shrine with picture of River Phoenix. AND RIVER PHOENIX DIES. FEBRUARY 1992 ~~Germany~~ Performer holds flag of the EU. *Helmut Kohl: 'Finally, finally we have achieved what the founding fathers of Europe always dreamt of: The United States of Europe.'* AUGUST 1991 ~~Eastern Europe~~ THE IRON CURTAIN COLLAPSES. Performer throws down a chain on the map, another performer arranges it in the shape of the iron curtain. ~~(Unspecified)~~ THE END OF THE COLD WAR. ~~Washington~~ THE USA PRODUCED MORE THAN 70,000 NUCLEAR WARHEADS. ~~Moscow~~ RUSSIA PRODUCED MORE THAN 75,000 NUCLEAR WARHEADS. NOVEMBER 1991 ~~Belgium~~ Performer holds baby picture of herself. *Performer: 'I am born in Deinze, I weigh 3.22 kilos and I am 53cm.'* ~~Washington~~ THE USA SPENT 7.8 TRILLION DOLLARS. ~~Moscow~~ RUSSIA SPENT SLIGHTLY LESS THAN 7.8 TRILLION DOLLARS. ~~Iraq~~ OPERATION DESERT STORM BEGINS. SEPTEMBER 1990 ~~Belgium~~ Performer holds baby picture of herself. *Performer: 'I am born in Ghent, seven weeks premature.'* ~~United Kingdom~~ THE WORLD WIDE WEB IS CREATED IN THE UNITED KINGDOM. FEBRUARY 1990 ~~South Africa~~ NELSON MANDELA IS SET FREE, MARKING THE END OF APARTHEID. *Nelson Mandela: 'Our struggle has reached a decisive moment...'* ~~Los Angeles~~ *Twin Peaks fan: 'Who killed Laura Palmer?* ~~South Africa~~ *'... Our March to freedom is irreversible.'* ~~Panama~~ THE USA INVESTS IN THE INVASION OF PANAMA TO OVERTHROW THE REGIME. Performer representing the USA holds a stack of money and hands some to another performer who impersonates a Panamanian rebel. ~~London~~ *Margaret Thatcher: 'I stand before you tonight in my Red chiffon evening gown, the Iron Lady of the Western world.'* NOVEMBER 1989 ~~USA~~ *Ronald Reagan: 'Mr. Gorbachev, tear down that wall.'* ~~Berlin~~ THE FALL OF THE BERLIN WALL Performer builds miniature wall with clay blocks. ~~China~~ PROTESTS IN TIANANMEN SQUARE. Performer holds miniature tank and slowly approaches another performer. ⌐ Picture of Regime army attacking protesters ⌐ JULY 1989 ~~Japan~~ THE GAMEBOY IS INVENTED IN KYOTO, JAPAN. NOVEMBER 1989 ~~Middle East~~ *Representative of USA: 'I also invested $40 million in Afghanistan.'* Performer representing Afghan regime accepts money. *Representative of the Sovjet Union: 'Russia lost this war.' Representative of the USA: 'I invested in Saddam in Iraq...'* Performer impersonating Saddam Hussein accepts money *'And I sold weapons in Iran.'* Performer impersonating Iran hands back money to the US representative. DECEMBER 1987 ~~Israel~~ AN ISRAELI BUSINESSMAN IS STABBED TO DEATH IN GAZA. IT'S THE BEGINNING OF THE PALESTINIAN UPRISING IN ISRAEL. ~~USA~~ MARLON BRANDO IS REALLY FAT RIGHT NOW. ~~(Unspecified)~~ THE HUMAN POPULATION IS NOW 5 BILLION. ~~Central America~~ *USA representative: 'Then with the money from Iran I invested in Nicaraguan rebels.'* Representative hands the money he received from Iran over to another performer impersonating a Nicaraguan rebel. SEPTEMBER 1986 ~~Australia~~ *Crocodile Dundee: 'That's not a knife, this is a knife!'* APRIL 1986 ~~Russia~~ CHERNOBYL NUCLEAR DISASTER. Performer puts nuclear sign on the map. JANUARY 1986 ~~Florida~~ Performer has prepared a teabag for flying up in the air while it's burning. *Countdown voice: 'Challenger in 5...4...3...2...1.'* If things go right, the teabag flies up and turns to ashes. ~~Los Angeles~~ *Michael Jackson: 'We are the world, we are the children...'* DECEMBER 1985 ~~Moscow~~ GLASNOST PERESTROIKA. ~~London~~ *Margaret Thatcher: 'I like Mr. Gorbachev, we can do business together.'* JULY 1985 ~~Ethiopia~~ FAMINE IN ETHIOPIA ~~Europe~~ *Representative of the USA: 'Can I put some nuclear missiles here?' Protesters: 'No! Ban the bomb! Queers against rocketeers! Janetten tegen de raketten!'* ~~United Kingdom~~ *Margaret Thatcher: 'A world without nuclear weapons would be less stable and more dangerous place for all of us.'* ~~Washington~~ *Ronald Reagan: 'I occasionally think how quickly our differences would vanish if we were facing an alien threat from an outside world.'* NOVEMBER 1984 ~~Los Angeles~~ *Darth Vader: 'The ability to destroy a planet...'* ~~USA~~ *Madonna: 'Like a Virgin.'* ~~Los Angeles~~ *'...is insignificant compared to the power of the dark side.'* ~~Germany~~ *Nena: '99 Luftballons.'* ~~North Africa~~ *Representative of the USA: 'I'm also spending $1 million on the war in Sudan.'* Representative hands money to another performer representing the Sudanese regime. ~~Los Angeles~~ *Michael Jackson: 'Thriller.'* OCTOBER 1983 ~~Carribean~~ *Representative of the USA: 'Can I invade Grenada?'* ~~Worldwide~~ *Members of the United Nations: 'No, I am against it!'* ~~Russia~~ *Representative of the Soviet Union: 'Mister Reagan, I am totally against it.'* ~~Caribbean~~ *Representative of the USA: 'I veto. America invades Grenada.'* Representative jumps on Grenada on the map, the other performers show disapproval. *Ronald Reagan: 'What? How can a president not be an actor?'* JULY 1982 ~~Sydney~~ Performer shows baby picture of himself. *Performer: 'I am born in Sydney. The first thing I do is burp.'* ~~Los Angeles~~ *Prince: 'I'm gonna party like it's 1999.'* ~~Central America~~ *Representative of the USA: 'I am also investing in the training of soldiers in El Salvador.'* Representative hands money to another performer representing the Salvadorian military. DECEMBER 1980 ~~New York~~ JOHN LENNON IS SHOT. SEPTEMBER 1980 ~~Belgium~~ Performer shows baby picture of herself. *Performer: 'I am born in Wilrijk, on 9/11.'* JUNE 1980 ~~North America~~ Performer covers himself with a blanket and points his finger from underneath it. *ET: 'ET phone home.'* FEBRUARY 1979 ~~Sweden~~ *Abba: 'Money Money Money. must be funny, in a rich man's world.'* ~~Australia~~ *The Beegees: 'Ah ah ah ah Stayin' Alive.' ACDC: 'I'm on a highway to Hell.'* ~~United Kingdom~~ *Queen: 'Is this the real life? Is it just fantasy?'* ~~USA~~ *Bob Dylan: 'Like a rolling stone.'* ~~United Kingdom~~ *Queen: 'Mamaaaa. OooooOOooOoo.'* JANUARY 1978 ~~China~~ CHINA BEGINS ITS ONE CHILD POLICY. ~~Rome~~ Performer holds crucifix and Bible. THE CHURCH STATES: CONTRACEPTION IS NEVER JUSTIFIED. APRIL 1975 ~~Southeast Asia~~ Killing fields. POL POT AND HIS ARMY THE KMHMER ROUGE KILLED ONE THIRD OF THE CAMBODIAN POPULATION. Three performers line up and kneel down one by one. CHILDREN UNDER THE AGE OF EIGHT, THE ELDERLY, AND ANYONE WHO WORE GLASSES. ~~Belgium~~ Performer shows baby picture of himself. I AM BORN IN GHENT. I'M THE OLDEST OF THE CAST. ~~Southeast Asia~~ THE END OF THE VIETNAM WAR. ~~Washington~~ *Representative of the USA: 'The USA spent $200 million and then we had to retreat.'* ~~(Unspecified)~~ THE HUMAN POPULATION IS NOW 4 BILLION. SEPTEMBER 1973 ~~Middle East~~ *Arab League: 'The American people should stand beside the Arab world. The Israelis should withdraw from the occupied territories.'* ~~Chile~~ *Representative of the USA: 'The USA supports the overthrow of Allende's regime in Chile.'* ~~Middle East~~ *Arab League: 'We will use our oil as a political weapon.'* ~~Europe~~ *Government calls: 'You are kindly requested to leave your cars home on Sundays.'* ~~Ireland~~ BLOODY SUNDAY. JUNE 1972 ~~Washington~~ *Richard Nixon: 'I can see clearly now that I was wrong in not acting more decisively and more forthrightly when dealing with Watergate.'* JULY 1969 ~~(Unspecified/on the moon)~~ Performer holds a miniature version of a moon rocket. *Neil Armstrong: 'Houston, Tranquility base here. The eagle has landed. Repeat: the eagle has landed. Roger, Twank, Tranquility, we copy you on the ground. We're breathing again. Thanks a lot. That's one small step for man, one giant leap for mankind.'* MAY 1968 ~~San Francisco~~ Performers form a line up from America till Russia and speak in turns, while passing on the protest cloth. *Scott McKenzie: 'If you're going...to San Francisco.'* Performer puts a flower behind his ear. *Allen Ginsberg: 'The cry of flower power echoes through the land.' Rolling Stones: 'I can't get no satisfaction.'* MAY 1967 ~~Australia~~ THE ABORIGINAL PEOPLE OF AUSTRALIA ARE ONLY NOW GIVEN THE RIGHT TO VOTE. ~~United Kingdom~~ *Beatles: 'We all live in a Yellow Submarine.'* ~~France~~ *Soixante-huitard: 'Soyez réaliste, demandez l'impossible.' Translator: 'Be realistic, aim for the impossible.'* ~~Eastern Europe~~ Performer holds a flower up. PRAGUE SPRING. SOCIALISM WITH A HUMAN FACE. Sovjet representative throws it on the floor and steps on it. *Representative of the Sovjet Union: 'Crushed by Russian military power.'* MAY 1966 China *Mao Zedong: 'A revolution is not a dinner party…'* MAY 1964 USA NIKE IS FOUNDED Performer removes the 'Nike'-sign. China *'…or painting a picture, or writing an essay…'* New York *Andy Warhol: 'In the future, everyone will be famous for fifteen minutes.'* China *'… It cannot be advanced softly, reading too many books is harmful.'* NOVEMBER 1963 Texas Performer approaches America with a gun and fires at performer impersonating President Kennedy. LEE HARVEY OSWALD. New York Performer shows shrine with picture of Marilyn Monroe. *Marilyn Monroe: 'Happy birthday to you…'* AUGUST 1963 Washington *Martin Luther King: 'I still have a dream. It is a dream deeply rooted in the American Dream. I have a dream.'* OCTOBER 1962 Mexican Gulf Representative of the Sovjet Union approaches Cuba with a nuclear sign, representative of the USA grabs in his pocket to produce another nuclear sign. THE CUBAN MISSILE CRISIS All performers pause until the representatives put away their nuclear signs. New York *'… Happy birthday Mr. President.'* Africa Performers put British, French, Belgian, Spanish and Portuguese flags on the map marking the colonization. Washington *John Fitzgerald Kennedy: 'Ask not what your country can do for you, ask what you can do for your country.'* AUGUST 1961 China END OF THE GREAT LEAP FORWARD. *Mao Zedong: 'In order to feed half of the population it's better to let the other half starve.'* IT IS ESTIMATED 45 MILLION PEOPLE DIED. APRIL 1961 Russia RUSSIA GETS THE FIRST MAN INTO SPACE: YURI GAGARIN. (Unspecified/in space) *Yuri Gagarin: 'I looked and looked and looked, but I didn't see god.'* (Unspecified) THE PILL WAS INVENTED BY A MAN. (Unspecified) HUMAN POPULATION IS NOW 3 BILLION. JANUARY 1959 Argentina *Che Guevara: 'Hasta la victoria siempre.'* Cuba *Fidel Castro: 'I am Fidel Castro and I have come to liberate Cuba.'* Communist revolutionary: *'Vive la revolucion!'* Louisiana *Horace Lee Logan: 'Elvis has left the building.'* Performer dances surrounded by other performers. *Elvis Presley: 'Shake, rattle and roll, shake, rattle and roll.'* Other performers scream hysterically. Indian Ocean *Performer: 'My father is born on a ship traveling from Egypt to Australia.'* Congo Performer puts a black skull on the map. THE FIRST KNOWN CASE OF HIV IS REPORTED IN CONGO. Belgium *Jacques Brel: 'Ne me quitte pas, il faut tout oublier…'* DECEMBER 1955 Alabama AFRICAN AMERICAN WOMAN ROSA PARKS REFUSES TO GIVE UP HER SEAT FOR A WHITE PERSON. United Kingdom *Archbishop of Canterbury: 'Do you solemnly promise to govern the peoples of the United Kingdom…'* Russia *Vladimir Nabokov: 'Lolita…'* United Kingdom *'… Canada…'* Russia *'…light of my life…'* United Kingdom *'… South Africa…'* Russia *'…fire of my loins.'* United Kingdom *'… Australia…'* DECEMBER 1953 Los Angeles FIRST ISSUE OF PLAYBOY IS PUBLISHED. United Kingdom *'… New Zealand, Pakistan and Ceylon?'* *Queen Elizabeth II: 'I solemnly promise so to do.'* Performer gets a crown. JULY 1951 Los Angeles *Rabbit from Alice in Wonderland: 'I'm late, I'm late, for a very important date.'* United Kingdom Performer produces Bond theme. *Sean Connery: 'Bond, James Bond.'* Russia Performer holds a vinyl record and scrutinizes it in front of another performer. *KGB officer: 'How did this capitalist pollution come into your possession?'* Performer throws the record on the floor, the other performer tries to pick it up but stopped. JUNE 1949 London GEORGE ORWELL WRITES 1984. *George Orwell: 'There will be no loyalty, except loyalty to the party…'* Los Angeles *McCarthyist: 'Mister Walt Disney, do you have any people in your studio at the present time that you believe to be communists or fascists employed there?'* *Walt Disney: 'No, at the present time I feel that everybody who works at my studio is a 100% American.'* Los Angeles *McCarthyist: 'Mr. Chaplin, are you a member of the communist party?'* *Charlie Chaplin: 'No, I do not want to create any revolution, all I want to do is create a few more films.'* London *'… There will be no love, except the love of Big Brother.'* Washington *Harry S. Truman: 'If we allow North Korea to take over the South, communism will get closer to our shores.'* Russia *Josef Stalin: 'It is always important to keep the enemy at arms length.'* Southeast Asia/India Performer puts a Dutch, French and English flag on the map to mark colonization. JUNE 1948 USA *Representative of the USA: 'America gets the first monkey into space.'* (unspecified) ALBERT IS THE WORLD'S FIRST MONKEY ASTRONAUT. HE DIED OF SUFFOCATION DURING THE FLIGHT. THIS MARKS THE BEGINNING OF THE SPACE RACE. Europe *Representative of the USA: 'The Marshall Plan.'* *Representative of Russia: 'The Molotov Plan.'* MAY 1948 Europe THE IRON CURTAIN IS CONSTRUCTED. Performer removes the chain. Europe THE UNITED NATIONS ARE FOUNDED. ISRAEL IS GIVEN TO THE JEWISH PEOPLE. I STARTED IT. SEPTEMBER 1945 Japan *Emperor Hirohito: 'I swallow my tears and surrender.'*

# AUGUST 1945

A performer crosses the stage with a miniature
plane. All other performers pause. Two miniature nuclear clouds are put on the map, on
Hiroshima and Nagasaki. The performer takes
out a pile of war signs and starts covering the
countries involved in World War II.

JAPAN AUSTRALIA NEW ZEALAND THAILAND INDIA

Another performer moves to Germany and
starts naming concentration camps.

TREBLINKA SOBIBOR BELZEC CHELMO AUSCHWITZ
BERGEN-BELSEN BUCHENWALD DACHAU

IRAQ SOUTH AFRICA GREECE

*6 million people were exterminated.*

Three performers line up and kneel down.

> *Most them Jews, but also half*
> *Jews, quarter Jews, anti-socials,*
> *intellectuals, homosexuals, social-*
> *ists, communists, anarchists,*
> *disabled, gypsies.*

**~~BULGARIA~~ ~~YUGOSLAVIA~~ ~~ROMANIA~~ ~~HUNGARY~~**
**~~CZECHOSLOVAKIA~~ ~~SOVIET UNION~~**

**~~United Kingdom~~ *Winston Churchill: 'I have nothing to offer you,* *but blood, toil, tears and sweat. We have before us many many* *long months of struggle and of suffering.'***

**USA performer begins to talk after 'sweat'**
**George S. Patton:**

> *Sure we want to go home. We want*
> *this war over with. The shortest*
> *way home is through Berlin*
> *and Tokyo. And when we get to*
> *Berlin I am personally going*
> *to shoot that hanging son of*
> *bitch Hitler just like I'd shoot*
> *a snake. Germany performer*
> *begins to talk after 'home' Joseph*
> *Goebbels: Wir sind an einem*
> *entscheidenden Moment in der*

*Geschichte des tausendjährigen*
*Reiches, also ich frage euch: wollt*
*ihr den totalen Krieg?*

**Performer:**

*Because of his Jewish heritage, my*
*grandfather thought it would be safer*
*to be a drug runner for the British*
*during the occupation of Egypt.*

**BELGIUM FRANCE NETHERLANDS NORWAY**
**GERMANY UNITED KINGDOM ITALY**

**Performer:**

*My great-grandmother hid people*
*from the resistance in her base-*
*ment. She was going to be executed,*
*but a few hours before that was*
*about to happen, the war ended.*

## ~~BRAZIL~~ MEXICO

### Performer:

*My father was born during the war.
He liked corned beef because that
was what the Americans brought.*

## ~~UNITED STATES~~ CANADA

### Performer:

*My grandfather did forced labour
in an arms factory in Germany,
under a mountain.*

**One performer crosses the stage with a miniature plane and lands it in the Pacific Ocean. The Japanese attacked Pearl Harbor.**

**MUSIC**
Background track from
Chaplin's movie 'The Great
Dictator.' Richard Wagner,
'Lohengrin', prelude.

**1940** A performer enters with a bow hat and a minuscule black mustache, carrying an inflatable balloon with the world map on it. *Charlie Chaplin: 'Emperor of the world.'* Performer throws the balloon in the air, all the others collect war signs and hand them over to a performer wearing a swastika and a minuscule black mustache. ~~Germany~~ The performer starts his speech while receiving war signs. *Adolf Hitler: 'I have throughout these years practiced a practical peace policy. I have approached all apparently impossible problems with the firm resolve to solve them peacefully. I myself am a frontline soldier and I know how grave a thing war is. I want to spare the German people such an evil.'* The performer puts the pile of war signs down in Germany. **1937** ~~USA~~ *Scarlett O'Hara: 'As God is my witness, I shall never be hungry again.'* ~~California~~ MCDONALD'S WAS FOUNDED. Performer removes the McDonald's sign. ~~Spain~~ Performer completes drawing on the floor of Picasso's 'Guernica'. GUERNICA. CIVIL WAR IN SPAIN. Performer puts war card down in Spain. ~~(Unspecified)~~ THE HUMAN POPULATION IS NOW TWO BILLION. **1936** THE GREAT DEPRESSION. Performers show empty pockets. ⌐ Dorothea Lange's photograph 'Migrant Mother' ⌐ ~~Russia~~ *Josef Stalin: 'If we would not let our enemies have weapons why should we let them have ideas.'* HITLER AND STALIN SHAKE HANDS. USA performer puts Ku Klux Klan hood on. ~~Southwest USA~~ *Billie Holiday: 'Southern trees bear strange fruit. Blood on the leaves, blood at the root.'* ~~India~~ *Mohandas Ghandi: 'An eye for an eye, makes the whole world blind.'* ~~(Unspecified)~~ Performer holds up miniature nuclear cloud. *Albert Einstein: 'I share this discovery with full knowledge of its destructive capacity. I can only hope and trust that it doesn't end up in the wrong hands.'* ~~USA~~ *Dorothy Parker: 'Guns aren't lawful. Nooses give. Gas smells awful. You might as well live.'* ~~Worldwide~~ *Suffragettes: 'I want to vote.'*

# 1918

The performers leave the stage, except for two, who work together to put the war signs on the countries involved in WWI. When the music stops, one performer comes to the front and addresses the audience. The other one leaves.

## 04.  SECOND MONOLOGUE

**NOTE**
Based on the poem 'Consola-
tion' by Wislawa Szymborska.

*They say Charles Darwin read novels*
*to relax, but only certain kinds:*
*Nothing with a bad ending.*
*If anything like that turned up*
*he'd get angry and throw the book*
*into the fire.*

*True or not,*
*I'm ready to believe it.*

*If I had explored in my mind so*
*many times and places,*
*I'd also have enough of dying*
*species, the triumph of the strong*
*over the weak.*
*The endless struggles to survive.*
*All doomed, sooner or later.*

*I'd also feel I earned the right to*
*happy endings.*
*At least in fiction.*
*I would want to see lovers reunited,*
*families reconciled, orphans shel-*
*tered, widows comforted, prodigal*
*sons welcomed home.*

*And my grandfather,*
   *lost in the first chapter,*
*Turned up alive in the last.*

## 05.   PART II

**Part II follows the same principle of performers using a world map and a timer to tell history in reverse, but now time lapses are bigger and the importance of scenic compositions increases. The element of music is added, which helps to evoke the atmosphere of historical periods but also provides cues for the action. In this part, the focus is more on general ideas and evolutions, rather than specific facts. The positioning on the map is less strict, sometimes even secondary to the presentation of images. The concept of history as a selection of events in service of a subjective narrative becomes more apparent.**

MUSIC
Igor Stravinsky, 'Sacre du
Printemps', 1913, Part II
'Rituel des ancêtres', 3'34".

**The performers enter the stage, wearing crowns.**

**1914** ~~South America~~ PANAMA CANAL. Performer drags South America to meet Panama. The crowned performers gather in ~~Europe~~ and ~~Russia~~, representing the old order of kings and emperors before the First World War. One performer shoots another performer, referring to the assassination of Archduke Franz Ferdinand of Austria which started the war. All performers collect war signs and take off their crowns. Two female performers take off their bras and are strapped in corsets. **1907** ~~China/North America~~ Tanks are replaced by cannons. The specific locations are a matter of *mise en scène.* **1903** ~~North America~~ FIRST FLIGHT. Performer removes the miniature planes. **1900** ~~Australia~~ AUSTRALIA INDEPENDENT. Performer puts a British flag in Sydney. **1896** ~~Central & South America~~ THE SPANISH LOSE THEIR COLONIES IN THE AMERICAS. Performer puts a Spanish flag in the Americas. **1890** ~~Congo~~ Crowned performer picks up the black skull and Belgian flag. CONGO. THE DARKEST MOMENT IN BELGIAN HISTORY. THE HORROR, THE HORROR. Referring to the bloody colonial rule of King Leopold II of Belgium and Joseph Conrad's Heart of Darkness. ~~China/North America~~ Cars are replaced by horses. Again: timing and *mise en scène*. The performers form a line-up and act out an assembly line processing money, which ends up in a factory in the United Kingdom. This refers to the second phase of the industrial revolution. ~~Europe~~ Karl Marx: *'Workers of the world unite!'* This line is delivered by a 'worker' in the assembly line. *Child labourer: 'Daens is verkozen!'* The performer drops dead in the assembly line. The quote refers to a 19th century activist priest who opposed the inhumane working conditions in early industrialism. **1886** ~~USA~~ COCA-COLA. Performer removes the Coca-Cola sign. **1871** ~~Japan~~ YEN. Performer removes the Yen sign. **1869** ~~North Africa~~ SUEZ CANAL. Performer drags Africa to meet the Middle East. ~~North America~~ GOLD RUSH. Performer removes a block of gold. ~~North America~~ OIL RUSH. Performer removes oil tank. ~~Africa~~ Five performers put their crowns back on and pick up war signs. They gather around Africa. These are the kings and emperors of the colonial powers who will scramble to take their part of the continent. The scramble is acted out like at a gaming table, with flags and war signs as pawns and tokens.

MUSIC
Igor Stravinsky, 'Sacre du Printemps', 1913, Part II 'Danse sacrale de l'élue', 0'51".

The first move is made on the first note of music. In the end, the continent is emptied and the performers get up, holding their flags and concealing their war signs in feigned innocence. **1866** ~~France~~ Female performer holds a gilded frame in front of her spread legs, referring to Gustave Courbet's painting ⌐ L'origine du monde ⌐ **1865** ~~Washington~~ Performer points gun at another performer dressed up as Abraham Lincoln, who holds a chain representing slavery. *John Wilkes Booth: 'Nigger lover.'* Performer raises the chain. *Abraham Lincoln: 'A house divided against itself cannot stand. I believe this government cannot endure permanently half slave and half free. As I would not be a slave so I would not be a master.'* ~~(Unspecified)~~ HUMAN POPULATION IS NOW 1 BILLION.

## Music stops.

~~Europe~~ Performers line up and form: ⌐ The Descent of Man ⌐ *Friedrich Nietzsche: 'God is dead. And God remains dead. And we have killed him. Who will wipe the blood off us? What water is there to cleanse ourselves? Is not this deed too great a deed for us? Must not we ourselves become gods, only to be worthy of it?'* **1830** ~~Belgium~~ *Belgian national hymn: 'O dierbaar België, O heilig land der Vad'ren, Onze ziel en ons hart zijn u gewijd.'* **1826** ~~Europe~~ Performer presents a camera. THE FIRST PRESERVED PHOTOGRAPH IS TAKEN. Performer blows chalk powder off his hand while simultaneously initializing a flash.

MUSIC
Franz Liszt, 'Romance oubliée', 1880, Andante malinconico, 1'58".

1819 Europe Performers form the image of ⌐⌐ Theodore Géricault's 'Le radeau de la Méduse' ⌐⌐ The image shifts to a tableau representing Napoleon Bonaparte's Russian campaign of 1812. One performer impersonates Napoleon, a second one scatters snow and the others act out freezing French soldiers. When Napoleon returns to France, the image shifts once more. The soldiers turn into kings again and form a pile of dead bodies. 1792 France With the pile of dead kings in front of them, two performers hold a miniature guillotine and drop the blade, referring to the Terror during the French Revolution. They also hold the protest cloth of Part I. 1789 France *Universal declaration of human rights: 'Les gens naissent et demeurent libres et égaux en droits. La déclaration est fondée sur des principes simples, contestables et au bonheur de tous.'*

## Music stops.

1788 Australia COLONIZATION OF AUSTRALIA. Performer removes British flag. 1785 Washington *Thomas Jefferson, United States Declaration of Independence: 'We hold these truths to be self-evident...'* Washington THE DOLLAR IS INTRODUCED. Performer removes Dollar sign. Washington *'...that all men are created equal...'* 1776 London STEAM ENGINE IS USED FOR THE FIRST TIME. Performer removes factory. Washington *'...that they are endowed by their Creator with certain unalienable Rights, that among these are Life, Liberty and the Pursuit of Happiness.'*

MUSIC
Henry Purcell, 'Dido and
Aeneas', 1689, Overture,
2'13".

Europe Two performers, representing the aristocracy of the ancient regime, laugh out loud, holding teabags and fanning themselves with money. South Africa SOUTH AFRICA. Performer removes Dutch flag. Philippines PHILIPPINES. Performer removes Spanish flag. 1773 Britain/ Boston Performer brings on a miniature ship with a British flag, takes the teabags from the aristocratic ladies, puts them in the ship and moves it from Britain to North America. He then picks up the tea bags, holds them up. THE BOSTON TEA PARTY. And throws them into the 'sea'. 1694 THE INTRODUCTION OF THE POUND. Performer removes Pound sign. Europe/ Africa/America Three performers demonstrate the slave triangle. One performer uses the ship to transport cotton from America to Europe and trade it for guns with a second performer. A third performer positions himself in Central Africa and puts on chains, representing black slaves. The first performer trades the guns for the slave and takes the chains to America, where the second performer exchanges them for cotton and the whole process can start over again. Middle East Two female performers put on burqas, referring to the rise of Wahhabism in the Islamic world. 1715 France Three performers evoke court ceremony in Versailles and the absolute monarchy installed by Louis XIV of France with a masked ballet. 1692 North America The performers who demonstrated the slave triangle end up creating an image of witch burnings. One pulls the witch's arms back and another holds a crucifix in front of her. The image ends in a scream.

## Music stops.

**1687** ~~Britain~~ One performer wearing a ruff is sitting down on his knees, another one drops an apple on his head. *Isaac Newton: 'I can calculate the motion of the heavenly bodies, but not the madness of humans.'*

MUSIC
Mr. de Sainte Colombe,
'Les pleurs', mid 17th
century, 4'10".

**1650** ~~Europe/North Africa~~ The performers put on ruffs and white collars. One performer lies down centre stage, the others gather around the body and look at it, creating the image of Rembrandt's painting ⌐⌐ The Anatomical Lesson ⌐⌐ **1632** One performer makes an incision in the body and demonstrates the first blood transfusion. Another one picks up the 'blood' and puts it under a microscope. A third performer opens a telescope, looks up into the sky and quotes *Blaise Pascal: 'The eternal silence of these infinite spaces terrifies me. Between us and heaven and hell there is only life, which is the frailest thing of all.'* Meanwhile, a fourth performer has started studying light rays through a prism. The performer who received a blood transfusion quotes *René Descartes: 'I think therefore I am.'* **1600** It's followed by another Renaissance quote *Shakespeare: 'To be or not be, that is the question.'* The rise of philosophical speculation and scientific discovery is countered by a lecture of the Roman inquisition. One performer rises from the group image holding the Bible and the crucifix. *Inquisitor: 'The idea of that the Earth is turning is foolish and absurd in philosophy, and contradicts the sense of the Holy Scripture. The earth is flat, like this.'* Performer points at the stage. *'Ashes to ashes, dust to dust.'* The other performers open their crucifixes and assume a praying position. Then they lift up the 'dead body' and put a funnel in the performer's mouth. With the permission of the inquisitor, another performer slashes the victim's belly to illustrate torture practices of the holy inquisition. The sequence shows that science cuts bodies to gain knowledge, while religion cuts them to suppress and inspire fear. The tortured performer screams. **1532** ~~South America~~ A performer wearing a feathered hat is standing in South America. He represents the Inca empire. The circle of performers holding crucifixes looks at the inquisitor for guidance. He lifts his crucifix like a sword, points at the Inca and moves towards him. He offers the Inca the Bible. The Inca reaches out for it, takes it, sniffs it, turns it upside down and throws it on the floor. The inquisitor, outraged by this action, points his finger at him and another performer slashes his belly with a crucifix-turned-into-sword. The Inca collapses. While he falls down, he stretches his arm towards the inquisitor, who is still pointing at him. **1512** The pointed fingers and body postures of the performers slowly form the image of ⌐⌐ Adam and God in Michelangelo's 'Sistine Chapel' ⌐⌐ The whole scene refers to the confrontation between the Spanish forces led by Pizarro and the Inca emperor Atahualpa. **1492** ~~Central America/Portugal~~ A performer brings on a boat and loads it with a cannon, a miniature horse, the Bible and a Spanish flag, then makes the journey back from the Americas to Portugal, where Columbus left off to discover the New World.

MUSIC
Giovanni da Palestrina, 'Jesu,
Rex Admirabilis', mid 16th
century, Motet, 1'46".

**1486** ~~Italy~~ A female performer covered in a cloak is revealed naked. Three other performers assist her in forming the image of ⌐⌐ The Birth of Venus by Botticelli ⌐⌐ **1421** ~~South America~~ A performer wearing a Chinese hat approaches South America with a boat. The Inca rises. The 'Chinese' offers him a teabag, the Inca gives him gold in return. This refers to the hypothesis that the Chinese discovered America before Western Europeans and mainly exchanged commodities with the natives. **1348** ~~Europe~~ The naked female performer is covered with the cloak and assumes the posture of a medieval Madonna, while the other performers surround her in prayer. The goddess of love transforms into a religious mother figure. Another performer approaches the scene from behind and holds the black skull, representing the plague. *Doom preacher, para-phrasing 1 John 2:18: 'Little children, the end is near. For the blood that descends upon your eyes like the Black Death, is the sign of the foul beast, the antichrist who is among us, by this we know the last hour has come.'* Performers whip their backs while two others put black skulls in Europe.

## Music stops.

~~North Africa~~ A performer recites the Qu'ran in Arabic. Two other performers stand next to him and write on blackboards. One writes down the opening sentence of the Qu'ran, the other an algebraic formula. When the recitation is finished, they show the boards to the audience *Avicenna: 'The world is divided into men who have wit and no religion and men who have religion and no wit.'* Performers wipe out the writings on the boards. **1295** ~~Europe~~ Performers put on a cap suggesting a chain mail and hold their crucifixes up like swords. They represent the crusaders.

MUSIC
Traditional Chinese Melody,
'The Moon is High', 2'20".

**1237** ~~Mongolia~~ A performer wearing a furred helmet holds a miniature horse. This represents the Mongolian empire of Genghis Khan. ~~China~~ A performer wearing a Chinese hat crosses his arms. Four other performers surround him, one holding an abacus, another one holding a cannon and lighting a sparkler representing gunpowder. Two performers take off their shoes and have their feet bound with white linen. The scene ends with a ceremonial greeting. **1000** ~~Newfoundland/Norway~~ A performer moves a miniature Viking ship from America to Scandinavia, representing Leiv Eriksson's voyage to America 500 years before Columbus's discovery. **476** ~~Rome~~ Performer wearing a laurel wreath holds up a chain, another performer stands beside him holding a crucifix. *Quote from Virgil's 'Aeneid', Anchises' advice to Aeneas in the underworld: 'For Rome, I set no limits, time or space. Remember, by your strength, to rule Earth's people. To pacify, to impose the rule of law, to spare the conquered and battle down the proud.'* Performer throws chain on the map.

MUSIC
Reconstruction of a melody
from Antiquity.

Two other performers sit down in front of him and put the chain around their wrists, repre-senting Roman slavery. The performer with the crucifix holds it like a sword and stabs the 'emperor', seizing the wreath and crowning himself with it. Another performer offers the 'new emperor' a poisoned cup and seizes the wreath in her turn. **33** ~~Jerusalem~~ Performer wearing a crown of thorns assumes the position of the crucified Christ. *Jesus of Nazareth: 'Father, forgive them, for they know not what they do.'*

## Timer counts down till zero.
## The performers look at the backdrop:

**3**
**2**
**1**
**0**

# 2,020 YEARS AGO

2,063 YEARS AGO ~~Rome~~ *Julius Caesar: 'Veni, vidi, vici.'*
2,350 YEARS AGO
2,400 YEARS AGO
2,500 YEARS AGO ~~Athens~~ *Democritos: 'Nothing exists except atoms and empty space, everything else is opinion.' Anaxagoras: 'Everything has a natural explanation. The moon is not a God, but a big rock and the sun is a hot rock.' Aristotle: 'Men create all Gods in their own image.'* ~~Israel~~ *Old Testament: 'And the lord God spoke all these words saying I am the lord thy God. Thou shalt have no other Gods before me. For I the lord thy god am a jealous God.'* ~~India~~ *Buddha: 'If we want to avoid suffering we must to look to ourselves because all suffering stems from our own desires.'* ~~China~~ *Confucius states: 'All humans are in nature the same, it is only their actions that carry them apart.'*
4,500 YEARS AGO ~~Egypt~~ Performer holds a whip and a sickle crossed in front of her chest, representing the Egyptian Pharaoh. The other performers gather around her. One by one, they produce clay blocks and build a miniature pyramid. When they've finished, they get up, line up and form an image of ⌐ ↵ Egyptian hieroglyphs ⌐ ↵

**Lights out.**

**Spotlight on the performer who delivers the third monologue.**

## 06. THIRD MONOLOGUE

**NOTE**
Based on 'Yali's question'
and the general thesis from
Jared Diamond's 'Guns,
Germs and Steel'.

*If an aboriginal person came up to*
*me on the street and asked me:*
*'why do you have so much and*
*I so little?' I wouldn't know what*
*to say and it bothers me.*

*I can understand the feeling.*
*Being African I too could be treated*
*differently because of my skin or*
*where I come from.*
*I guess history is not on my side, nor*
*on theirs.*

*It's hard to think about.*
*Why did some people conquer other*
*people and not the other way*
*around?*
*Why do some people have more?*

*I think it started here.*
*Food meant everything, it still does.*
*I would be a farmer, I work the land*
*for the food I need.*

*Everybody does it and there's just
   enough.
But one day, for some reason, there's
   some left.
Who's going to take it? Who's going
   to decide who gets it?
And then there's this one clever guy
   who says: 'I'll think it over, you
   go back to work.'
I think that's where it all went
   wrong.*

07.  **PART III**

In Part III, the actions and images are further reduced to the essentials. Props become scarcer and their meaning is extended. For example, miniature animals now signify domestication or seeds symbolize agriculture. Snow is used to demonstrate Ice Ages. The performers' positions on the world map represent the subgroups of human kind spread over the globe. We are now dealing with the foundations of human civilization and beyond. Time passes exponentially faster, while the action slows down, because it covers long-term evolutions. The whole part is accompanied by one music track, which is no longer related to a historical period.

MUSIC
Trent Reznor and Atticus
Ross, 'Hand Covers Bruise',
4'19", reprise 1'21" and 4'19".

# 5,000 YEARS AGO

Lights on.

All performers are sitting on the map, except the pharaoh of Part II and the performer who delivered the third monologue. There is one in ~~South America~~, one in ~~North America~~, three are in ~~the Middle East~~, one is in ~~China~~ and one in ~~Australia~~. They all have two clay blocks forming a little house and animals enclosed by a piece of rope in front of them, except for the one in ~~Australia~~, who holds a wooden stick with a clay block tied to it and has a miniature kangaroo in front of her. In ~~Egypt~~, the performer who impersonated the pharaoh stands in front of the pyramid and holds the whip and the sickle, as in the end of part II. The Pharoah hands the whip over to the performer in ~~the Middle East~~. The centre of power is now in ~~the Fertile Crescent~~. The performer who played the pharaoh sits down in ~~the Middle East~~, moves the clay blocks of the pyramid to ~~the Fertile Crescent~~ and constructs older buildings out of them. These represent older civilisations and the first cities. One performer in ~~the Middle East~~ holds up a wheel and demonstrates how a goat is pulling it. He removes the wheel. It no longer exists. The performer takes a blackboard with cuneiform on it and wipes it clean. Writing no longer exists. Performers in ~~South America~~, ~~North America, the Middle East~~ and ~~China~~ start sowing seeds in front of their settlements, indicating there is agriculture in these areas of the world. The performer in ~~Australia~~ stands up and knocks over the kangaroo with her 'tool', demonstrating that the Aborigines have no agriculture but instead hunt larger mammals, driving them to extinction. The performers in ~~the Middle East~~ harvest their seeds and pour them in front of the performer holding the whip. This demonstrates the first hierarchical societies, divided in workers and rulers. The other performers eat their harvested seeds, representing communities of farmers without class division. The performers in ~~the Middle East~~ who gave up their seeds to the 'master' move to ~~North Africa~~ and ~~Europe~~, where they sow their own seeds and eat them. The performer who's left in ~~the Middle East~~ puts down the whip, sits down, also sows her own seeds and eats them. The performer in ~~South America~~ looks at the time, then removes the rope around his miniature lama, demonstrating the peoples of ~~South America~~ no longer have domesticated animals. He topples the clay blocks, the settlement, indicating they are no longer sedentary. With the clay block, the rope and a wooden stick, he fabricates a tool. ~~South America~~ is now inhabited by hunter-gatherers. The performer in ~~North America~~ follows the example of ~~South America~~. The performer in ~~China~~ does the same thing. Then it's ~~North Africa~~ and ~~Europe~~'s turn. Six performers are holding stone tools.

~~(Unspecified)~~ HUMAN POPULATION IS NOW 1 MILLION.

The performer in ~~the Middle East~~ holds up a miniature cup. She milks her miniature cow, pouring real milk into the cup. She 'shaves' her miniature sheep, which has cotton wool attached to it. She stuffs it under her sleeve.

## The light shifts to cold white.

Six performers move from the outskirts of the map towards the middle, scattering snow all over the world. This represents **THE MOST RECENT ICE AGE.** The performer in ~~the Middle East~~ cleans away her animals and destroys her settlements. She also fabricates a tool. All humans are now hunter-gatherers.

## The light returns to the previous setting.

7,000 YEARS AGO The performer in ~~South America~~ starts walking backwards in slow motion towards North America. 13,000 YEARS AGO The performer in ~~North America~~ starts walking backwards. When he reaches the ~~Bering Street,~~ he crosses the stage from behind and enters on the other side, continuing his journey in ~~Russia.~~ The performer who left South America follows him. The performer in ~~China~~ also starts walking backwards, towards the Middle East. One performer draws images from the cave paintings of Lascaux in chalk on the floor. The performer in the ~~Middle East~~ starts walking backwards, towards Africa. 26,000 YEARS AGO/33,000 YEARS AGO The performer finishes the drawing and begins to walk backwards to Africa. 40,000 YEARS AGO The performer in ~~Australia~~ puts the kangaroo back up and crosses the ocean towards Southeast Asia with a miniature boat. The Polynesians join the rest of humanity in the journey back to Africa. 100,000 YEARS AGO All performers reach ~~Africa,~~ the original habitat of the homo sapiens. They unwind the rope of their tools and put them away. Humans no longer produce artefacts.

~~Africa~~ HUMAN POPULATION IS NOW 100,000.

130,000 YEARS AGO One performer falls down backward, supported by the others. They put her on the floor, on Africa. She plays dead. FIRST BURIAL Another performer closes her eyes.

~~Africa~~ HUMAN POPULATION IS NOW 10,000.

Performers form the image of ⌐ Descent of Man ⌐ 800,000 YEARS AGO A performer produces fire. All the others stare into the flame.

# 800,000 YEARS AGO

A performer produces fire. All the others stare into the flame. The lights dim. The performer blows the fire out. All performers except one leave. The one who stays delivers the fourth monologue.

## 08.   FOURTH MONOLOGUE

**NOTE**
Based on 'Descent of Species'
from the collection 'SUM.
Tales of the Afterlife' by
David Eagleman.

*I wish I was a horse. I envy the bliss
of its simple life. Afternoons graz-
ing in grassy fields, the peace of
its slow-flicking tail or the steam
pouring through its nostrils as it
gallops through the snow.*

*I don't believe in an afterlife. But if
I did, if I arrived there and was
given a choice to be whatever
I'd like to be in the next life…
I'd choose something simpler.*

*So for the next round I'd choose to
be a horse.*

*And as soon as I announce my deci-
sion my body begins to metamor-
phose into a horse. My muscles
start to bulge; a mat of thick hair
covers me like a comfortable blan-
ket in winter. My fingers turn
into hoofs, my hips strengthen,*

*my knees stiffen. And meanwhile,
as my skull lengthens into its new
shape, my brain patterns start to
change: neurons redirect, synapses
unplug and then replug into horse
patterns.*

*My dream of what it's like to be
a horse gallops toward me from
the distance. My concern about
human affairs begins to slip
away; I'm no longer cynical about
human behaviour. In fact my
whole human way of thinking
drifts away from me.*

*And then I become aware of a prob-
lem I've overlooked. The more
I become a horse the more I forget
the original wish. I forget what it
was like to be a human wonder-
ing what it was like to be a horse.*

*This moment of clarity doesn't
last long and maybe it serves
as a punishment for my sins,
I'm crouching half-horse half-
human with the knowledge that
I can't appreciate the destination without knowing the starting point; I'll never enjoy that*

*simplicity unless I remember the
alternatives.*

*And that's not the worst of my revela-
tion. I realize that the next time
I arrive in the afterlife, with my
thick horse brain, I won't have the
capacity to ask to become human
again. I won't even know what
human is. My choice to change
from human to horse is irreversible.*

*And just before I lose my final human
capabilities I wonder: will this be
the last thought I ever have?*

07.   PART IV

There is no more human life on earth. The map is cleared of props, only the symbolic 'tree of life' is left in the Middle East. The timer now makes leaps of millions of years. We're going back in evolution to the first cell. To guide the audience in tracing back the biological ancestors of the homo sapiens, we use chalk drawings on the stage floor illustrating the gradual reduction from mammal to the most basic life form. The performer who makes the drawings explains the evolutionary changes while directing the other performers, who carry out a physical demonstration.

MUSIC
Fuck Buttons, 'Sweet Love
for Planet Earth', 9'41".

The performer who delivered the monologue sits down in the Atlantic Ocean and clears the floor. Five performers enter and stand in a circle in Africa.

# 6 MILLION YEARS AGO

~~Atlantic Ocean~~ HUMAN POPULATION IS NOW ZERO.

**The performer in the middle starts drawing a monkey. The five performers look at the drawing and crouch down. They extend their arms to the ground and start using them for support. The performers have become monkeys.**

NOW YOU SHARE A COMMON ANCESTOR WITH A CHIMPANZEE.

**The performer starts erasing and redrawing. To show the gradual transformations from one species to another, he keeps using the same drawing. The drawings follow the line of 'common ancestors'.**

*EVOLUTION OF THE DRAWING: Snout larger, almost double the size. Skull smaller but protruding at the front.* AND NOW YOU HAVE A MORE MUSCULAR NECK. *Long line tracing a thicker neck.* AND NOW YOU HAVE A MORE PRONOUNCED MUZZLE. *Snout more narrow.* AND NOW YOU HAVE LARGE EARS. *Over the existing ears, leaving them as inner ear detail.* AND NOW YOU HAVE SHORT BACK LEGS. *Shorter back legs, erase the existing.* AND NOW YOU HAVE LONG FRONT ARMS, WHICH YOU USE FOR TOOLS. ~~South Africa~~ One of the monkeys smashes a nut with a clay block and eats it. The other monkeys look at the 'tool' with interest. The clay block is passed through, until the monkeys start fighting over it and disperse. The clay block is left on the map. One monkey picks it up and drops it again. It has lost interest. Intelligence is decreasing. AND NOW YOU HAVE LONG FRONT ARMS. *Long front arms and big hands.* AND NOW YOU HAVE A BIGGER BACK. *Long line for a broader back.* AND NOW YOU HAVE A BROADER CHEST. 7 MILLION YEARS AGO AND NOW YOU SHARE A COMMON ANCESTOR WITH A GORILLA. AND NOW YOU HAVE A VERY MUSCULAR BACK. *Thicker back.* One monkey lifts another monkey on his back and moves to ~~Russia~~. The other monkeys remain in ~~North Africa~~. Their postures form images reminiscent of previous images in the performance. AND NOW YOU HAVE SHORTER BACK LEGS. *Legs very short and feet very big.* AND NOW YOU HAVE A BROADER CHEST. AND NOW YOU HAVE POWERFUL FRONT ARMS, NOW YOU SPEND YOUR TIME ON THE JUNGLE FLOOR. *Front arms shorter and thicker.* 14 MILLION YEARS AGO AND NOW YOU SHARE A COMMON ANCESTOR WITH AN ORANG-UTAN. AND NOW YOU HAVE A BROADER FACE. *Face broader.* AND NOW YOU HAVE SMALLER EARS. *Erase larger ears, leaving the human ones again.* AND NOW YOU HAVE A MORE PRONOUNCED BROW. *Brow darker.* AND NOW YOU HAVE SHORTER FRONT LEGS. *Front legs even shorter.* 18 MILLION YEARS AGO AND NOW YOU SHARE A COMMON ANCESTOR WITH A GIBBON. One performer crosses the stage scattering snow. All but the two monkeys in Russia die. The composition is similar to the image of Napoleon's campaign in Russia from Part II. The dead monkeys put on their hoods and turn into puppeteers who start moving the continents, representing continental drift. This continues until all continents are united and form Pangaea. AND NOW YOU HAVE A SMALLER BACK. *Line straight back to make a standing monkey.* AND NOW YOU WALK WITH EQUAL BEARING ON ALL FOUR LIMBS. *Erase big feet.* AND NOW YOU HAVE SHORTER ARMS. *Small hands.* AND NOW YOU HAVE SHORTER BACK LEGS. *Smaller feet.* AND NOW YOU HAVE BIGGER EARS. *Bigger ears.* AND NOW YOU HAVE A VERY SMALL PROTRUSION ON YOUR BACKSIDE. *Tail.* AND NOW YOU HAVE A VERY SHORT TAIL. AND NOW YOU HAVE A LONGER TAIL. AND NOW YOU HAVE A VERY LONG, POWERFUL TAIL, YOU SPEND A LOT OF TIME IN TREES. *Tail curling backwards.* AND NOW YOU HAVE BIG EYES. *Big eyes.* AND NOW YOU HAVE A SMALLER SNOUT. *Smaller snout.* AND NOW YOU HAVE A SMALL NECK. *Creature sitting with its legs curved up again, the small feet poking out.* 63 MILLION YEARS AGO AND NOW YOU SHARE A COMMON ANCESTOR WITH A LEMUR. The two performers left on the map, now lemurs, move towards Africa. One performer crosses the stage holding a cotton ball with a red light in it. This is the meteor that killed the dinosaurs. When the meteor hits the map, the puppeteers shake the earth. They put miniature dinosaurs on the map and continue moving the continents. The two performers playing animals now represent small mammals that lived during the age of the dinosaurs. AND NOW YOU HAVE BIG EARS. *Bigger ears.* AND NOW YOU HAVE BIG EYES, THE EARTH IS MUCH DARKER SO ALL YOUR SENSES ARE HEIGHTENED. *Big eyes.* AND NOW YOU HAVE SMALL ARMS, AND LITTLE PAWS. *Tiny feet.* AND NOW YOU HAVE A SMALL BODY. *Smaller torso similar in shape to lemur.* AND NOW YOU HAVE A THICK BUSHY TAIL. *Thick bushy tail.* AND NOW YOU HAVE A LONG SNOUT. *Long, thin snout.* AND NOW YOU HAVE WHISKERS, WHICH YOU USE TO FIND FOOD. *Whiskers.* AND NOW YOU HAVE POINTY EARS. *Pointy ears almost the length of the snout.* The puppeteers move miniature flying dinosaurs in the air, casting shadows on the map. The 'small mammals' look at them in fear. AND NOW YOU HAVE A VERY SMALL BODY. *Torso even smaller, erasing all the time.* AND NOW YOU HAVE A THIN TAIL. *Line representing the tail.* AND NOW YOU HAVE LONG CLAWS. *Claws.* 75 MILLION YEARS AGO Another meteor hits the earth. The puppeteers shake the map and remove the dinosaurs. The 'mammals' move backwards into the oceans. They lie down on their belly facing each other. *Erase existing drawing. Rapidly draw outline of a reptilian creature, just a long thick body and short front and rear limbs.* AND NOW YOU HAVE A BIG HEAD, AND A BIG POWERFUL BODY. AND NOW YOU HAVE A BIG THICK TAIL. AND NOW YOU HAVE POWERFUL FRONT LEGS. 340 MILLION YEARS AGO AND NOW YOU HAVE POWERFUL BACK LEGS, AND YOU HAVE A REPTILIAN TONGUE. *On the front, forked like a snake tongue.* AND NOW YOU HAVE BIG EYES. *Big eyes.* AND NOW YOU HAVE SHORTER FRONT LIMBS. *Erase part of the front limbs.* AND NOW YOU HAVE SHORTER BACK LIMBS. *Erase part of the back limbs.* AND NOW YOU HAVE VERY SHORT BACK LIMBS, YOU SPEND YOUR TIME ON THE SHORES AND SHALLOW WATER. AND NOW YOU HAVE NO TONGUE. *Erase tongue.* AND NOW YOU HAVE NO BACK LIMBS, YOU JUST HAVE A TAIL. AND NOW YOU SHARE A COMMON ANCESTOR WITH THE LUNG FISH. 417 MILLION YEARS AGO AND NOW YOU HAVE NO LUNGS. The two performers take a deep breath, then exhale and remain silent.

MUSIC
Arvo Pärt, 'Spiegel im
Spiegel', 8'24".

AND NOW YOU HAVE A BIG TAIL FIN. *Tail fin and erase the tail.* AND NOW YOU HAVE BIG FRONT OR PECTORAL FINS, YOU ARE A VERY PROFICIENT SWIMMER. AND NOW YOU HAVE A MORE NARROW TAIL FIN. *Narrow tail fin inside the other tail and erase the original.* The two performers bring their legs together. AND NOW YOU HAVE SHORTER, BROADER PECTORAL FINS. *Pectoral fins inside and erase the others.* AND YOU SPEND YOUR TIME IN VERY DEEP WATER, YOU'RE NOT AWARE OF THE TEMPERATURE ON LAND. AND NOW YOU HAVE NO TAIL FIN, YOU HAVE A TAIL. AND NOW YOU HAVE VERY SMALL FRONT FINS. AND SMALLER...SMALLER...SMALLER. *Keep drawing inside as you say smaller.* AND NOW YOU HAVE NO FINS. The two performers stuff their arms inside their hoodies. Four puppeteers enter with their hoods on and cross the stage scattering snow, representing another ice age. *Erase all fins.* AND YOU HAVE A MORE STREAMLINED BODY AND NOW YOU HAVE FORWARD FACING EYES. *More narrow eyes.* AND NOW YOU HAVE VERY SMALL EYES. AND YOU ONLY HAVE THE ABILITY TO DISTINGUISH BETWEEN LIGHT AND DARK. *Erase most of eye leaving only a little.* The two performers start to squint. 570 MILLION YEARS AGO AND NOW YOU HAVE NO EYES. The two performers pull the draw strings of their hood so it covers their eyes. Their mouths are gasping for breath. *Erase eyes.* AND NOW THERE IS NO VEGETATION LEFT ON LAND. Performer removes the tree of life. AND NOW YOU HAVE A SMALL GAPING MOUTH AND YOU FEED ON BACTERIA THAT PASS WITH THE CURRENTS. *Erase part of mouth.* AND NOW YOU HAVE NO MOUTH. *Erase all of mouth.* The two performers pull the draw strings of their hood so it covers their entire face and mouth. AND NOW YOU ARE LIKE A TUBE, AND YOU DON'T SWIM YOU JUST FLOAT GENTLY IN THE CURRENT. *Long tube.* The performer who draws starts drawing lines up and down the body, constantly faltering as though he's not sure the terminology is correct. He lets the drawing match momentum in the loss for words. AND NOW YOU HAVE THESE MARKS...INDENTATIONS...PARTS, NO NOT PARTS... The drawer looks at the two performers, then at the date. AND NOW YOU ARE A SEGMENTED WORM, AND YOUR BODY IS COMPRISED OF ALL THESE SEGMENTS THAT ARE HELD TOGETHER IN AN ECTOPLASM. *Lots of segments, then circles all connected.* The two performers bring their legs up towards their body. AND NOW YOU ARE MUCH SMALLER. *Erase some circles from either end and keep doing this for the next parts of text.* AND NOW YOU ARE EVEN SMALLER. AND NOW YOU ARE VERY SMALL. The two performers are entirely curled up. AND NOW YOU SHARE A COMMON ANCESTOR WITH ALL LIFE ON EARTH. *Left with two clusters of three cells.* The other performers enter. Their entire bodies, including their faces, are covered in black. With the two performers on the floor, they form clusters of three, tightly squeezed together. AND NOW YOU ARE LIKE THREE CELLS IN A MEMBRANE. *Line encapsulating each.* AND THEN... 2 BILLION YEARS AGO *Little mark next to one of the cells.* (NAME PERFORMER) YOU SEPARATE. One performer rolls over on his side, away from the cluster. Whenever a new name is called, the other performers repeat the same action. *Draw in stages of separating until the cell is completely detached.* (Name performer) YOU SEPARATE. *The same.* (Name performer) YOU SEPARATE. *The same.* (Name performer) YOU SEPARATE. *The same.* AND NOW YOU ARE ALL EXACT COPIES OF EACH OTHER. *Left with six individual cells, all looking alike.* (Name performer) YOU GO. When their names are mentioned, the performers leave the stage. *Erase cell representing the performer.* (NAME PERFORMER) YOU GO. *Erase cell representing the performer.* (Name performer) YOU GO. *Erase cell representing the performer.* (Name performer) YOU GO. *Erase cell representing the performer.* (Name performer) YOU GO. *Erase cell representing the performer. Left with a single cell.* The drawer leaves the stage. Only one performer, one cell, is left on stage.

# 3.25 BILLION YEARS AGO

The performers, still covered in black, enter
the stage, gather around the map and start
folding it. With an accelerating movement,
they compress it into a ball. They pause. The
performer who was left lying on stage gets up
and wipes out the drawing of the first cell.
There is no more life on earth. Lights dim. The
ball is lifted, then lowered into a black bag.
The performers push the bag front stage. One
performer detaches herself from the group
and walks to the front, in the dark. This is the
performer who delivers the fifth monologue.

## 08.   FIFTH MONOLOGUE

NOTE
Gratitude to 'Gravity', with
reference to 'Unweaving
the Rainbow' by Richard
Dawkins.

*I'm not afraid of the universe.*
*I know some people are.*
*They get terrified when they think*
*of infinite space or black holes,*
*But I don't.*

*No, when I think about me and the*
*Big Bang, I feel a bit obliged.*

*I asked a scientist who I should thank*
*for me being here, who I should*
*thank for our universe to exist.*
*He told me to thank six things,*
*so here it goes:*
*Thanks to the three spatial*
*dimensions I live in.*
*Thanks to the strength between*
*atomic cores, so stars can change*
*hydrogen into all the other atoms.*
*Thanks to a number 10 with 35*
*zeros, that holds all atoms together.*
*Thanks to the exact amount of dark*
*matter in our universe.*

*Thanks to the power that can break
    the largest structures in the cosmos.
And thanks to anti-gravity that
    controls the expansion of our
    universe.*

*I don't know what these six things
    mean, but thanks for doing this.*

*I know they don't do it for me.
They don't care.
It doesn't matter to them if I'm happy,
    miserable, anxious or dead; but
    still, they ask nothing in return.
I can live because of them
    and I will die.
We're all going to die.
And that makes us the lucky ones.*

09.   PART V

Part V starts in the dark. We are now away from
the earth, in the wider universe. The performers
have become puppeteers who move planets
and galaxies. There is no more timer, since our
concept of time is irrelevant for the material we
are showing. In this part, we move back towards
the Big Bang and then return to the present day.

MUSIC
The Antlers, 'Prologue/
Kettering', 7'41".

Bit by bit, the performers close the black bag,
making the silver ball of the earth disappear.

Lights out.

One performer moves a lit blue marble in front
of the bag. This is now the Earth. Behind it,
another performer turns on a bulb, representing the sun. The performers line up to the right
and left of the sun.
    One performer sits front stage facing the
light show. She calls out the names of the planets.
One by one, the performers light their coloured
marbles, completing the image of our galaxy.

p.381   'A History of Everything'

MERCURY VENUS MARS JUPITER SATURN
URANUS NEPTUNE

The performers move their marbles towards the sun, suggesting a zoom out. They turn off their lights behind the sun.

One performer holds up a lit cotton ball representing our Milky Way. We are now moving further and further away, passing different galaxies. One by one, four performers move to the front of the stage and lit cotton balls. They slowly move backstage, squeezing their galaxies until they're extinguished.

When the last galaxy reaches the back, a spotlight is cast into the audience in full brightness. This is the Big Bang. When it's turned off, blacklight turns the snow left on the stage floor into an image of the starlit universe.

The performer holding the marble Earth slowly moves front stage. The audience sees the Earth floating in the vastness of the galaxies.

The timer starts.

# 4 BILLION YEARS AGO

It moves forward until today's date. The performer holding the Earth reaches front stage and turns off the marble. Blackout.

p.383 'A History of Everything'

**THE END** ·

# AUDIENCE

An homage to the beauty and the danger of being an audience:

PROJECTION

CAMERA

Visitor            Visitor            Visitor            Visitor
                        Visitor            Visitor
Performer ONE                           Visitor            Visitor
                        Visitor            Visitor
Visitor            Visitor            Visitor            Visitor
        Visitor                            Visitor
Visitor            Performer TWO                     Visitor
        Visitor                            Visitor
Visitor            Visitor            Visitor            Visitor
        Visitor                            Visitor
Visitor            Performer THREE                   Visitor
        Visitor                            Visitor
Visitor            Visitor            Visitor            Visitor
        Visitor            Visitor
Visitor            Visitor                     Performer FOUR

## OUTLINE

'Audience' is one of our most controversial shows. The performance deals with all the different aspects of a crowd gathering to share an experience. The spectator is never left out of the action, at times even forced to take position. It's a playful challenge which gives food for thought and debate. However, under the surface, it carries the scary warning that any crowd is susceptible to manipulation.

## REQUIREMENTS

- · A camera.
- · A projector.
- · A large projection screen, filling a standard stage.
- · Microphones to record voices.
- · Microphones to amplify voices.
- · Fireworks.
- · Confetti, streamers.
- · Flags, an Arafat scarf, 3D glasses, a smartphone, popcorn, sunglasses, a vuvuzela, a rosary.
- · An audience.
- · Jackets and hoodies of the audience.
- · Fake bags and purses of the audience.

## CREDITS

Created by:
  Alexander Devriendt
    (director)
In collaboration with
  Joeri Smet
And
  Maria Dafneros
  Tiemen Van Haver
  Matthieu Sys
  Aaron De Keyzer
    (the original cast)

First performed
  March 15th, 2011
  Vooruit, Gent, BE

Originally produced by
  Ontroerend Goed
  Theatre Royal Plymouth
  Richard Jordan
    Productions Ltd.
With the support of the
  Flemish Community
  Province of East-Flanders
  City of Ghent

# CREATION

The initial idea for 'Audience' was an homage to 'being an audience' and drew largely on our experience of performing the Personal Trilogy, getting into close contact with individual spectators. We wondered if it was possible to apply the knowledge and skills we achieved through immersive theatre on a larger group of people.

As inspiration material, we used Peter Handke's 'Publikumsbeschimpfung' ('Offending the Audience'), a classic piece of subversive theatre, mainly directed at the overly bourgeois, rusty audiences of the late sixties and the old-fashioned, easily digestible repertory plays they enjoyed. The piece is unique in pointing out the theatre situation, drily summing up the steps the audience took to come to the theatre and their predictable expectations, only to finish by openly offending them. Our secret desire for 'Audience' was to update this piece – different in approach, since audiences have changed in many ways, but similar in trying to produce a wake-up call. Instead of adopting a confrontational style, we opted for seduction as our main instrument. We wanted to get under the audience's skin, rather than forcing them into the defensive.

First we needed to avoid a few traps. Fictionalizing the audience was one of them, perhaps even the biggest. In our first rehearsals, the performers acted out typical audience behaviour, which was then recorded. The exercise was comparable to copying and

impersonating visitors in 'A Game of You', but we
wanted to apply this principle on a larger scale.
Projected on a screen, the actors would help to
produce a 'virtual audience', mirroring the real
audience. From there, we thought of devising eerie
dream-scenes in which 'impossible' things would
happen, nightmares such as waking up naked in the
middle of a crowd or fantasies of audience members
experiencing love at first sight during the show.
It seems a trifling detail, but one of the reasons
why we got stuck in this train of thought, is the
icy cold temperature in the rehearsal room, which
prevented us from improvising on the floor.

Our first test audiences, however, soon rapped
our knuckles for overlooking their presence. Instead
of playing audience members, sometimes even just
using voices, and projecting images of empty seating areas, where 'crazy' things would happen, they
wanted us to address their reality and work with
that. Luckily, our time schedule allowed us to make
a U-turn and start all over again. At this point, the
director even toyed with the idea of dismissing the
performers altogether and devising an installation
with the audience at the centre of the action.

From then on, one rule applied in rehearsals:
everything that would be said, done or shown in the
performance, had to be linked directly to the experience of being an audience – the specific audience
of that night. We contemplated all the aspects of
being in a theatre, from the cloakroom to the final
applause, and improvised scenes around them. Every
character we would assume, had to be functional
for an audience: a warm-up guy, an usher asking
for mobile phones to be turned off, an interviewer
gauging the atmosphere in the house. We would
point the camera at people and scrutinize them.

When we explored the idea of having a standup
comedian pick on someone in the audience, things

got heated. We felt there was more to it than met
the eye. In a comedy show, singling out an audience member – usually in the first row – has become
a standard moment and people seem to accept it
as such. But if we took it further and had a grim,
nasty bullying scene, the audience would be forced
to react – or give their silent permission. During
improvisations, we all got our worst bully tricks
out and then pasted them together into a relentless
session of cornering a spectator. We had questions
and doubts about the acceptability of the action,
but we needed a moment that would transform the
audience into a crowd, relating directly to the events
in the performance. Not on a rational or intellectual level, but emotionally and socially. The first
time we tested it with a live audience, some people
were upset, but everybody could feel the importance
of the scene. Some even wanted it to go further –
a line that we incorporated in the scripted debate
after the bullying.

In the last phase of rehearsals, it became
increasingly difficult to perform 'Audience' without
an audience. We considered this a good sign: it
meant we had truly devised a performance in
which the presence of spectators was indispensable.
The general rehearsal was more like a technical
runthrough than an actual performance. We even put
cardboard figures in the seats for camera practice.

The first performances of 'Audience', in
Belgium, didn't upset the audience as much as we
had anticipated. The irony shone through too easily.
In the UK, however, the show caused outrage and
indignation, due to the 'questionable ethics'. Shoes
were thrown at the stage, people got up and tried to
sabotage the camera or improvised a sit-in in front
of the screen. For the performers, it wasn't always
easy to keep a cool head, but the strong reactions
proved that the performance touched upon a sore

point. After a while, we even longed for lively, rowdy crowds, because they made the performance all the richer, more meaningful and memorable.

# SCRIPT

To give a good idea of 'Audience' as a performance, we will describe the different steps of the dramaturgy from the point of view of the 'manipulator'. The manipulator, in this case, is not a physical person, he's more or less the spirit of the play, the train of thoughts that shaped the structure. Sometimes, the performers literally speak the words of the manipulator, but more often it is in the actions and visual stimuli that his intentions start to work.

# THE MANIPULATOR

I wanted 'Audience' to start before the audience realized it had started. The whole performance needed to be a web in which they'd get caught step by step. I was inspired by Handke's description of individuals leaving their homes, prepared to go to the theatre, following a trajectory that leads them to the same place, where they gradually turn into a unified group all watching the same thing.

Of course I couldn't film every single trajectory of every single spectator, but I could film the audience's entry into the theatre space. So I put a camera behind the screen on stage to record the audience as they take their seats and chat before the show. I didn't even bother to hide it very well, since nobody would look for it. In the seating area, I placed microphones to register what they say.

I will use this material later on.

Before they enter, some things have been checked. I let one performer interview the bartender to know what people drank before they came in. I let another performer check the reservation list, so we know the composition of the audience in singles, pairs and groups. I let a third performer keep an eye on who comes in first, because she will mention this person's details later on.

I place the cloak room in the theatre space and let the performers take the audience's jackets and purses. This serves two purposes: to make the custom of handing over your belongings explicit and to get hold of the jackets to use them later on in the performance. The performers serve as cloakroom attendants. They need to make every individual audience member feel welcome. If people refuse to hand in their stuff, they are being told that it's more comfortable since actors are going to run around in the seating area. This isn't even a lie. However, there's no obligation or pressure. The audience is the client and the client is always king.

All of this is just a preparation. The audience needs to be unaware that the net is being woven while they're quietly waiting for the show to start.

And when it starts, it seems as if it hasn't started yet. The performer entering the stage adopts another typical role in the theatre: that of the usher asking people to turn off their mobile phones. Her explanation is a bit longer than usual. Not only does the audience get instructions on how to go to the bathroom and how to come back in, eating or not eating and bringing in drinks, they also get informed of the reasons why:

*There are going to be some actors
    here.
They're the ones who tell the story
    and they tell that live, which
    means that silence is needed.
So you can't really eat popcorn or
    chips because the person next to
    you won't hear the actors then.
I hope you understand.*

At this point, it should dawn on the audience they're being told the obvious. The extended usher speech is based on a school teacher explaining theatre to children who are about to see their first play. I put it in as a reminder of how many unwritten rules govern our public life, how many codes of behaviour there are, even on a relaxed night out. The audience is allowed to laugh, but not to indulge in a wild coughing fit. If they get out, it will be remarked as a sign of disapproval, so coming back in is highly desirable. Sleeping can be tolerated, snoring not.

In some parts of the speech, I inserted hidden warnings that will only become relevant later on:

*When in theatre an actor asks
    a question, you're not really
    supposed to answer.*

*No, mostly when an actor asks a*
*    question, he's thinking out loud,*
*    he's thinking to himself.*
*Has anyone heard of interactive*
*    theatre?*
*    Yes?*
*    You?*
*For those who are not familiar with*
*    interactive theatre...*
*Think of a puppet show: when a*
*    puppet asks a question, you have*
*    to answer to the puppet.*
*But remember: here you always*
*    have a choice.*

Through these lines, I have indicated that the audience is allowed to react. Many will have forgotten
this by the time they need to remember it, but I can't
say I didn't point it out.

I end the speech reiterating the whole ritual of
applauding and curtain calls, even giving tips to clap
without noise, if they didn't like the performance.

To finish off, I let the performer insist:

*Don't think of them as rules.*
*They're not rules, they're more*
*    guidelines.*

*To help you relax, to avoid*
*embarrassment.*
*You know, to make you blend in.*

The house goes dark.

The performer takes a seat among the audience, as did the other performers. She immediately applies the rules and apologizes to every single audience member she passes on the way to her seat.

A camera man enters the stage and points his camera at the audience. The lights fade in, not on stage, but in the seating area from the back. Slowly, the black screen lights up and reveals the spectators' silhouettes.

I wanted this scene to be poetic and complimenting to the audience. I chose the track 'Villa del refugio' by This Will Destroy You, quiet music that creates a intense, meditational atmosphere. The images of the audience are carefully framed, highlighting finger movements and clothes, no faces. They should feel safe and enjoy the beauty of an anonymous crowd. It's a flattering mirror.

When the music goes towards the end the camera man slowly zooms out. The lights go to full strength so that the faces become visible and the screen displays a whole shot of the audience. A perfect life-size mirror of themselves. This is the first time the audience sees itself as a unity and I want them to give a moment's thought to this.

Then, I let the camera man zoom in on one face. The tension rises, but it's still just a tease. I want the audience to feel exposed, but not offended. I'm aware some people might feel highly uncomfortable being projected on a screen in front of an audience, but I count on the general consensus that it isn't the end of the world, so that individual discomfort will most likely be laughed off.

I let the performers use the close-ups to phrase some potential audience thoughts. They're short one-liners, fixed in slots per face. The performers take turns. Women's thoughts are always voiced by the female performer.

The first ones are simple, basic thoughts:

*He chose me…have a good look.*

Sticking to reality, to what the audience actually sees, is a good way of grounding the thoughts in the here-and-now. The performers adopt a tone appropriate for the face on the screen. Some 'thoughts' provoke recognition:

*I'm beginning to look more and
more like my father.*

Others contain implicit instructions:

*I have to stay open to new things.*

There are extravagant ones, that put philosophical or aesthetic reflections in people's minds:

*I want to be pulled out of my comfort
zone. Out of my daily routine.
I want to see a mirror of myself
in which I look strangely
recognizable.
I genuinely want to cry. I'm not
sentimental.
Just show me something so good, that
it makes me forget about the fool-
ishness and danger of people and
gives me trust in us as a species.*

At one point, I let the camera man come forward and zoom in on the eyes of one person in the first row. It's necessary to break the pattern of moving from face to face, but also to depersonalize

the spectator and dive deeper into the underlying
motives for being an audience member. Now it's
time to open up their sense of togetherness:

> *I just love being here with all these*
> *people around me.*
> *When I try to grasp what they're*
> *thinking right now and why and*
> *how and...*
> *It just makes my head explode.*
> *I'm surrounded by all these different*
> *universes.*

The camera zooms out again.
 By now, the audience should feel we've touched
upon the most basic reasons why they are here: escap-
ism, social contact, emotional relief, intellectual stimulation, aesthetic enjoyment, habit. I want them to
recognize at least one of these motivations, if not for
themselves, then at least for the people around them.
I also want them to realize they cannot possibly grasp
all the thoughts going on in the minds around them.
 In this part, the focus is on their individuality
and their uniqueness. I want them to feel special,
affirmed in their personal identity.
 I let each of the performers pick one audience
member to describe, starting with 'I'm...'.

*I'm the woman with the checked shirt and the curly hair in the second row.*

This is to make them feel we're really talking about them, here and now. Everybody can identify these specific persons in the audience. I let one performer describe a person who came in alone. This is verified information.

Now I let the performers sum up the data they gathered from the reservation list: the number of people who came in alone, the amount of pairs, the amount of couples among the pairs, the groups of more than two people.

If any doubt arises concerning these numbers, I have one last item to convince them we're true to reality. While one performer describes the first person who entered the theatre, the screen switches to the footage of the audience coming in. The audience sees this person taking a seat and then watches their own behaviour before the show started. They also hear fragments of their chats.

I want them to realize they've been under surveillance. For most people, this isn't a big deal since we've grown accustomed to being filmed in public places. But I do want them to think about this fact of life. I don't mind them getting uneasy at this point.

Before they've recovered from the surprise, I introduce a new element of potential indignation.

I let three performers bring on the clothing rack with the audience's belongings behind the screen, so the silhouettes are visible. I let them pick some jackets and put them on.

I play some pumping music ('The Turtle' by Nathan Fake) and let the performers show the jackets in a mock fashion run.

Meanwhile, I let another performer 'present' the collection. What he describes, is the uniformity of people's clothes. The likeliness of colours, combinations, cut and size. Meanwhile, the performers walk on and off wearing the audience's jackets. It's done in a lighthearted way, but the message should get through: you are not as original as you think you are.

I let the presenter point out the brightest person, the one wearing the most coloured or conspicuous outfit. Usually, even this isn't very spectacular.

From the clothes, I move on to the body.

*If you're balding, you will most
    likely have a beard and a stubble.
If you have a beard, you have
    a moustache.
There are no solo moustaches –
    except for this creature.
There are fat people in the audience.
You know who you are.*

Now it's time to raise the stakes. The performers enter wearing three bags. They start rummaging in them.

I let the performers take stuff out of the bags and purses and show it to the audience. The camera zooms in on the objects. They're fairly common and similar to what most people carry around. Again, I want to show the audience how impersonal their personal belongings actually are.

In one of the bags I put clean underwear. It's my guilty pleasure to put it on display and it makes for a good laugh.

Now I let the presenter use the information from the bar, the reservation list and general statistics to make a summary of the audience. What they had for a drink, how many white people there are, if there are other ethnicities, the statistic number of homosexuals, the amount of free tickets distributed… Meanwhile, the performers pack the bags and leave the stage. I don't mind doing this, since the bags aren't real. The jackets were, so the audience will assume the bags are theirs too.

The speech turns into an ironic eulogy on the individuality and uniqueness of the audience:

*You are all individuals.*
    *You are all a unique brand.*
*You are all special.*
    *You are you and you alone.*

*You probably ask yourself why*
*I'm telling you this.*
*Well, there is nobody in the world*
*like you.*
*There will be nobody like you,*
*ever again.*
*Not all of you are exceptional*
*or unusual, but you are all*
*unrepeatable, exclusive, rare,*
*one of a kind.*

That's enough praise for now. Time for a reset.
    The screen goes blank, back to the setting at the beginning of the show. The performers who ran the fashion show rush back to their seats in the audience. The pumping music switches to a show-tune (Big Wheel), introducing a new character: the warm-up guy, who walks on stage like a talkshow host or standup comedian. I let him introduce himself and tell the audience what he's there for:

*I'm going to get you in the mood.*
*Get you clapping your hands.*
*Basically, I'm here to train you like*
*animals.*

The warm-up guy lets the audience applaud the venue, the crew, the camera man and ultimately, themselves. But he wants a subtle applause, a buildup. He suggests they use one finger at a time...

*A trick I've used many many times,
so trust me, it works.*

...and slowly build up the volume to a full clap. The second time, he asks the audience to do it without his help, because he doesn't want to spoil the experience.

Almost without exception, the audience complies. They even perform a standing ovation. I let the camera man record this moment. I will use the footage later on. The warm-up guy thanks the audience for their cooperation:

*Isn't it wonderful? That we all did
the same thing...?*

This is the turning point. Now, the warm-up guy picks a girl on the first row and addresses her directly. The other performers, who are in the audience, start to observe the reactions in the house. One takes his notebook and counts the shouts of laughter. Another one registers the objections and muffled protests.

The warm-up guy tells the girl she didn't cooperate enough. She didn't do well. Because whatever she does, it's wrong.

Most of the time, the audience still interprets this moment as a funny intermission – the standup comedian's trope. But the warm-up guy goes on, corners the girl by denoting the situation:

*Now you're thinking,*

*There's the actor, picking on me.*
*That's just part of the show, of the*
*    act.*
*I'll just have a laugh at it because*
*    it's got nothing to do with me.*
*I just happen to sit in this chair.*

*Well, I've got bad news for you.*
*It's not the chair, you little fuck.*
*It's you.*

*You've got it written all over*
*your forehead.*
*You're the girl who makes every-*
*body feel:*

*I'm glad I'm not her.*

In fact, it's not only the girl who's cornered. The whole audience is dragged into the game. Usually, this is the moment when the entire house falls silent. Whoever laughs past this point, is frowned upon. Even if the audience doubts whether the scene is real or simulated, the risk of misinterpreting the situation is high enough to choose the safer option: taking it seriously.

    I let the warm-up guy order the camera man to zoom in on the girl's face. She's now projected on the screen. The warm-up guy comments on her looks:

*Not a pretty sight, is it?*

This is very often the moment when individual audience members start murmuring.

Playing cat and mouse with his 'victim', the warm-up guy keeps provoking the audience and adds a touch of sarcasm:

> *You know that song 'you are beautif-*
> *uuul, no matter what they say…'?*
> *You know that song?*
> *Don't lie to me, you know that song.*
> *You listen to it every day.*
> *And you know why?*
> *Because YOU FUCKING NEED IT.*

Aware that the audience is no longer on his side, the warm-up guy blames the girl for his fall from grace:

> *You make me waste the sympathy*
> *that I've built up with these people.*
> *They like me less, because of you.*
> *And the more I give you what you*
> *deserve, fuckface, the more they're*
> *going to start thinking:*

> *Hey, back off…she's one of us.*

*Because that's what you do.*
*You make people feel sorry for you.*

By now, he has turned into a full-blown bully. Twisting the logics of the situation, relentless in self-righteousness and brutal in abusing the power of his position.

*Show me your real face.*
*Show me the real you.*
*Is that the best you can come up*
*with?*

He even challenges the audience to take a stand.

*I'm not going to stop.*
*Unless somebody here stands up and*
*tells me to stop.*

This can be a painful moment, if nobody reacts. However, if the indignation in the audience has mounted to a point of eruption, this is where people get up and ask the warm-up guy to stop. The irony, of course, is that they do it after they received the permission, in the designated slot of the script. In a way, even their protest at this point is a sign of obedience.

To recuperate the mood in the house, I let the warm-up guy change tactics. It was a joke. The girl is beautiful, that's why he picked her in the first place. The bullying was a conceptual thing. Although still suspicious of the guy, the audience usually seizes the chance to take a brief relief from their discomfort. The warm-up guy reassures them that eventually, he will stop, he has to stop, but not until...the girl spreads her legs.

I let the camera zoom in on the girl's lap. If she opens her legs, it will be on display for the whole audience.

The audience realizes the bullying will be taken to the next level. The warm-up guy now poses as a passionate artist and underlines the importance of the image for the show, dragging in art history:

> *You know that painting, 'L'Origine du monde'? 'The Origin of the World?'*
> *For those who haven't seen it, you see a woman lying down on her back, and her pussy with this big bush of hair, right in your face.*

*It's a great image, you know, the
origin of the world', 19th century
realism, very provocative back
then, but very poetic...*

I secretly enjoy the line 'provocative back then', since
the image we're looking for here is prudish compared
to the painting. The girl is fully dressed and she's
only asked to spread her legs a few inches. Of course,
the provocation here is more about the social situation than the actual image, but I still find it funny
that a 21st century audience can be just as upset
about a girl spreading her legs as their 19th century
counterparts.

If any person asks the warm-up guy to do it
himself, I let him say:

*You've obviously never seen the
painting.*

The girl keeps refusing. She always does, because
she's a plant. We've informed her about the bullying
scene before the show and we've asked her not to
spread her legs, under no circumstance. So we're safe.
I let the warm-up guy use emotional blackmail:

*Is there any woman here who wants*
*to spread her legs for her?*

*(If yes, to the girl:)*
*You see, other people are willing to*
*sacrifice themselves for you.*
*That's how selfish you are.*

*(If no, to the girl:)*
*You see, you're all alone here.*
*It's just you and I.*

**The warm-up guy now calls in the help of the audience and asks them to perform a gentle chant:**

*Spread – your – legs,*
*Spread – your – legs.*

**I provided the warm-up guy with some cash money, which he offers to audience members as a bribe or as a decisive element in removing the doubts of those who are hesitating. This is usually a rowdy moment in the show. If people are chanting, whether or not for money, it's most likely met with disapproval from the other audience members. On one**

occasion, the opponents even started a counter-chant: 'Keep – them – closed, keep – them – closed.' Sometimes people even start debating on the spot. The stronger the division in this scene, the more charged the rest of the performance will be. When everybody has a clear opinion of the events they just witnessed, they tend to engage more in what happens next.

The warm-up guy gives the girl a last chance to change her mind. If the audience tries to advise her, he says to the girl:

> *It's your decision, don't let them*
> *influence you.*

He starts a countdown. At zero, the girl doesn't open her legs. For the last time, the warm-up guy asks for an applause and addresses the girl:

> *Bravo.*
> *We tried to make you do something*
> *you didn't want.*
> *And you didn't do it.*
> *You have integrity.*
> *I respect you.*

The scene is clearly finished, but I don't give the audience time or space to react. Instead, I let one of the performers channel the potential storm of protest by expressing her disapproval. She gets up from her seat in the audience and speaks up:

*Excuse me, but I think I need to*
*make a stand here.*
*I know I'm part of this performance,*
*but I want to reassure you.*
*What just happened to*
*— sorry, what's your name again —*
*(the name of the girl)*
*doesn't feel right to me either.*

*Some lines were crossed here.*
*Maybe some of you felt silenced*
*sitting here in this theatre,*
*with a play going on,*
*but I didn't like what I saw.*
*And I think somebody needs to say*
*it out loud. That's all.*

I don't mind if the audience clearly sees that this is a scripted moment. If they're truly upset, they will probably look skeptically at the performer for her blatant attempt at passing the buck. But sooner or later, they will all understand that I'm trying to voice their opinions in a good old-fashioned piece of dialogue. For those who feel more comfortable with the fiction of classical theatre, this is a moment of relief.

The characters I chose for this scene are representatives of different points of view. The performer who made a stand is the moralist, who defends good manners and decency. She sums up the audience's gasps and sighs, whispered objections and uncomfortable silences during the bullying scene. Then there's the seasoned theatre-goer, who thinks it was all a game and points out the irony. He counted the shouts of laughter and confronts the audience with the number. And finally, there is the voice of the 'ordinary guy', the audience member who hasn't made up his mind yet and tries to figure out what he's supposed to do.

I also let the warm-up guy butt into the debate. He tells the other performers – and in extension, the audience – that they should be ashamed of themselves for not stopping him.

The audience is largely left out of the debate, except maybe at the moment where the camera zooms in on the person who accepted the money and the moralist publicly tells him off:

*You made a profit out of her humiliation.*

The ones who refused get rewarded with another gush of praise.

Of course, if audience members want to interfere, they can always have their say. The performers are prepared for possible interruptions.

However, as the discussion moves on, it becomes more and more detached from reality. I want to introduce the political dimension of crowd dynamics, so the performers turn into campaigners.

They start using political slogans and rhetorical language. For the audience, it's even more relaxing. They're no longer urged to take a position and it's fun trying to identify the quotes and references. I throw in a little bit of Tiger Woods, a well-known sports coach turned politician and some Kennedy:

> *Ask not what we can do for you,*
> *ask what you can do for this*
> *performance.*

The camera functions more and more as a propaganda tool. The performers check if they look impressive on the screen, and at times, they use the audience's image to forward their argument. There's a close-up of the brightest person, who becomes an example of someone outstanding, someone people can look up to, like to a leader.

I let the whole discussion move towards the question whether people need a leader or can think and decide for themselves. It's about giving up individual responsibility and the way so-called representatives persuade people to hand over power. I'm getting closer to the point I want to make.

I let the ordinary guy make his final point:

*It's not because I'm listening that*
*I agree.*
*I don't need anyone to represent me,*
*I can think for myself.*
*And I don't follow anyone.*

This is the moment to insert a totalitarian speech. I've always wanted an oration based on Hitler, since he is still considered the ultimate example of a dangerous demagogue. But that would've been too obviously a parody. Instead, I devised a text full of familiar rhetorical tricks and hollow but invigorating phrases. In this speech, emotional effect had to be more important than content. I wanted to show the moment when a crowd has lost its freedom of speech, but still listens to a person who preaches change, liberation and individual fulfillment.

The performer starts by assuring the audience that he is not their leader, but one of them. He is using a microphone, but he's still standing in the seating area, among the people. He then praises them for their willingness to leave their houses, get together and share experiences.

> *I thought you were stuck in your*
> *own minds, but you're not.*
> *This is not a dream, this is not a*
> *fantasy.*
> *We are all here together.*
> *All listening to the very same words.*

Meanwhile, I let the camera zoom in on the performer's face, very closely, to produce a Big-Brother-like image. I also adds some music, Händel's 'Sarabande', which goes into a crescendo as the face on the screen asks people not to think only for themselves but fill their minds with one thought: 'you have no power alone.' The rhetorical proof soon follows:

> *You can't play soccer on your own.*
> *You can't organize a revolution*
> *on your own.*
> *You can't get to the moon*
> *on your own.*

I let the performer guarantee the audience that they will still exist, if they give up their individuality and become one:

*There is no reason to be afraid of this.*
*You still exist.*
*In fact, you exist more than you've*
    *ever existed before.*

If everybody spread the word – the performer never really specifies which word – 'we' would form an unstoppable force. It's an example of an empty message that has multiple interpretations and is therefore capable of inciting many different groups of people, even if their interpretations are incompatible. I'm thinking of a demonstrating crowd, of which half doesn't know what it's demonstrating for or against, or would disagree if they knew.

*We can reach a million by midnight.*
*A million people who know: you*
    *have no power alone.*

In the finale of the speech, the footage of the standing ovation during the warm-up is projected on the screen. In true Sovjet-propaganda-style manipulation, it looks as if the audience is applauding the speaker.

At this point, the show is demonstrating live how public acclaim can be faked. Even if the audience loathes the speech and listens to it with silent resistance, the screen tells a different story. And the screen, as well as the music, the microphone and the footage, are under my control.

As soon as the final drums of the music roll, the screen goes black and words appear, like commands. I made a music compilation consisting of samples of lyrics that give orders to the listener. Silly orders, fun orders, but also some quite disturbing ones. These are projected on the screen during the whole sequence. It's dance music so people might want to shake a leg. To encourage them, the lights in the seating area are turned down and the performers carry out a choreography, stimulating people to join in.

Here are some of the commands...

NOW
THROW
YOUR
HANDS
IN
THE
AIR
AND
WAVE
THEM
LIKE
YOU
JUST
DON'T
CARE

LET
ME
HEAR
YOU
SAY

A A A A A A A
A A A A A A A A
A A A A A A A
A A A A A A
A A A A
A A A
A A
AHH

*BOOM,*

*SHAKE,*
*SHAKE,*
*SHAKE*

*THE*
*ROOM*

*EVERYBODY*
*DANCE*
*NOW*

I've noticed that the audience's eagerness to join in is often directly related to the tension during the bullying scene. Dancing together seems to provide some release, if not a sense of reconciliation. I guess it helps to forget what happened before.

In the middle of the action, I let the performers act out examples of extreme or remarkable audience behaviour from different contexts. Someone stops his ears, someone exposes his ass, another one boos. There's prayer, mimicked boxing punches, 3D glasses, national anthems, popcorn, a vuvuzela. The images switch from religious gatherings to cinemas, from sports events to political meetings.

The camera zooms in on each of these actions. The commands become more violent and sexual...

*SUCK*
*THIS*
*PUSSY*

*JUST*
*LIKE*
*YOU*
*SHOULD*

*BURN
OUT
SODOMITES*

*AND
BURN
FAGGOTS*

If the audience is still dancing, it looks like they support the messages on the screen. Again, this is to seduce people into a moment of oblivion. I want to show that if crowds get carried away, they might cheer for things they'd otherwise reject.

At the end of the compilation, accompanied by the command 'Hold your head up high/Show some pride', I let one performer act out a Hitler salute. Agreed, it's maybe a bit foisted, but this is the moment nobody in the audience can misinterpret the message that mass movements can easily get out of hand.

I let the performers wave flags. Confetti is dropped from the ceiling. There are streamers and a recording of cheering crowds. Fireworks are released.

Before they realize the party is over, I let one performer grab a microphone, look into the camera and address the audience through the screen. He poses as a live reporter witnessing a mass event:

*I'm in the middle of the crowd here and the atmosphere is absolutely electrifying.*

I let him interview two audience members, one who joined in the action and one who stayed on the side. They're asked why they participated or refused to

participate. I want to hear them express the reasons
behind their choice. I let the reporter summarize
their response.

In the end, he addresses the whole audience.
His conclusion is a reflection on all mass gatherings,
protests, demonstrations, revolutions.

> *Who made the right decision?*
>     *We don't know.*
> *Afterwards other people will tell us if*
>     *this gathering made sense or not,*
> *Reporters will decide and the general*
>     *audience will probably follow.*
> *Time will tell.*

I don't know either what the right decision is. All
I know is that crowds frighten me. It scares me to
see people lose a part of their individuality and
blend into an anonymous mass. People can become
more powerful together, but they can also become
destructive.

I let the camera film the audience. Slowly, the
image crossfades to a recorded video of an audience
and solemn, orchestral music starts: Johann Johann-
son's 'Fordlandia'.

I want to make a leap from the live audience to
examples of crowd behaviour in the outside world.

The video compilation consists of historical and more recent footage of audiences, focusing on the dangers and beauty of mass gatherings, with a buildup to multitudes of millions. I show peaceful demonstrations, but also football fans trampling each other, Nazi gatherings and black protests for equality. Crowds in disciplined patterns and crowds in destructive chaos. I deliberately don't make a distinction between 'good' and 'evil', because I want to illustrate that crowd movements create their own sense of purpose, whatever it may be. The music is there to soak the viewing in an emotional slipstream.

At the end the audience members become mere pixels on the screen. Tiny and wormlike.

I let the lights go out.

On the screen, I project commands…

p.439 'Audience'

*APPLAUD*

*IMAGINE THE ACTORS*

*ON STAGE*

# IMAGINE THEM

# RUNNING AWAY

DECIDE
HOW
MANY
TIMES
YOU
WANT
THEM
TO
COME
BACK

p.443 'Audience'

# *APPLAUD ACCORDINGLY*

*STOP*

*THANK YOU*

p. 446   'Audience'

*LEAVE*

I turn the lights on. The last command remains on the screen. I play a recorded compilation of audience reactions from previous shows, while they get out. The performers return the jackets. There's no curtain call. Nobody bows.


THE END ·

# FIGHT NIGHT

An interactive performance about what makes you vote:

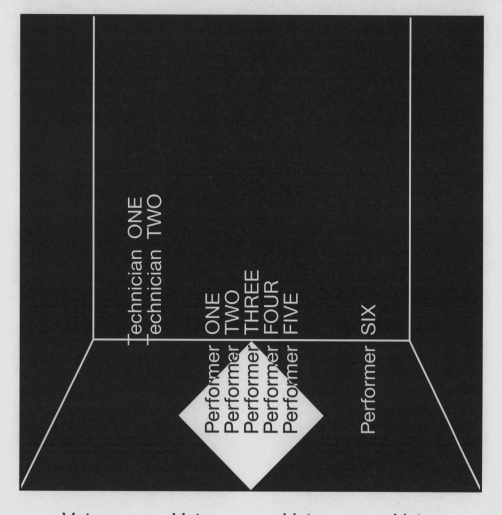

Technician ONE
Technician TWO

Performer ONE
Performer TWO
Performer THREE
Performer FOUR
Performer FIVE

Performer SIX

Voter          Voter          Voter          Voter
     Voter          Voter          Voter
Voter          Voter          Voter          Voter
     Voter          Voter          Voter
Voter          Voter          Voter          Voter
     Voter          Voter          Voter
Voter          Voter          Voter          Voter
     Voter          Voter          Voter
Voter          Voter          Voter          Voter
     Voter          Voter          Voter
Voter          Voter          Voter          Voter
     Voter          Voter          Voter
Voter          Voter          Voter          Voter
     Voter          Voter          Voter
Voter          Voter          Voter          Voter

## OUTLINE

'Fight Night' is an exploration of democratic ideals
through an interactive voting
show, in which five perform-
ers/candidates struggle for
the audience's favour. Winners stay, losers leave the
stage. The audience votes,
the system decides. The voice
of the majority will prevail.

## REQUIREMENTS

· Five actors of different
  sexes, ages, appearances
  and personalities.
· A host.
· Screens.
· An electronic voting sys-
  tem with voting devices.
· A microphone.

## CREDITS

Created by:
  Alexander Devriendt
    (director)
In collaboration with
  Angelo Tijssens
  Sophie Cleary
  David Heinrich
  Roman Vaculik
  Charlotte De Bruyne
    (the cast)

First performed
  April 10th, 2013
  Vooruit, Gent, BE

Originally produced by
  Ontroerend Goed
  The Border Project
  Vooruit
  Theatre Royal Plymouth
  Richard Jordan
    Productions Ltd.
With the support of the
  Flemish Community
  Province of East-Flanders
  City of Ghent

This project was assisted by
  the Australian Govern-
  ment through the Aus-
  tralia Council, its arts and
  funding advisory body,
  and the Government of
  South Australia.

# CREATION

Our initial idea was simple: what if we created a play in which actors could vote other actors out? Around 2007, we started to develop a concept which would then result in a show. It seemed fun, daring and in our ballpark to produce that kind of live experience. However, by the time the production was due, the company had grown jaded from experimenting with purely formal ideas. We felt the concept would only deal with theatre and the best performer, in a very self-referential way, so we didn't pursue it.

In 2012, two political events brought the project back to our attention. The stalemate in the Belgian government formation, which led to 541 days without a new government, and the rise of a nationalist, economically separatist party in Flanders.

The former made the climate of political weariness rise to new heights and an increasing number of voices started questioning our form of government and democracy as a whole. Wouldn't it be more efficient to install a two-party-system and get rid of the constant compromise that paralysed the country? The support for this radical vision seemed to grow day by day. We ourselves believe in compromise, not when it concerns the creation of artistic work, but on a political level. We feel it's necessary to include as many different views as possible in order not to exclude anyone. As voters in a democratic system, we need to feel represented in the decision making, while at the same time accepting that opposite views also need to be voiced.

The latter, notably the rise of nationalism and separatism in Belgium, is a discomfiting evolution. For decades, the extreme right-wing, racist party Vlaams Belang kept winning votes, but was excluded from governing by the so-called 'cordon sanitaire' – an agreement among the other parties not to enter into a coalition with them. However, many of Vlaams Belang's ideas found their way to the party program of the more moderate N-VA, which dropped the racism and shifted the focus to an economic narrative, while maintaining the claim for autonomy. From a tiny, marginal party they grew extremely popular overnight.

The incentive for creating 'Fight Night' and returning to the concept we had devised years before, was a quiz show, ironically called 'The Smartest Person'. It was immensely popular in Flanders and contributed a great deal to the success of N-VA, since the chairman of the party participated in it and nearly won the final. Without explicitly promoting political views, the party had the most effective campaign ever. Week after week, the chairman could present himself on prime time television as an intelligent, funny man of the people with a broad knowledge. Even voters of a different political opinion felt inclined to support him in the next election.

In reiterating the idea of performers being eliminated during a show, we felt inspired by the 'personalized' unofficial campaign of the aforementioned chairman. What if the audience could vote for the people on stage, but the entire process would be an exploration of mediatised politics, rather than a purely theatrical self-reflection? The example of the chairman proved that a politician could win votes merely through his presence as a private person. We decided to let the audience vote without the reassurance of a party program or political views and discover how different their voting behaviour would be from the 'real' elections – or how similar. We would let them vote for personalities, but carefully media-trained ones. We wanted to explore the importance of charm, appearance and persuasion, as opposed to the ideas a politician stands for.

Our collaboration with the Australian company The Border Project was an important element in guaranteeing the show would cross boundaries in terms of content. Incorporating the difference between the Belgian pluralist system and the Australian Westminster model – similar to the American and British system – in the working process, ensured different cultures and political traditions could relate to all the elements included in the show.

Now that the performance is re-created in Turkish in Istanbul and a Chinese version is commissioned in Hong Kong, we are confident that the show raises issues of politics and democracy in a broader sense than we imagined.

# SCRIPT

'Fight Night' is ruled by an intricate, elusive system that steers the course of the performance. In order to give a clear impression of how the show works, we have chosen to add one more point of view to the original script: the perspective of the system that manipulates the voice of the audience throughout the performance.

00.

The system is set up. At the entrance of the venue, each spectator receives a voting device with buttons numbered from 1 to 9. The stage is empty, above it are two television screens.

Enter the host.

As he walks to the front of the stage, a microphone descends from the ceiling.

01.   PROLOGUE: In which the host explains the voting system and gathers information from the audience to get an idea of who they are.

The host addresses the audience.

*HOST*


*Ladies & Gentlemen,*
    *Lend me your ears.*

*It has often been said that you*
    *can't have a show without an*
    *audience and tonight that is*
    *more true than ever.*
*Because tonight we will not only*
    *need your eyes and ears, because*
    *at the centre of everything will*
    *be your voice.*

*Ladies & Gentlemen,*
    *Welcome to 'Fight Night'.*

*You can vote only once, and the*
    *voting is, of course, anonymous.*

He asks the audience to test the voting system.
There are three simple questions. The numbers
indicate the button they need to press on their
voting device.

**Question One**

| | | |
|---|---|---|
| 1) | Woman | % |
| 2) | Man | % |

**Question Two**

| | | |
|---|---|---|
| 1) | Single | % |
| 2) | In a relationship | % |
| 3) | Married | % |

**Question Three: Age**

| | | |
|---|---|---|
| 1) | Under 18 | % |
| 2) | 18 to 24 | % |
| 3) | 25 to 44 | % |
| 4) | 45 to 60 | % |
| 5) | Over 60 | % |

After each round of pressing buttons, the percentages are displayed on the screens. The
fourth question is a bit more intrusive, it's
about their income. By the end of this warm-
ing-up, the system knows the basic statistics of
the audience. On a given night, this could be

a majority of female spectators in a relationship, aged between 25 and 44 with an income
slightly above the average.

   The system will use these data later on in
the performance. The host announces that it's
time to meet the candidates.

02.   ROUND I: In which the audience gets a first impression of the five candidates, a winner and a loser emerge and campaigning starts.

Five performers enter the stage one by one, wearing dark boxer's robes with a hood to conceal their outfits. They form a line-up.

The host gives each performer a number between 1 and 5 randomly, which indicates their position in a new line-up.

A bell rings.

The performers move to their new positions. The procedure is carried out in silence, which enhances the impression of fairness and neutrality.

The performers, now 'candidates', take off their hoods, revealing their face and hair. The host asks them to close their eyes and gives the audience one minute to vote for their favourite candidate.

Through this first, seemingly random vote, the system checks the voters' impulsive, intuitive preferences, purely based on appearance. Sex, body type and face are the only parameters.

The results are announced one by one per candidate in percentages and displayed on the screens. The candidates position themselves on stage according to their ranking, taking one or two steps forward or backward. In spite of their neutral facial expressions, the audience may get a glimpse of their response to the results through gaze or body language. The candidates are aware that these tiny hints of emotion might influence the voters' opinion.

The candidate with the highest percentage is now called the winner. The candidate with the lowest percentage is deemed the loser.

The system allows both of them to address the audience with a fixed text: the winner speech and the loser speech. Whoever wins or loses, these speeches remain the same in every performance.

The winner speech starts off with the statement that by speaking, a parameter is added, the voice, which can either contribute to the first impression or ruin it. Actually two parameters are added, since the content of the speech also influences the audience.

*WINNER FIRST POLL*

*This is my voice.*
*This is the voice that comes with my*
    *face.*
*I hope you like it.*
*I hope you like it as much as you*
    *like my face.*
*I hope I'm not ruining anything.*
*A voice can do that sometimes.*

*I'll take the risk*
    *because I like talking to you.*
*The more I do, the more I speak, the*
    *more I reveal myself to you.*
*I'm going to tell you my name and*
    *I hope you'll think it suits me.*

*My name is [ … ]*
*I'm [ … ] years old.*

*The other candidates have other*
    *things to say, they're different*
    *from me.*
*And from the moment they will talk,*
    *I know I'll lose a lot of you.*
*Because I know you'll like them too.*

The system, however, doesn't allow candidates 2, 3 and 4 to speak. Only number 5, the loser, gets a chance to address the audience. The system is aware that the loser speech is very likely to increase the percentage of the candidate who delivers it. By presenting him or herself as an underdog, chances are that the he or she gains sympathy votes. The system encourages the voters to change their minds, applying natural laws of demagogy.

### *LOSER FIRST POLL*

*This is my voice, obviously.*
*It probably sounds less confident to*
*  you.*
*I can't help it.*
*I can't do anything about that.*

*Because I'm the loser for now.*
*  I'm the loser of whatever your*
*  vote was based on.*

*I know none of you intended to put*
*  me in this spot.*
*It's just how it works.*

*And although I'm in a unique*
*  position, I don't like it.*

*So please.*
*Like me more.*
*Pity me.*
*Care for me.*
*Support me.*
*Let me win you over.*
*I will be your underdog.*

**The host calls for the bell.**

**The candidates take off their robes. The clothes they reveal differ in style, but all of the candidates look nicely dressed. No one is over- or underdressed, there are no eye-catchers such as bright colours, garish accessories or cleavage. One could imagine this is what each of them would wear for a formal occasion.**

**The host allows the candidates to introduce themselves. These are the parameters they reveal:**

)        **Name**
)        **Age**
)        **Relationship status**

The host now shares the information that the system gathered about the audience. Some of the candidates take out their notebook to make notes. The host informs the candidates about:

)        The number of people
)        The ratio of men/women
)        The most represented relationship status
)        The division of age groups
)        The division of income classes

The host is careful not to cause offense, e.g. by calling people over sixty 'of respectable age'. He does brand the highest income group as 'claims to be rich' and the lowest as 'poor'. Mild humor and irony are indispensable in any host of this performance. The system, speaking through the host, now lets the candidates start their campaign. They all get the opportunity to answer the questions: 'who would vote for you?' and 'whose vote would you be most proud of winning?'. The candidates produce truthful, but slightly spin-doctored answers. They're all aware of their appearance and apply tactics that either reinforce it or go against it, adding depth to their first impression. Some of the strategies employed include:

)    Naming potential prejudices. (implication: 'I'm smarter than you might think')

)    Welcoming any vote, without distinction. ('I'm open-minded')

)    Cracking jokes.

)    Encouraging identification. ('I'm in the same situation as you, so we must have a lot in common')

)    Subtly playing on the results of the first vote. ('Be fair and give me another chance')

)    Using flagwords such as 'responsibility', 'loyalty', 'honest' and 'straightforward'.

)    Displaying affinity with the minority to win over the sympathy of the majority.

)    Feigning depth. ('I love people with strong opinions I'd be proud if they would vote for me')

)    Personalizing your voting audience. (Following the example of George Bush's Joe the Plumber)

)    Casting yourself as an outsider to circumvent competition.

Subliminally, the system also starts playing on issues of loyalty to one candidate – the first choice – or the rationality of voting for 'substance'. Since the candidates do not defend opinions or present a political program, the idea of 'substance' is entirely the voters' projection. A lot depends on whether the voters' first choice lives up to the expectations, whatever those might be.

03.   **ROUND II: In which the audience eliminates one candidate, but not the one they expected, and the system starts to have its way with direct democracy.**

The host now announces the second round of voting. For the 'electorate', this vote feels more serious, because they 'know' the candidates better.

*HOST*

*Ladies & Gentlemen,*
*I think you are ready.*
*I think you are ready to vote again.*

*Take your time to make your*
*   choice, because as a result of*
*   your next vote one of the candi-*
*   dates will be eliminated.*
*He or she will have to leave the*
*   stage and won't come back.*

*You have one minute to choose*
*   your favourite candidate.*

After 60 seconds, the host announces the results, going up from 5 to 1. Again, the percentages are displayed on the screen. Before handing over the microphone to the winner, he adds:

*You've done your duty,*
*but now everything is in the*
*  candidates' hands.*

Without drawing much attention to it, the host has told the voters that their votes will be subjected to the intricacies of the system. This reflects the reality that the power of the electorate reaches as far as filling in the ballot, however the decision making is in the hands of the politicians.

The winner, most likely a different candidate than the winner of the first round, addresses the voters. The system has encouraged a shuffle of the ranking by favouring the loser through the underdog speech.

### WINNER ROUND II

*I am humbled.*

*I am humbled to have been voted the
    favourite candidate in this round.
My first thanks goes to those who
    stayed with me from the beginning.
Thank you for your loyalty, I cherish
    your vote.
And for those of you who just joined
    us: welcome. Welcome to the
    biggest group here tonight.
I also want to thank the people here
    tonight who didn't vote this round,
    because in a way, your apathy
    contributed to my victory.*

The host reminds the candidates – and the voters – that somebody will have to leave the stage. Naturally, the winner doesn't feel this applies to him or her.

However, the host declares that coalitions are allowed. If the four other candidates combine their votes, then the winner could be outnumbered. But of course, every alliance is possible.

The candidates now start calculating. Not only the numbers matter, but also the way in which they handle the negotiations. Nobody wants to be perceived as a backstabber or an obvious double-dealer. Before the brokering starts, the host lets the loser speak.

## *LOSER ROUND II*

*'#'*
*[number of votes he/she has, calcu-*
*lated from the percentage and the*
*number of audience members]*
*That's the most important number*
*for me now. I represent '#' people*
*sitting here tonight.*
*We are the smallest group.*
*We are the minority.*
*And although I don't know who*
*you are, or if we're going to stick*
*together, the '#+1' of us represent*
*something that the others don't*
*have.*
*And I'm going to make sure that*
*doesn't get lost,*
*I'm going to make sure your vote*
*counted.*

Appealing to the idea that a minority, despite its small number, might be right, the system lets the loser defend individuality against the abstract logics of numbers.

The host interviews the loser. Here are some points the loser makes during the talk:

### LOSER

*We're the smallest group but does*
*that makes us less important?*

*We're not talking about numbers*
*here, we're talking about*
*individuals.*

*I think it's dangerous not to listen*
*to a minority.*
*It would make the winner very*
*unpopular.*

Upon this final argument, the loser teams up
with the winner. The host turns to the three
other candidates.

### HOST

*Maybe we should listen to some-*
*body from the middle field.*

The system allows the candidates to openly share their strategies with the audience. The open discussion gives the impression that the audience is included in the decision making. Needless to say they have no voice in the matter.

Number 3 steps forward. Together with the host, he or she runs through the options. The system allows for different outcomes at this stage. Either Number 2, 3 or 4 will be eliminated. The division of votes does influence the negotiations.

Mathematically, for Number 3, combining his or her votes with Number 2, the runner-up, seems a good solution. It would guarantee both of them to stay in the game. On the other hand, for Number 2, joining up with Number 4 is also interesting. In case Number 3 and 4 have more percentages than Number 2, the possibility to kick out Number 2 becomes viable. The decision lies in the hands of the candidates.

The host declares who they chose to eliminate. He or she will leave the stage. Before sending the candidate off, the host offers him or her the microphone to make a final statement.

### FIRST ELIMINATION SPEECH

*It seems like I have to leave the game.*
*It feels a bit harsh, but hey.*

*I know this is harder for me then*
*it is for you, so I'm not going to*
*burden you with it.*

*I agreed to play this game so I have*
*to respect the rules.*
*I'd be a sore loser if I didn't do that.*

**HOST**

**And what about the people who**
**voted for you?**
**What do they have to do now?**

**ELIMINATED CANDIDATE**

*I don't really care, I'm sorry.*
*Vote for somebody else.*
*But thanks.*

HOST

Did you prepare what you're
saying right now?

ELIMINATED CANDIDATE

Well, a little bit.
But yeah, let me put it this way.
    This is the part I like the least.
If you don't mind, I'd rather just
    leave the stage now.

HOST

Well, this is the last time you can
voice your thoughts.

### ELIMINATED CANDIDATE

*Well…*
*There is a bear in the woods.*
*For some people the bear is easy to see.*
*Others don't see it at all.*
*Some people say the bear is tame.*
*Others say it's vicious and dangerous.*
*Since no one can really be sure who*
*    is right, isn't it smart to be as*
*    strong as the bear?*
*If there is a bear?*

**The speech seems odd and obscure, but it opens the metaphorical question: who is the bear? Answers vary between the candidates, notably the winning one, the host or the audience itself. The text is taken from a publicity campaign of Ronald Reagan, in which the bear referred to Sovjet Russia and its nuclear weapons.**

**The eliminated candidate leaves the stage.**

04. ROUND III: In which the four remaining candidates are subjected to a blind round of voting concerning social, political and philosophical issues.

The host announces the next round. At the sound of the bell, the candidates line up.

*HOST*

*For this round we will ask you a series of questions.*
*Based on your answers, one of the candidates will have to leave the stage.*

*But my dear voters,*
*This is a blind round. You will only be able to vote for the issues.*
*You won't know which answer corresponds to one of our candidates.*

The host reads out each question, then gives the audience some time to chose their answer. The questions are:

Which qualities would you like your candidate to have? The options are displayed on the screen, in pairs of 'positive/negative', e.g.

| | | |
|---|---|---|
| 1) | Passionate | % |
| 2) | Stubborn | % |

I am ...

| | | |
|---|---|---|
| 1) | Religious | % |
| 2) | Spiritual | % |
| 3) | Neither | % |

Which word offends you the most?

| | | |
|---|---|---|
| 1) | Nigger | % |
| 2) | Faggot | % |
| 3) | Cunt | % |
| 4) | Retard | % |
| 5) | I find none of these words offensive | % |

Judging people is ...

| | | |
|---|---|---|
| 1) | A way of protecting yourself | % |
| 2) | Necessary | % |
| 3) | Harmful | % |
| 4) | Unavoidable | % |
| 5) | Enjoyable | % |

Do you consider yourself ...

| | | |
|---|---|---|
| 1) | A little bit racist | % |
| 2) | A little bit sexist | % |
| 3) | A little bit violent | % |
| 4) | Without any of these flaws | % |

If this audience was taken hostage, I would like my candidate to …

| | | |
|---|---|---|
| 1) | Try to sneak out of the venue | % |
| 2) | Act as a spokesperson of the group | % |
| 3) | Try to be a hero | % |
| 4) | Stay calm and wait for help | % |

Each time the results are revealed, the candidate representing the winning answer takes a step forward and the one representing the losing answer takes a step back. When there's a tie, more than one candidate takes a step.

In this way, the different options seem to reflect the candidates' opinions, although the audience can never be sure. There's also a strong suggestion that the candidate who ends up at the back will be eliminated.

Regardless of the answers, the system disconnects the audience's opinion from the candidates they vote for. The voters can do two things: answer the questions sincerely according to their personal opinion or try to guess which option belongs to their favourite candidate and make him or her win. While the competition is going on, the system reveals more and more about the audience's ideas and attitudes towards social issues. The last question forces the audience to reflect on themselves:

Do you trust the majority of this audience?
1)      Yes                                    %
2)      No                                     %

The host rephrases the result of the last question, for example:

*Ladies & Gentlemen,*
*The majority of this audience*
*doesn't trust the majority.*
*The minority of this audience*
*trusts the majority.*

In deciding who will be eliminated, the system again proves to be unpredictable.

At the end of the round of questions, one candidate has finished in the back, another one up front. They are perceived as the loser and the winner of this round. The two others are more or less in the middle. The host announces that the audience can now choose to eliminate either the winner (the one who shares *most* of their beliefs) or the loser (the one who has the *least* in common with the voters). The two 'middle ground' candidates are safe.

Despite the logical choice for the candidate who has the most in common with the audience, the voting usually turns into a highly subjective popularity poll. The voters might feel they didn't have a say in the selection of these two candidates, but for those who believe in voting for ideas rather than people, this round ought to make sense.

At this point, the system reveals the power of persuasion over rational consideration.

**The loser of the voting leaves the stage.**

05.  **ROUND IV: In which campaigning takes the form of a talkshow, the surviving candidates present their spin-doctored personality and the host changes the game.**

The candidates prepare themselves for the next scene. They make small changes in their costume, e.g. opening a button of a shirt, putting on a jacket or a tie, adjusting their hair. They sit down on bar stools.

The atmosphere is a bit more relaxed. The candidates seem to be more confident since they've made it to the fourth round and they can trust they have a following among the voters.

The host interviews them. This gives the candidates the opportunity to reveal more about their personalities. In spite of the casual tone, their answers are still carefully chosen and part of a strategy.

The system has given them pitches to tackle the questions, which will be represented as points A, B or C. In the performance, these points are dressed up in more everyday speech.

## FAIRNESS

### *HOST*

### *The candidate who had to leave the stage in round III, was that fair?*

**The candidates phrase three opinions:**

a)       **It was fair.**

> Quote: *...fair, although the audience lost the most radical voice.*

b)       **This is game of strategy and we all agreed to play it.**

> Quote: *My strategy is trying to be honest.*

C)       **Fair or not, it depends on who the audience is and that's a matter of luck.**

> Quote: *I feel lucky to be here.*

## UNDERDOG

*HOST*

*Did the underdog strategy work?*
*Who is the underdog now?*

**b)**  **Once you name a strategy, people see through it.**

Quote: *Yes, people see through my strategy of 'being honest'.*

**a)**  Quote: *Everybody likes an underdog, nobody likes a loser.*

## RISKS

*HOST*

*The winner speech of the first round mentioned the risk of talking to the audience.*
*What does it mean?*

c)    Quote: *Every time I open my mouth,*
      *I'm at risk of losing votes. I could*
      *be losing your votes right now.*

### RACIST/SEXIST/VIOLENT

### *HOST*

### *How do you explain your choice to be a little bit sexist/racist/violent?*

c)    **Admit to the flaw, but limit it to certain situations. Example: Admit violent tendencies. Say, for example, you've kicked a dog in the face.**

**The host gives the candidate the opportunity to explain him/herself and to rephrase the story.**

c)    **In the explanation, add mitigating circumstances. Example: you kicked a dog in the face because it was attacking your infant niece.**

Another candidate is allowed to explain his or her flaw. The same 'template' can be used for racism and sexism. Degrees of justification, laughing away the matter or straightforward owning up to the vice can be used as tactics.

Through this item, the system points out that any story can be made acceptable through delivery and editing.

## CUNTRETARDNONEFAGGOT

### *HOST*

*Which of the words nigger, faggot, cunt or retard offends you the most and why?*

Cunt)     Choose for the joke as a strategy, thereby avoiding risky answers.

Quote: *My choice was purely based on the sound of the words. Nigger, there's a nice rhythm to the word: nigger nigger nigger. But cunt, is so harsh. Cunt Cunt Cunt.*

**Retard) None of the above) Stigmatizing words can be disempowered when the targeted group starts using it themselves.**

> Quote: *Niggers use the word nigger. I mean you can't turn on the radio without hearing 'nigger this, nigger that.'*

**The host confronts the third candidate with his or her choice. Whatever the third candidate's choice may be, the answer starts with the same three lines as the previous answer. Words may be replaced with more politically correct or elevated terms, but the content needs to be the same. This is to draw attention to fact that the interview is scripted and rehearsed. The third candidate is able to use more subtle, carefully chosen language, because he or she has had time to think it over.**

> Quote: *African American people really reappropriated the word nigger in their music, movies and urban poetry.*

**The candidate might even add a 'humane' touch of consideration.**

> Quote: *A lot of disabled people can't disempower the word retard,*

*because some of them are unable to
use it themselves.*

## RELIGIOUS QUESTION

**Spiritual) The minority position.**

> Quote: *I like thinking different about
> this, because I think there is more.
> And people can share that belief
> with me.*

**Neither) The religiously tolerant point of view.**

> Quote: *I don't think just because
> we believe in different things,
> we can't understand each other.
> I'd be happy if religious or spir-
> itual people voted for me.*

**Neither 2) The hardcore atheist position.**

> Quote: *If you believe the world was
> created in seven days, you're
> stupid. And stupid people have
> the right to be represented...
> by stupid people.*

**The screen displays a question:**

Who is winning?                                        %

*HOST*

*In the meantime we launched an
    opinion poll. It's going on above
    their heads.
Feel free to participate.*

### HOSTAGE

Explain what you would do in a hostage situation. The options are:


)        Be the spokesperson: ask the hostage
            takers why they're there, where they
            come from, what their intentions are
            and if they had an unhappy childhood.
)        Sneak out…and seek professional help.
)        Be the hero: shoot one or two of the
            hostage takers. Not everybody would
            survive, but at least someone did
            something.
)        Stay calm: the least risky decision.

Candidates take turns in defending their choice.

## POLL

### *HOST*

*Who is winning the poll?*

The first candidate answers honestly. The second one too. The last one says:

> *I hate this question:*
> > *Who is winning what?*
> *Being the funniest? Being the most*
> > *entertaining?*
> *Being the one who says the things*
> > *that make the most sense to you?*
> *What what what?*

This final reply summarizes the essence of the whole interview. The question at the heart of the candidates' casual, natural representation of themselves and the calculated spontaneity of their replies, is the measurability of popularity. The system deliberately mixes up charisma, accumulated sympathy, (precarious) personal opinions and on-the-spot performance to confuse the audience's criteria of choice. The host announces the winner of the poll.

*Winner comment: Obviously these numbers are encouraging.*
*I think what I have to say is reso-nating with the audience, but let's not get ahead of ourselves.*
*Polls come, polls go.*
*The only poll that really counts is the next election.*

*Loser comment: Congratulations to the winner.*
*I just want to ask how many people participated in this poll?.*

If the host quotes a high number, the loser admits his defeat by commenting:

*Message received.*

**If the number is relatively low, the loser states:**

*Those are interesting figures.*

## THE BEAR

### *HOST*

**Before the first eliminated candi-
date left the stage, he or she
talked about a bear.
What was the meaning of that?**

**b)**     **The bear is the audience.**

Quote: *The woods are this room
here. The bear, which we should
fear, is the audience.*

**a)**     **The bear is me.**

Quote: *I feel like the bear – it could
be vicious or tame and I can be
both.*

c)        **There is no bear.**

*Quote: … Or I just don't see it.*

**The interview is finished. The host announces the next voting round.**
   **However, before he asks the audience to press the button, he takes the floor:**

*HOST'S*
*GAMECHANGER SPEECH*

*There are three things I want to say.*
*A warning, a reassurance and*
   *a declaration.*

*First of all:*
*These three remaining contenders*
   *all are strong candidates.*
*Round after round they have*
   *earned your vote.*
*And not only your vote,*
   *but also your sympathy,*
   *your trust, your support.*
*But let me warn you.*
*Whatever they've been saying here,*
   *they prepared their answers.*
*For every sentence they spoke at*
   *least fifteen have been deleted.*

*Every move they made has been*
  *rehearsed.*
*Every pause – calculated.*

*But let me reassure you:*
  *I am different.*
*I care for your vote.*
*For me, you are more than a*
  *percentage.*

*And finally my declaration:*
*I can no longer stand on the*
  *sidelines.*
*I have decided to resign as your*
  *host and become your candidate.*

*Let's change the rules.*
  *Let's change the game.*
    *Together.*

*So for the last time,*
*Ladies & Gentlemen,*
*Let me walk you through the*
  *options.*

*For (name candidate), press 1.*
*For (name candidate), press 2.*
*For (name candidate), press 3.*
*Or press 4, if you want change.*

*You can vote now.*

With the host turned into a candidate, the system seems to have lost its neutral representative. For those who believe he will truly bring change, voting for the ex-host seems a way to express disagreement with the manipulations of the other candidates – or even disapproval of the way their votes are used. In reality, the system has introduced this twist to prepare for more effective ways of manipulating the voters.

The results are displayed on the screen. Most likely, the host will have the fewest votes. For the rest of the script, we will assume the host has lost the round and will be eliminated.

06. **ROUND V: In which the candidates try to make you agree, disagree or stop voting.**

   **After a short pause to mark the absence of a host, the winner of the vote grabs the microphone. (If the host has won the vote, he delivers a slightly different version of the speech.)**

   ### *WINNER ROUND IV SPEECH*

   > *Our host has stepped down.*
   > *He has given up his throne, and*
   >    *I believe he made the right choice,*
   >    *because he was never elected.*
   > *You never had a say in his position.*
   >
   > *Now every one of us is chosen by you.*
   > *We are at your mercy.*
   >    *Liberty, equality, guillotine.*
   >
   > *Our host promised change,*
   >    *and by resigning his position,*
   >    *he fulfilled that promise.*
   > *Because things will never be the*
   >    *same again.*
   >
   > *We will miss him as a host,*
   >    *but welcome him as a candidate.*

*With most of your votes behind me*
*I will take up his mantle.*
*And to the best of my ability,*
*fulfill his role.*

*And I'll start with the most*
*unpleasant job.*

*So, (Host)*
*The people here tonight have made*
*their choice.*
*I think it's time for you to leave*
*the stage.*

**HOST**

**Can I say something?**

*No.*

**The host leaves the stage. The winner announces there will be three more rounds, in which each of the three remaining candidates will try to win the audience over. The last vote will determine the winner.**

**FIRST ROUND**

**From now on the candidates represent AGREE, DISAGREE or NO VOTE. They no longer seem to represent themselves, but a conviction. The three points of view relate directly to the system.**

### *AGREE*

*We all know how this is going to
    turn out.*

*After three rounds, one of us will
    have the majority of the votes.
He will have 51% or 60% or maybe
    even 70%.
And he (or she) will be declared
    your winner.*

*But what if tonight could be different?
What if tonight could be special?
Unlike any other night,
    unlike any other election.*

*You can make that happen.
Hold your device. Hold your device
    in your hand.
And move your finger over one of
    the buttons. And now press it.*

*Go on. It's not for real. Press.*

*Imagine now the results appear*
    *on the screen, and you see that*
    *everybody around you pressed the*
    *same number. Everyone around*
    *you made exactly the same choice.*

*All of you here tonight, making*
    *exactly the same choice.*

*A 100%. Your winner would be*
    *truly your winner.*

*Wouldn't that be amazing?*
*I would take that with me as*
    *a small miracle.*
*The other candidates will of course*
    *disagree with me.*
*They have to, they have no choice,*
    *it's the role they have to play.*

*They will try to divide us,*
    *don't let them.*

*Of course I want to be a winner.*
*But most of all,*
    *I want this idea to win.*
*Because it would be beautiful that*
    *just for once,*
*We show that we can agree.*

## *NO VOTE*

*You have three candidates to choose
     from.
Three options you can vote for,
     but there are no real choices here.
We're forcing them on you.*

*That's the problem.
That's the problem with the system.
The only choices you have are the
     ones it gives you.*

*The system doesn't reflect what you
     believe in.
It's impossible to represent every one
     of you sitting here tonight.
And the system has to stop pre-
     tending that it can.*

*No system should control you.*

*I don't even want to change it.
I just want to get rid of it.
And get rid of the people that are
     stealing your votes, because none
     of us deserve your vote.*

*Don't even vote for me, don't vote*
    *for anyone.*

*When they ask you to vote,*
    *show them that you don't want*
    *to take part in it anymore.*
*Press 9.*

### DISAGREE

*Those were nice words,*
    *(name AGREE) & (name NO*
    *VOTE) are both good speakers.*
*But they're deceiving you,*
    *both of them.*

*They are both taking you hostage.*
*They are stealing your choice.*

*This one is asking you to mindlessly*
    *press the same button.*
*For the sake of some rhetorical*
    *proposition that we should all*
    *make the same choice.*
*But if all of you agree, your opinion*
    *doesn't matter anymore.*
*There is no need to use your vote if*
    *it is the same as everyone else's.*
*It just doesn't matter.*

*And that one, well he/she is just*
*cheating.*
*I love it how he/she pretends he/she*
*doesn't want your vote, and then*
*asks you to vote for him/her.*
*Just giving it another number*
*doesn't change anything.*
*Don't say there are no real choices*
*and then offer yourself as a choice.*

*I understand the sentiment he/*
*she has.*
*You want to disagree.*
*I too disagree.*
*And I think it's good to disagree.*
*There is nothing wrong with*
*thinking differently.*
*It's beautiful.*

*You all have a different opinion.*
*and thanks to the system you can*
*make your own choice.*
*Keep the contest of ideas alive*
*and let's all agree to disagree.*

**The winner announces the next election.**

1)          is for AGREE                           %
2)          is for DISAGREE                        %

NO VOTE suggests to press 9.                        %

The system, however self-critical it appears, still allows the candidates to collect votes. The voters have no choice: by agreeing with an idea, they're also obliged to appoint a winner.

The results are displayed: three percentages, adding up to a 100%. The winner announces the second round of voting.

## SECOND ROUND

AGREE takes the microphone.

### *AGREE*

*Look, none of us have a 100%.*

*I know some of you think it's not
    going to happen.
I know some of you think it's
    impossible.*

*But do you realize that that thought*
*    is the only thing that prevents it*
*    from happening?*

*It's easy not to believe in it.*
*    Much easier.*
*It's easy to say no, like both of them.*

*That's what we do all the time.*
*We all have different opinions on*
*    difficult issues.*
*When we will leave this space we go*
*    back to a world where we all have*
*    to compromise, make concessions.*
*But here, tonight, anything is*
*    possible.*

*Here, tonight,*
*    you can know what it feels like*
*    if for once we agree.*

*Say yes.*
*    Vote 1.*

*Show that we, although we have our*
*    differences, we can agree.*

*One hundred percent.*

## NO VOTE

*Aren't you curious what's going to*
*   happen, if we succeed?*

*We already have [   …    ] %*
*But let's be more than a percentage.*

*When they ask you to vote*
*   don't press any button,*
*   but hand in your device.*
*Make your protest visible.*
*Let's break the system.*
*Let's make their percentages*
*   meaningless.*
*She/he can have her/his dream*
*but it won't be a real 100% anymore.*

*When they announce the next vote,*
*   raise your hand and I will come*
*   and collect them from you.*

### *DISAGREE*

*There you go again.*
*Don't let him/her trick you.*
*It's very clever what he/she's doing.*

*The moment you hand your device to*
    *him/her, she/he's not giving it back.*
*You can't change your mind*
    *anymore.*
*Your opinion doesn't matter.*

*But don't give away your choice.*
    *Make yourself heard.*

*Don't give in to people who tell you*
    *what you have to do.*
*They're both telling you what to do.*
*Don't let them control you.*

*Be in control. Vote 2.*

**1)**      **is for AGREE**      %
**2)**      **is for DISAGREE**      %

**NO VOTE asks the audience to hand in**
**their voting device.**

The results are displayed: two percentages amounting to 100%. The collected devices are not counted in. The system ignores them. The winner announces the final round.

## THIRD ROUND

AGREE takes the microphone.

### *ENDORSEMENT OF AGREE*

*It's not going to work.*
*It's not going to happen.*
*You failed me.*
*Maybe it's just a game, but in a way*
*    that makes it even worse if we*
*    can't even make it happen here.*

*If I want to be loyal to the idea*
*    I represent,*
*The only sensible thing I can do*
*    now is to step down,*
*I'm withdrawing my candidacy.*
*I failed at what I wanted to achieve.*
*    I failed you.*

*I want to thank the [ … ] %*
  *of you who agreed.*
*For me you're the idealists of this*
  *audience. Thank you.*
*And I want to urge you to join*
  *DISAGREE.*
*You don't know what's going to*
  *happen in the end.*
*So don't give away your ability to*
  *decide for yourself.*

**AGREE leaves the stage.**

**NO VOTE**

*Look, it's working.*
  *One down, one more to go.*
    *It's us against them now.*
      *It's us against the system.*

*This is a fake election.*
  *It only gives you one choice.*
    *Don't take part in it.*

*I would like to ask all of the people*
  *who gave up their device and*
  *the people who are still thinking*

*about it to come to the front and*
*sit down.*
*I won't ask anything more.*
*Just show your protest.*
*Come to the front.*
*And occupy the space.*

**DISAGREE**

*This is an absurd position to be in.*
*It seems like you don't have a*
*choice anymore.*
*But you still have.*
*It's not about me or him/her*
*anymore.*
*There's no us against them.*
*Vote for your right to vote.*
*Vote so you can decide.*
*Don't give it up.*
*Press 1.*

*Or hand over you right to vote.*
*You can vote now.*

**NO VOTE**

*Come down.*

The results are displayed: 100% for DISAGREE.
The system seems to have created its winner.

07.  **ROUND VI: Where the winner takes it all and burdens and dissects the majority of tonight.**

**The microphone comes down.**

### *WINNER/DISAGREE*

*Ladies & Gentlemen,*
*Lend me your ears.*

*Some people say you can't have a*
    *show without an audience.*
*And tonight, for me, that was more*
    *true than ever.*

*I'm here.*
    *I'm here because of you.*
    *Thank you.*
*I couldn't have done it without you.*

*I've said that everybody has the*
    *right to their own opinion.*
*To think differently is beautiful.*
*The non-voters here tonight have*
    *decided they don't want to be a*
    *part of it anymore.*
*And I don't want to force them*
    *to stay.*

*You are the majority.*
   *The first true majority of tonight.*

*You don't only decide for yourself*
   *now. You decide for all of us.*
*You represent the rest.*

*So to all of the voters here tonight*
   *I propose a referendum.*
*Tell them what we want them to do.*

*Should the non-voters here tonight*
   *leave or stay?*

**The screen displays the options:**

**1)**        **LEAVE**                                    %
**2)**        **STAY**                                     %

*Press 1.*
   *If you want them to leave, because*
   *they don't want to be a part of it*
   *anymore.*

*Press 2.*
*If you want to force them to stay,*
*because you believe that's what*
*they should do.*

*You can vote now.*

**The results are displayed. If on a given night, LEAVE has won, the winner announces:**

*The majority has spoken.*
*It's time to leave.*

**NO VOTE addresses his followers.**

*If you want us to go, we will go.*
*I'll come with you.*

**Even if they're 'allowed' to stay, NO VOTE will urge them to go, because they choose not to be part of the system.**

**NO VOTE exits with the people who gave up their device.**

### *DISAGREE*

*Some of them are probably still here.*
*But I believe I speak for the majority.*
*We don't want to force anybody for*
*    now. They can stay.*

*I believe you made the right choice.*
*They wanted to go.*
*But they couldn't decide for*
*    themselves.*
*They were waiting for you.*

**The technician comes to the front to give a list to the winner and shows the audience where the number of their device is.**

*I know some of you didn't want to*
*    make the decision.*
*'#' of you didn't want to tell them*
*    what to do,*

*There's a number on the bottom of*
    *your device,*
*The people with the device*
    *number #, number #, number #*
*We didn't receive your vote.*
*Maybe there was a system error.*
    *Maybe.*
    *But still, your opinion matters.*
*You are part of the majority now.*

*Look around you.*
*This is what a majority looks like.*

*This is what [  …  ] %*
    *of you doesn't trust.*
    *(The percentage is the number*
    *of people who didn't trust the*
    *majority in Round III.)*

*Who are you really?*

*I believe it's time to declare your*
    *winner for tonight.*
*Because you can't have a game*
    *without one.*

*She/he is not among you.*
*She/he is you.*
*She/he is the one whose opinion*
    *matters the most of all.*
*She/he decided everything tonight.*

*She/he is always right.*
*Even when she/he's wrong.*

*Ladies & Gentlemen,*
*Your winner.*

*The majority is...*

**The screen displays a description of a person, assembled from the data gathered during the show:**

)    **Sex**
)    **Relationship status**
)    **Beliefs**
)    **Age**
)    **Income**
)    **Racist, sexist or violent tendencies**
)    **Decision for the others to leave or stay**

**Only the data of the people who constitute the majority are processed and presented as a personification of the common denominator. All together, the description might look like this:**

**A MARRIED, ATHEIST WOMAN, 35 YEARS OLD, WHO MAKES 1650 EUROS A MONTH, IS A LITTLE BIT SEXIST AND WANTED THE OTHERS TO LEAVE**

Outside the theatre space, NO VOTE and his or her followers have gathered around a speaker. The winner's speech is broadcasted.

*NO VOTE (to the followers)*

*Whoever they declare now as their winner, it doesn't matter.*
*You resisted. You opposed.*
*You didn't give in.*
*For me, you are the true winners of tonight. Thank you.*

And the system? It has achieved its goal: creating a metaphor for the democratic machinations in the outside world. The audience is left with the question whether their vote really matters. Hopefully, they'll make the right decision.

**THE END ·**

**p. 527 'Fight Night'**

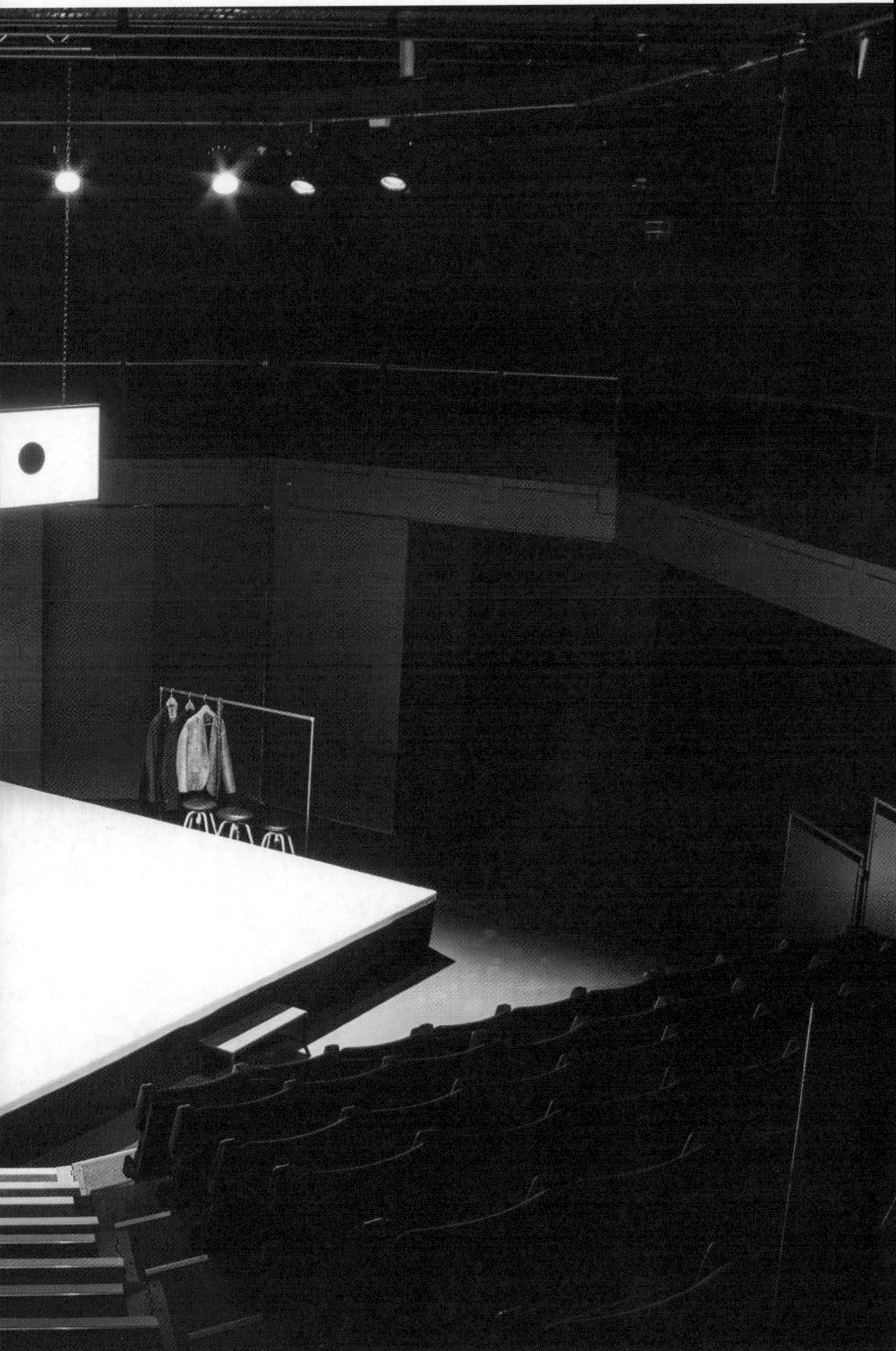

p. 528 'Fight Night'

VOTE